# High-Growth Firms

# High-Growth Firms

Facts, Fiction, and Policy Options for
Emerging Economies

Arti Grover Goswami, Denis Medvedev,
and Ellen Olafsen

 **WORLD BANK GROUP**

ISBN (paper): 978-1-4648-1368-9
ISBN (electronic): 978-1-4648-1370-2
DOI: 10.1596/978-1-4648-1368-9

*Cover art:* Remedios Varo, *Papilla Estelar (Star Maker)* (1958). Used with the permission of the artist's estate. Further permission required for reuse. The painting was photographed by Gallery Wendi Norris, San Francisco.
*Cover design:* Bill Pragluski, Critical Stages

**Library of Congress Cataloging-in-Publication Data has been requested.**

# Contents

## Boxes

## Figures

## Map

## Tables

# Preface

Productivity accounts for half of the differences in GDP per capita across countries. Identifying policies to stimulate it is thus critical to alleviating poverty and fulfilling the rising aspirations of global citizens. Yet productivity growth has slowed globally in recent decades, and the lagging productivity performance in developing countries constitutes a major barrier to convergence with advanced-country levels of income.

The World Bank Productivity Project—an initiative of the Vice Presidency for Equitable Growth, Finance, and Institutions—seeks to bring frontier thinking on the measurement and determinants of productivity, grounded in the developing-country context, to global policy makers. Each volume in the series explores a different aspect of the topic through dialogue with academics and policy makers, and through sponsored empirical work in our client countries. The first volume, *The Innovation Paradox*, developed a blueprint for reshaping many aspects of innovation-related productivity policies in developing countries. The second volume, *Productivity Revisited*, framed cutting edge thinking on measuring and understanding productivity dynamics within the agenda of developing-country policy makers.

This volume, the third in the series, focuses on the disproportionate contribution to overall growth by a relatively small share of firms that quickly scale their employment and output and generate positive spillovers along the value chain (high-growth firms). Policy makers across the world are keen to identify and support such firms in an effort to boost development. However, episodes of high growth are typically short-lived, and the empirical support for the ability to successfully target these firms is, at best, lukewarm. The analysis in this volume sheds new light on key features and drivers of high-growth firms in developing countries and leads to rethinking of public policy priorities to support firm growth.

William F. Maloney
Chief Economist
Equitable Growth, Finance, and Institutions
World Bank Group

## Other Titles in the World Bank Productivity Project

*Productivity Revisited: Shifting Paradigms in Analysis and Policy*. 2018. Ana Paula Cusolito and William F. Maloney. Washington, DC: World Bank.

*The Innovation Paradox: Developing-Country Capabilities and the Unrealized Promise of Technological Catch-Up*. 2017. Xavier Cirera and William F. Maloney. Washington, DC: World Bank.

All books in the World Bank Productivity Project are available free at https://openknowledge.worldbank.org/handle/10986/30560.

# Acknowledgments

This book was prepared by a team led by Arti Grover Goswami (World Bank Finance, Competitiveness, and Innovation Global Practice), Denis Medvedev (World Bank Finance, Competitiveness, and Innovation Global Practice), and Ellen Olafsen (World Bank Finance, Competitiveness, and Innovation Global Practice) under the guidance of Paulo Correa (Practice Manager, World Bank Finance, Competitiveness, and Innovation Global Practice) and Ganesh Rasagam (Practice Manager, World Bank Finance, Competitiveness, and Innovation Global Practice). Anabel González and Klaus Tilmes (Senior Adviser, World Bank Equitable Growth, Finance, and Institutions cluster) provided direction to the team during the initial stages of the book preparation. The team is indebted to Najy Benhassine (Director, World Bank Equitable Growth, Finance, and Institutions cluster), Mary Hallward-Driemeier (Senior Economic Advisor, World Bank Equitable Growth, Finance, and Institutions cluster), William F. Maloney (Chief Economist, World Bank Equitable Growth, Finance, and Institutions cluster), and Ceyla Pazarbasioglu (Vice President, World Bank Equitable Growth, Finance, and Institutions cluster), who linked the team to the World Bank Group's overall strategy and steered them in that direction.

The book's findings and analytical insights draw on a set of background papers commissioned for this report. The papers' authors were Paulo Bastos and Joana Silva (Brazil); Xavier Cirera, Roberto Fattal Jaef, and Nicolas Gonne (Côte d'Ivoire); Arti Grover Goswami (Ethiopia); Balázs Muraközy, Francesca de Nicola, and Shawn Tan (Hungary); Kay Kim and Siddharth Sharma (India); Ruchita Manghnani (India); Esteban Ferro and Smita Kuriakose (Indonesia); Luis Sanchez Bayardo and Leonardo Iacovone (Mexico); Marcio Cruz, Leila Baghdadi, and Hassen Arouri (Tunisia); Izak Atiyas, Ozan Bakis, Francesca de Nicola, and Shawn Tan (Turkey); Chanont Banternghansa and Krislert Samphantharak (Thailand); José-Daniel Reyes, Arti Grover Goswami, and Yahia Ziad Abuhashem (financial development); Johanne Buba, Julio Gonzalez, and Deeksha Kokas (targeting entrepreneurs); and Sameeksha Desai, Ellen Olafsen, and Peter Alex Cook (entrepreneurship policies). William R. Kerr provided major contributions and insights on firm dynamics in the United States, Mulalo Mamburu did so for South Africa, and Umut Kilinç for Turkey. Yue Li added to the discussion on place-based policies, and Maja Andjelkovic did so for the entrepreneurial ecosystems. Marcio Cruz made substantial contributions to the analytical framework, and Anwar Aridi and Danqing Zhu contributed to earlier versions of the book.

Yahia Ziad Abuhashem, Nuria Tolsá Caballero, Peter Alex Cook, and Ndirangu Warugongo provided valuable research assistance. Rachel Fano, Susan Mandel, Orlando Mota, Patricia Katayama, Jewel McFadden, Alloysius Ocheni, and Susana Rey provided production and logistical support. Dina Elnaggar, Elena Gex, Nicola Vesco, and Nina Vucenik provided communications support. William Shaw organized, streamlined, and edited the narrative.

The peer reviewers were Alex Coad (CENTRUM Católica Graduate Business School, Lima, Peru), Alvaro Gonzalez (World Bank), Ivailo Izvorski (World Bank), David McKenzie (World Bank), Esperanza Lasagabaster (World Bank), David Audretsch (Indiana University), Donna Kelley (Babson College), and Fadi Ghandour (Aramex).

# Abbreviations

| | |
|---|---|
| BS | backward spillover |
| FDI | foreign direct investment |
| FS | forward spillover |
| GDP | gross domestic product |
| GQ | Golden Quadrilateral |
| HGF | high-growth firm |
| HS | horizontal spillover |
| IFC | International Finance Corporation |
| M&E | monitoring and evaluation |
| MNE | multinational enterprise |
| MSMEs | micro, small, and medium enterprises |
| NBER | National Bureau of Economic Research |
| NESTA | National Endowment for Science, Technology and the Arts |
| NS-EW | North-South-East-West |
| OECD | Organisation for Economic Co-operation and Development |
| R&D | research and development |
| ROA | return on assets |
| RPQ | relative prevalence quotient |
| SMEs | small and medium enterprises |
| STI | science, technology, and innovation |
| TFP | total factor productivity |
| TFPQ | total factor productivity, quantity based |
| TFPR | total factor productivity, revenue based |
| VC | venture capitalist |
| VS | vertical spillover |
| WBES | World Bank Enterprise Surveys |
| ZBTIC | Zone Franche de la Biotechnologie et des Technologies de l'Information et de la Communication |

# Executive Summary

The cover of this book features a painting by the Spanish surrealist artist Remedios Varo (1908–63), *Papilla estelar* (*Celestial Pablum*, also known as the *Star Maker*). Stars, superstars, elephants, gazelles, gorillas, unicorns, and other monikers for high-performing firms abound in the economic and financial literature, as well as in popular discourse. Targeting such firms, in an effort to boost policy selectivity and efficiency, has become an increasingly appealing goal for policy makers in high-income and developing countries alike. Yet the making of stars, a process by which a venture capitalist or policy maker identifies high-potential businesses and puts in place processes and policies to accelerate firm growth, remains mostly art rather than science. This is particularly true for developing countries because the evidence base in this field has thus far been largely limited to high-income economies.

What difference do high-growth firms (HGFs) make to growth, productivity, and job creation in developing countries? How do they do it? And what is the appropriate role for public policy? Inspired by these questions, this book sets out to quantify the importance of HGFs for employment and output growth, considering both the dynamics within HGFs and their impact on other firms in the economy (chapter 1). It contrasts a popular perception of HGFs as high-tech start-ups with evidence, focusing particularly on those characteristics of HGFs that have been or can be used as filters for policy action (chapter 2). The book then draws policy makers' attention away from outward characteristics of firms and toward factors that establish a solid foundation for rapid firm growth, including innovation, agglomeration and networks, skills and managerial experience, global linkages, and financial development (chapter 3). Finally, it reviews the public policies used in developing countries to support the creation and scaling up of HGFs and the evidence on the effectiveness of mechanisms to screen and identify high-potential firms, concluding with a blueprint for a reorientation of public policies aimed at facilitating firm growth (chapter 4).

The book's insights are based on detailed analysis of high-quality longitudinal data sets in Brazil, Côte d'Ivoire, Ethiopia, Hungary, India, Indonesia, Mexico, South Africa, Thailand, Tunisia, and Turkey. The selection of countries reflects in large part data availability, given that there are simply not many panel censuses or surveys of firms in developing countries, and accessing the existing ones is often a challenge. Even so, the data sets in this book cover all six World Bank regions, as well as diverse income levels and very different growth performances (figure ES.1). Despite the heterogeneity of data sources and underlying country characteristics, the main findings and conclusions

**FIGURE ES.1   Country Coverage of the Book**

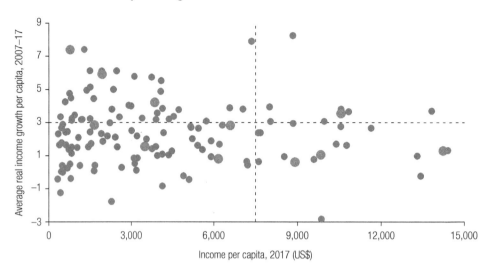

**MAP ES.1   Countries Covered by the Book**

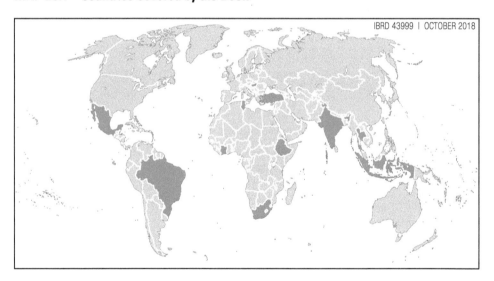

tend to be quite robust across the various cases, supporting the general insights and policy recommendations developed in the book.

## The "80/20" Rule of Firm Growth

HGFs are powerful engines of job and output growth. In the countries studied in this book, HGFs make up about 20 percent or less of firms in manufacturing and services, yet they create as much as 80 percent of all new sales and jobs in these sectors taken together. Another way to appreciate their disproportionate impact is to recognize that, in nearly all cases, the net change in employment and output would have been negative without the positive contribution of these firms (that is, in aggregate, non-HGFs destroy more jobs than they create, and decline rather than grow in terms of sales). These dynamics are similar to what has been previously observed across a range of high-income economies, such as Sweden, the United Kingdom, and the United States. To paraphrase Paul Krugman's famous quote, high-growth firms are nearly everything when it comes to determining an economy's overall performance.[1]

Curiously, HGF incidence does not appear to be systematically related to per capita income, rates of sectoral growth, or market concentration. The share of HGFs in the United States—a benchmark dynamic economy in studies such as Hsieh and Klenow (2009)—is in the middle of the range of developing countries studied in this book. This suggests that there may be no "desired" incidence of HGFs in an economy, and policies targeting a specific share of HGFs could be misguided.

In addition to their critical role in job and output growth, HGFs also create positive spillovers. Whereas evidence for horizontal (same sector) spillovers is mixed—since HGFs may transfer knowledge or create networks but also may raise competition and push down prices—the evidence on vertical spillovers is stronger. In the two countries where this book was able to follow HGF spillovers, being a buyer from or a supplier to an HGF improved firm performance across a wide range of indicators in Hungary and also, in some cases, in Turkey. These extraordinary abilities of HGFs are what make them an interesting subject for academics and an attractive target for policy makers keen to boost economic performance.

## Facts versus Fiction of High Growth

A common view of a typical HGF is a small start-up in a high-tech sector that grows quickly over a sustained period through some favorable quality inherent to the firm. Thus, the policy challenge is framed as determining which firms have the potential for high growth and providing these firms with access to financial and technical resources to realize this potential. However, the new analysis in this book, as well as the economic literature it surveys, shows that this view is a misconception.

First, although HGFs tend to be younger than the average firm, most will have been in business for at least a couple of years before embarking on a high-growth trajectory. HGFs are not necessarily small either; many already are larger than the average firm at the beginning of a high-growth episode and, depending on the definition, the average HGF is anywhere from 4 percent larger to six times as large as an average firm after three years of high growth. HGFs also do not appear in the same sectorss across countries, and are not necessarily more common in high-tech industries. Finally, they operate across a range of locations, although proximity to infrastructure plays an important role in facilitating high growth.

Second, the achievement of high growth in one period does not mean that firms are more likely to grow rapidly in subsequent periods—evidence shows that HGFs mostly turn out to be "one-hit wonders." As many as 50 percent of firms that experienced a high-growth event in the previous three years are likely to exit the market altogether in the following three to six years, whereas fewer than 15 percent are likely to repeat a high-growth episode—illustrating the short-lived and episodic nature of firm growth. Some firms move in and out of high growth, while others achieve high growth after a decade or more of subpar growth performance. This evidence casts doubt on whether high-growth—or any growth at all—is a permanent characteristic of any firm and suggests instead that a "high-growth episode" is something that select few firms experience at some point in their life cycles. Because all of the benefits of HGFs take place only within these narrow windows, the fragile and elusive nature of high-growth events means that targeting them may be neither feasible nor advisable.

## Quantity versus Quality of Firm Growth

The evidence in this book shows that policies that seek out potential HGFs based on outward characteristics or target some desired share of HGFs are likely to be misguided. This is because the link between productivity and high growth is often weak since firms may grow for a variety of reasons, with the growth driven by high efficiency but also demand shocks, uncompetitive markets, or political connections (the second volume of the World Bank Productivity Project, Cusolito and Maloney [2018], presents the latest advances in productivity research). For example, data from Côte d'Ivoire indicate that there is little overlap between a set of "efficient" HGFs (those firms that would attain HGF status if resources across the economy were allocated according to firms' productivity) and the observed HGFs. Thus, productivity-limiting distortions may not only reduce the number of firms that could attain high growth but are also likely to misallocate resources in a way that allows less efficient firms to achieve high growth—obscuring the relationship between high growth and productivity. And when it comes to policy, these results suggest that using past performance as a guide for supporting specific firms may exacerbate distortions rather than reduce them (in the absence of real-time data on firm productivity).

Instead, the findings in this book call policy makers' attention to factors such as innovation, agglomeration and network economies, managerial capabilities and worker skills, global linkages, and financial development, which contribute significantly to increasing the probability of a high-growth episode. For instance, evidence from India shows that the link between innovation and firm-level growth strengthens along the growth distribution of the firm's turnover and operates via an interplay between innovation and accessing foreign markets. Agglomeration and network economies offer learning and specialization opportunities due to greater firm density, which in turn plays an important role in determining the likelihood of being an HGF. For example,

Ethiopian plants located in or close to large urban centers have a greater probability of attaining high-growth status compared with ones located farther away, while in Thailand, firms that are more connected with others via ownership networks are also more likely to experience high growth.

External market linkages—measured by a firm's own exporting status, share of exporters or FDI recipients in a given location or sector, or imports of technology—significantly increase the probability of a high-growth event for firms in India, Hungary, Mexico, and Tunisia. Firms that pay higher wages have a greater likelihood of subsequently attaining high growth, reflecting the key role that human capital plays in firm performance. In particular, the contribution of founding managers and employees (as measured, for example, by experience in the formal sector, in a larger firm, and in management) is found to be critical in determining future firm growth in Brazil. Finally, the likelihood of attaining high growth also depends on firms' ability to access finance, although given the large number of other potential distortions in the business environment, the link can be robustly identified only in countries with well-developed financial markets.

## New Directions for Policies to Support Firm Growth

The search for the "right" firms to target is not new. However, the evidence presented in this book shows that most public initiatives to identify and target HGFs are likely to be misguided—buttressed by findings on the venture capital industry that show that even in the hands of professional investors, success is most often random and most projects lose money.

Existing efforts to support HGFs—identified through a review of 54 interventions in 14 developing countries—are constrained by weak empirical foundations, poorly articulated logical frameworks, and largely absent monitoring and evaluation systems (including impact evaluations and cost-benefit analyses). Evidence also shows that it is difficult to consistently identify high-potential firms before or at early stages of a high-growth episode: the strike rate of predicting success for any set of methodologies, including scoring by judges, predictive models, and machine learning approaches, is between 2 and 12 percent. And the few characteristics that have some explanatory power in predicting high growth, for example, age, gender, and IQ scores, can lead to investment strategies that select the already better-off beneficiaries and may widen rather than reduce existing inequities.

This book's findings therefore suggest an important reorientation of policies to support firm growth from searching for high-potential firms toward the ABCs of growth entrepreneurship: improving Allocative efficiency, encouraging Business-to-business spillovers, and strengthening firm Capabilities. A large body of existing literature shows that interventions aimed at supporting these ABCs are positively correlated with furthering desirable outcomes such as firm productivity, whereas the evidence presented in this book shows that they are also associated with a greater likelihood of a high-growth episode. Rather than searching for the next unicorn, policy makers wishing to reap the benefits of high firm growth may find greater returns in policies that support and encourage good practices, such as healthy firm entry, exit, and resource reallocation; improved access to finance and flexible labor markets; better flows of knowledge across firms through tighter linkages to external markets, denser networks, and agglomeration; and stronger firm capabilities, including innovation, managerial, and entrepreneurship skills.

In order to improve *allocative efficiency*, policy makers may wish to structure the issue in terms of the standard productivity decomposition approaches, which consider the three margins of entry, exit, and reallocation. Policies along the *entry* margin seek to improve allocative efficiency by making it easier for new, potentially more productive firms to enter the market. Conversely, policies along the *exit* margin seek to ensure that less productive firms release their resources for more efficient use. Finally, policies along the *reallocation* margin seek to improve the ability of existing firms to access resources through more flexible factor and product market policies. For example, flexible labor market policies that facilitate the ability of employees to bring their experience from one firm to the next, as well as further steps in the financial reform agenda, can have important positive implications for the ability of more efficient firms to grow.

To facilitate *B2B spillovers* through positive agglomeration economies, spatial policies can encourage more efficient land use, while transport policies can improve connectivity and reduce input costs—although agglomeration gains in some locations may come at the expense of displacement in others. Similarly, policies to attract high-quality FDI and connect firms to export markets can encourage learning and quality upgrading, leading to a greater likelihood of high firm growth. Direct instruments to facilitate knowledge spillovers—such as science and technology parks, clusters, and network initiatives—can also enhance the benefits of such connections for firm growth.

Policies to strengthen *firm capabilities* help firms innovate (which in the majority of developing-country firms occurs in the absence of formal research and development), improve managerial practices and access to technology, and acquire soft skills that are being increasingly recognized as critical to firm success. Governments can utilize a range of instruments to resolve market and coordination failures that may prevent firms from making these investments. *Financial incentives* include direct instruments, such as vouchers, grants and matching grants, equity financing, and public procurement, and indirect interventions, such as fiscal incentives and loan guarantees. *Inducement instruments and recognition awards*, for example, prize competitions, are nonmarket mechanisms to encourage efforts by firms and entrepreneurs to address specific challenges. Government can offer various kinds of *extension advisory services* to strengthen firms' use of technology or to provide advice on business issues, including the well-known examples of the Manufacturing Extension Partnership in the United States,

Fraunhofer Institutes and Steinbeis Centers in Germany, Japan's Kohsetsushi Centers and Productivity Centers, and SPRING and A*STAR agencies in Singapore. Finally, *incubators* and *accelerators* provide access to physical space, advisory services, mentorship, and perhaps access to finance at an early stage of a firm's life cycle.

Given the wide menu and complexity of the available instruments, a key factor determining success is the ability to match the instruments with the needs of firms and the ability of public institutions to deliver these programs. In the first volume of the World Bank Productivity Project, Cirera and Maloney (2017) develop the concept of the "capabilities escalator," which helps match policy challenges with firm and institutional capabilities, and provide some examples of practical applications of such an approach.

In addition, three crosscutting themes are a necessary condition to the success of the ABCs of policy interventions. First, given the critical importance of accurately measuring productivity and other variables that matter for policy choices, this book is also a call for improving the quality and accessibility of firm-level data to enable evidence-based decision making in developing countries. Second, there is an urgent need to radically expand the use of rigorous evaluations of policy interventions. Despite the large number of initiatives underway to support firm growth, very few programs—whether in developing countries or advanced economies—have undergone rigorous impact evaluations or cost-benefit analyses. Embedding impact evaluations into program design and implementation is critical to ensuring that public resources achieve the desired outcomes efficiently and effectively. Third, institutional capabilities to implement policies need to be strengthened. In line with the "capabilities escalator" approach, countries and agencies should gradually build their institutional capabilities to match the ambition of policy instruments, which are currently often taken from high-income countries without adaptation to local context. Ensuring that the relevant institutions have the necessary human and financial resources and the right mandate, and communicate effectively in implementing the ABCs of growth entrepreneurship, will be critical to the success of the new generation of policies to support firm growth.

## Note

1. "Productivity isn't everything, but in the long run it is almost everything" (Krugman 1994, 11).

## References

Cirera, X., and W. F. Maloney. 2017. *The Innovation Paradox: Developing-Country Capabilities and the Unrealized Promise of Technological Catch-Up.* Washington, DC: World Bank.

Cusolito, A. P., and W. F. Maloney. 2018. *Productivity Revisited: Shifting Paradigms in Analysis and Policy.* Washington, DC: World Bank.

Hsieh, C.-T., and P. J. Klenow. 2009. "Misallocation and Manufacturing TFP in China and India." *Quarterly Journal of Economics* 124 (4): 1403–48.

Krugman, P. 1994. *The Age of Diminished Expectations.* Cambridge, MA: MIT Press.

# 1. The Appeal of High Growth

High-growth firms (HGFs) are the dynamic core of an economy, set apart by their disproportionate ability to generate output and create jobs. Evidence for high-income countries shows that these firms form a small share of the total number of businesses—often less than 10 percent—but account for more than half of the entire change in employment and output. This chapter establishes the foundation for the overall book by quantifying the contribution of HGFs to growth in developing countries, starting with definitions of high growth and its incidence, and moving on to the importance of HGFs in generating jobs and output and creating spillovers to non-HGFs.

Just as in high-income countries, the chapter's findings confirm that HGFs—whether defined by absolute growth thresholds or relative top performers, and whether using employment or revenue as the main variable of interest—are a small group in emerging market economies. For the 11 developing countries covered by this book, the share of HGFs according to one of the most common definitions (from the Organisation for Economic Co-operation and Development [OECD]) varies between 3 and 20 percent, similar to the range observed in high-income countries. But the diversity in size, growth, and overall level of development across these economies is well above that of the group of high-income countries, suggesting that HGF incidence may be more akin to a statistical regularity in the distribution of firm growth rates rather than a function of per capita incomes, sectoral growth rates, or measures of market concentration.

Although their share in the overall firm count is small, it is difficult to overstate the importance of this group of firms to economic performance. More than half of all new jobs and sales in the economies studied in this book are created by HGFs.[1] In fact, in nearly all cases, net employment and output growth would have been negative without the positive contribution of these firms (that is, the non-HGFs destroy more jobs than they create and decline rather than grow in terms of sales). Although the group of firms making these disproportionate contributions to employment and to sales are usually not the same (correlation coefficients between the two sets are 0.4 or lower), to paraphrase Paul Krugman's famous quote, high growth is nearly everything when it comes to determining an economy's overall performance.[2]

In addition to their disproportionate contribution to job and output creation, HGFs are capable of generating significant spillovers that benefit other firms. The evidence for horizontal (same sector) spillovers is mixed since HGFs may transfer knowledge and create networks but may also raise competition and push down prices. The evidence for vertical spillovers—benefits from being a buyer from or a supplier to an HGF—is stronger. These extraordinary abilities of HGFs are what make them an interesting subject for academics and an attractive target for policy makers keen to boost economic performance.

## Definitions

HGF definitions could fill a small zoo with real and fantastical creatures. Birch (1981) defines a "gazelle" (or HGF) as a firm that has at least US$100,000 (roughly US$250,000 today) in annual revenues and sustains 20 percent annual revenue growth over a four-year period. SBA Office of Advocacy (2008) differentiates between mice (small firms with fewer than 20 employees), elephants (large firms with more than 500 employees), and gazelles by using employment as an indicator for growth. Nightingale and Coad (2014) introduce "muppets" to contrast with gazelles, and Ferrantino et al. (2012) discussed "gazillas"—large firms that continue growing rapidly and make a large contribution to employment growth. There are also "stars" (Ayyagari, Demirgüç-Kunt, and Maksimovic 2018; Furman and Orszag 2018) and "superstars" (Autor et al. 2017; World Bank 2019), defined as firms in the top tier of the distribution of returns on invested capital, productivity, and market share. Finally, Lee (2013) defines "unicorns" as privately held start-up companies valued at more than US$1 billion.

The various definitions of HGFs can be broadly grouped into three sets:

- The *absolute* definitions, such as Birch (1981) and the often-used OECD definition, set a minimum rate and duration of growth. According to the *OECD-Eurostat Manual on Business Demography Statistics* (2007), an HGF is a firm that (1) initially possesses 10 or more employees or that has at least four times national per capita income in annual revenues, and (2) experiences average annualized employment or revenue growth of greater than 20 percent over a three-year period.
- The *relative* definitions classify HGFs as those in the top percentiles of firms in the distribution of employment or revenue growth (Haltiwanger et al. 2017) or top percentiles of firms in the distribution of the Birch index (United Kingdom, Department of Business Innovation and Skills 2014).[3]
- The *distributional* definitions are based on specific properties of the distribution of firm growth, most often attempting to identify a threshold at which the right tail of the (usually Laplace) distribution of firm growth rates converts to a power law distribution (Halvarsson 2013). They combine certain features of absolute and relative definitions but are computationally intensive to implement.

This book studies HGFs using high-quality longitudinal data sets in Brazil, Côte d'Ivoire, Ethiopia, Hungary, India, Indonesia, Mexico, South Africa, Thailand, Tunisia, and Turkey. The selection of countries reflects in large part data availability since tracking down HGFs requires wide national coverage and the ability to follow firms over time, whereas panel surveys of firms in developing countries remain rare and accessing the existing ones is often a challenge. Even so, the data sets used here cover all six World Bank regions as well as diverse income levels and very different growth performances (figure ES.1).

To study HGFs in these countries, this book uses both definitions of high growth: absolute (OECD) and relative (firms above the 90th percentile of the Birch index of employment and sales growth).[4] The advantages of the absolute definition are that it is simple, easy to apply, and ensures that the set of HGFs in one country is similar (at least in terms of growth rates) to the set of HGFs in another. The disadvantages are that the growth threshold is arbitrary and that in some cases (for example, during economic downturns or in smaller surveys) there may be too few, or no HGFs because the right tail of the firm growth distribution thins rapidly. Moreover, using the rate of growth (as in the OECD definition) biases the sample of HGFs toward smaller firms that, even as a group, may contribute little to economywide job creation but can achieve rapid growth by adding just a few employees. To maximize cross-country comparability and minimize the variation in including micro firms, this book (as in the OECD definition) imposes a minimum size threshold of 10 employees for all countries (including the United States), except in Côte d'Ivoire (where the cutoff is five employees), and Indonesia and Turkey (where the data are collected only for enterprises with more than 20 employees).[5]

For the absolute high-growth indicator based on sales, this book similarly limits observations to firms with 10 or more employees, rather than introducing yet another (sales-based) threshold. However, there are two countries, India and Thailand, for which no employment data are available. The case of India is simpler because the data set is a sample of firms that are listed on the stock exchange and, by definition, these are relatively large firms. In the case of Thailand, where the data set is composed of all registered firms, including some micro firms, this book uses an estimated cutoff that approximates a distribution of firms with 10 or more employees.[6]

When comparing employment-based with revenue-based HGFs, studies for different countries reach varying conclusions: the two sets identify similar firms in the United States (Haltiwanger et al. 2017) but substantially different ones in the United Kingdom (Du and Temouri 2015). Between the two options, this book emphasizes employment-based definitions of high growth because creating good-quality jobs is a major pathway for reducing poverty and boosting shared prosperity. Thailand and India are two exceptions, where the book relies exclusively on a revenue-based definition because employment information is not available in the data sets used here (annex 1A provides details on the data sets). Where relevant, the book also notes when using revenue-based definitions leads to important changes in findings.

Unlike absolute definitions, relative concepts of HGFs ensure more balanced coverage across countries. And the Birch index favors larger firms, so the HGFs are more likely to have a significant impact on job creation. Nonetheless, the average growth rate of HGFs in one country may differ substantially from that of HGFs in another, and in some cases HGFs may grow very little if at all (for example, if all firms are contracting, then a relative definition will assign HGF status to those firms that contracted the least).

In summary, the definitions of HGFs used in this book are as follows:

1. *OECD*. HGFs are firms that employ more than 10 workers (including owners but excluding unpaid workers) and whose employment grows at an average annual rate of 20 percent or more over a period of three consecutive years.[7] As a further robustness check, a variant of this definition imposes an additional restriction that employment growth must be positive in each of the three years.
2. *Birch*. HGFs are firms that employ more than 10 workers (including owners but excluding unpaid workers) and whose employment growth places them above the 90th percentile of the Birch index of all firms in the economy, with the index defined over a period of three consecutive years.[8] As a further robustness check, a variant of this definition imposes an additional restriction that employment growth must be positive in each of the three years.

## Incidence

Regardless of the specifics, all HGF definitions seek to identify firms that are high performers and are "sufficiently" far apart from the average or median firm. As such, it is perhaps not surprising that there is enough commonality across definitions and studies, at least when it comes to the incidence of high growth. For example, Bravo-Biosca, Criscuolo, and Menon (2016), following the OECD definition, show that the share of HGFs in 10 high-income economies varies between 3 percent in Austria and Norway to some 6 percent in Spain, the United Kingdom, and the United States. Other studies establish a similar if somewhat broader range: HGF incidence has been documented to vary from less than 2 percent in Austria, Germany, Italy, the Netherlands, Norway, and Poland (Goedhuys and Sleuwaegen 2010) to 5 percent in Finland (Deschryvere 2008), 6 percent in Sweden (Daunfeldt et al. 2013) and the United Kingdom (Anyadike-Danes et al. 2009), up to 10 percent in the Republic of Korea, and between 5 and 15 percent in the United States (Choi et al. 2017; Decker et al. 2014).[9] Using a variation of the OECD definition that requires annual growth of 20 percent per year or more and a minimum threshold of 15 employees, Hoffmann and Junge (2006) and Petersen and Ahmad (2007) find that HGFs account for 5–6 percent of all firms across 17 high-income countries. Interestingly, the few available studies on developing countries also suggest a similar range; for example, a study of 11 African nations using the World Bank's Enterprise Surveys finds that the HGF incidence for these economies is about 6 percent (Goedhuys and Sleuwaegen 2010).

Figure 1.1 plots the incidence of HGFs across the 11 country data sets analyzed in this book and benchmarks the results against the United States. For each country and

## FIGURE 1.1 Incidence of High Growth

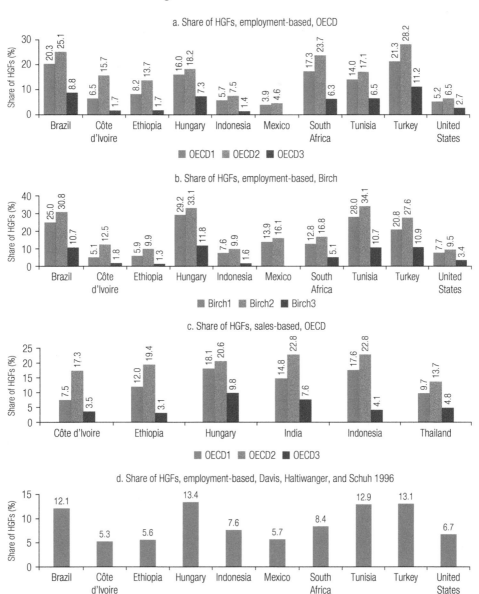

a. Share of HGFs, employment-based, OECD

b. Share of HGFs, employment-based, Birch

c. Share of HGFs, sales-based, OECD

d. Share of HGFs, employment-based, Davis, Haltiwanger, and Schuh 1996

*Source:* Elaboration using national survey and census data.

*Note:* OECD1 and Birch1 incidence are calculated as the number of high-growth firms (HGFs) in time $t$ (based on either definition) divided by the total number of firms with nonzero employment in time $t$. OECD2 and Birch2 are calculated as the number of HGFs in time $t$ (based on either definition) divided by the total number of firms with nonzero employment in time $t$ and $t$–3 (only firms that are three years of age or older are included in the numerator and denominator). OECD3 or Birch 3 are calculated as OECD1 or Birch1, with the additional requirement that a firm can be classified as HGF only if it registers positive employment or sales growth in t, $t$–1, and

$t$–2. The Davis, Haltiwanger, and Schuh (1996) approach calculates growth rates as $g_{i,t} = \dfrac{L_{i,t} - L_{i,t-3}}{\left(L_{i,t} + L_{i,t-3}\right)/2}$, $g_{i,t} \in [-2,2]$. Firms that

employ more than 10 workers (including owners but excluding unpaid workers) are ranked by values of $g_{i,t}$ from smallest to largest, and those with values of $g_{i,t}$ above the 90th percentile are classified as HGF (that is, $HGF_{i,t} = 1$ if $g_{i,t} > P^{90}(g_t)$). In each panel, incidence is calculated for each year and then an unweighted average is computed over the entire sample period. See annex 1A for more details. OECD = Organisation for Economic Co-operation and Development.

definition, the figure shows three sets of columns: the first column, labeled OECD1 (panels a and c) or Birch1 (panel b), divides the number of HGFs by the total number of firms in a given year (more precisely, it divides the number of firms that experienced a high-growth episode between periods $t–3$ and $t$ by the number of firms that are observed in period $t$). This is perhaps the most intuitive measure, although it is clearly biased downward because it includes all firms that started in periods $t–2$, $t–1$, and $t$ in the denominator but not in the numerator.[10] The second column, labeled OECD2 or Birch2, corrects for this bias by limiting the denominator to firms that entered the market in $t–3$ or earlier, ensuring that a three-year growth rate can be calculated for each firm in the sample. For example, for a three-year window from 2015 to 2018, this metric would cover only firms that have nonzero employment in both the starting and ending year. The final column, labeled OECD3 or Birch3, imposes an additional requirement that firms must register a nonnegative growth rate in each year during the three-year period and divides this number by all firms operating in the current period (that is, uses the same denominator as OECD1 or Birch1). For each country, the shares in each column are averaged over the entire period for which data are available in order to minimize the impact of business cycles. However, similar results are obtained if averages are calculated for a common period of 2005–08, which covers most of the data sets analyzed for this book.[11]

Several insights emerge from figure 1.1. First, there is relatively limited variation in the share of HGFs across countries, particularly when taking into account the wide range of income levels and country characteristics of the economies considered. Indeed, the incidence of HGFs observed in developing economies is within the range reported in the literature for high-income countries.[12] Second, there is no obvious relationship between a country's level of development (measured by per capita income) and the incidence of high growth (see also the discussion later in this section). Third, firm entry and exit play a large role in most countries; using the OECD2 or the Birch2 variant, which does not consider recent entrants, substantially increases the incidence, and in one case, Côte d'Ivoire, more than doubles it. However, as shown in panel d, which plots the Davis, Haltiwanger, and Schuh (1996) growth rates that capture the entry and exit margins, the first two points remain valid regardless of how one accounts for the impact of entry and exit. Fourth, firm growth is highly volatile. Limiting the definition of HGFs to only firms that do not experience negative growth during the three-year window brings down the incidence by half or more, suggesting that most HGFs attain the threshold through a high-growth event in just one year, or at most two years.[13] The patterns are similar regardless of whether one uses the absolute (OECD) or relative (Birch) definitions of high growth, although the incidence calculated with the Birch definition is generally lower because the metric is biased toward larger firms.[14] Fifth, similar to high-income countries, sales-based incidence is well above employment-based incidence, suggesting that most firms find it easier to increase sales than raise employment.[15]

How similar are the sets of firms captured by various definitions of high growth? Studies usually find low correlation between the set of HGFs captured by indicators based on absolute versus relative growth in variables such as sales, employees, profit, productivity, equity, assets, and so on. For example, using data on all firms registered in Sweden between 1994 and 1998, Shepherd and Wiklund (2009) find that some pairs of growth measures were highly correlated (for example, the growth of sales and of employees, defined in absolute terms), whereas others were not (for example, the growth of sales and of assets, defined in relative terms). Another analysis of Swedish data by Daunfeldt et al. (2013)—defining HGFs as the top 1 percent of the fastest growing firms—found that firms selected on the basis of employment growth were inversely correlated with those selected on productivity growth. In South Africa, Mamburu (2017) shows that the correlation coefficients between the samples generated by 10 alternative definitions of HGFs—based on growth in employment, revenue, or both—were generally in the 0.1–0.3 range. Similarly, using firm-level data from Vietnam, Moldova, and Morocco, Aterido and Hallward-Driemeier (2018) also find that the overlap across firms selected using 18 different definitions of high performance is at most 25 percent, and often a lot smaller than that.

In the country data sets analyzed for this book, the exact definitions of high growth (for example, OECD versus Birch) appear to be less important than the choice of the underlying metric (employment versus sales). This is illustrated in table 1.1, which shows the correlations across alternative definitions of HGFs for a select set of diverse countries. In all instances, the correlation across definitions for the same set of metrics (employment or sales) is much higher than the correlation across metrics.

Although the results in figure 1.1 hint at a lack of relationship between a country's level of development and its HGF incidence, it is difficult to formally test this hypothesis with only 11 countries studied in this book, plus the United States, which is included in the figure as a benchmark. As an alternative, this book uses the HGF incidence observed in the World Bank's Enterprise Surveys (WBES) to explore the relationship between the share of HGFs and per capita income (HGF shares tend to be highly correlated across national data sets and the WBES; see box 1.1 for a more detailed discussion). Figure 1.2 plots the results for all developing countries, as well as showing them separately by income groups. In all cases, there is no clear relationship between the incidence of HGFs and a country's level of development.

This finding may come as a surprise (for example, for policy makers who may wish to target the HGF share of some benchmark country), but it underscores a broader point of the potential false equivalence between greater incidence of high growth and healthy firm dynamics. Consider an example of two firms in different countries receiving a positive demand shock. One firm, operating in a relatively distortion-free environment, can instantly scale its operations and hire more workers to meet new demand; in the data, this firm will show at most one year of rapid employment growth. The second firm, operating under significant factor and input market constraints, can add

**TABLE 1.1  Correlations across HGF Definitions**
*(partial correlation coefficients)*

| | HGF Definition | | | |
|---|---|---|---|---|
| | **OECD employment** | **OECD sales** | **Birch employment** | **Birch sales** |
| *Côte d'Ivoire* | | | | |
| OECD employment | 1 | | | |
| OECD sales | 0.240 | 1 | | |
| Birch employment | 0.441 | 0.142 | 1 | |
| Birch sales | 0.120 | 0.350 | 0.293 | 1 |
| *Ethiopia* | | | | |
| OECD employment | 1 | | | |
| OECD sales | 0.215 | 1 | | |
| Birch employment | 0.539 | 0.133 | 1 | |
| Birch sales | 0.146 | 0.461 | 0.218 | 1 |
| *Indonesia* | | | | |
| OECD employment | 1 | | | |
| OECD sales | 0.227 | 1 | | |
| Birch employment | 0.641 | 0.187 | 1 | |
| Birch sales | 0.203 | 0.478 | 0.281 | 1 |
| *Hungary* | | | | |
| OECD employment | 1 | | | |
| OECD sales | 0.484 | 1 | | |
| Birch employment | 0.651 | 0.398 | 1 | |
| Birch sales | 0.318 | 0.576 | 0.409 | 1 |

*Source:* Elaboration using national survey and census data.
*Note:* HGF = high-growth firm; OECD = Organisation for Economic Co-operation and Development.

workers only slowly over time (growing from, say, 10 employees in year $t$ to 12 workers in year $t+1$, from 12 to 15 in year $t+2$, and from 15 to 20 in year $t+3$). This firm will be recorded in the data as HGF, even though it is clearly not operating as efficiently as the first. Hence, it is possible that some rates of high growth over prolonged periods capture difficulties in adjusting to optimum scale and may therefore be reflective of resource misallocation rather than efficient dynamics.

If per capita incomes do not drive the variation in HGF incidence, it may be the case that sectoral variables play a role. For example, increased market concentration may be associated with greater HGF incidence if it is indicative of "up-or-out" dynamics in which unsuccessful firms exit or are bought out by more successful competitors who absorb the labor and capital released by exiting firms. By comparison, high rates of entry and entrepreneurship (for example, due to a good business environment) may simultaneously lead to a decline in market concentration and an

## National Firm Data versus Enterprise Surveys

Most of the data sets used in this book are drawn from national surveys and census data, gaining in the depth of country coverage at the expense of cross-country comparability afforded by instruments such as the World Bank's Enterprise Surveys (WBES). To test the comparability of the two sources, figure B1.1.1 plots the incidence of high-growth firms (HGFs) in the national surveys and census data against the incidence calculated using the WBES.[a] The solid green line in the figure is a 45-degree line: when a point appears below the line, it means that high-growth incidence in national surveys is lower than in the WBES.

**FIGURE B1.1.1    HGF Incidence in National Data Sets and Enterprise Surveys**

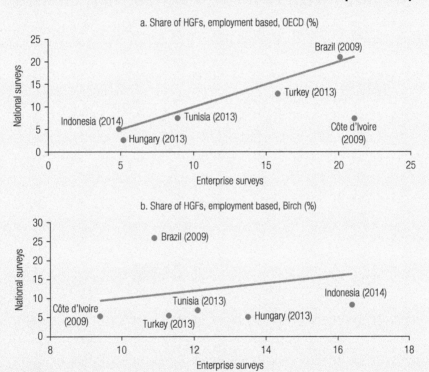

*Source:* Elaboration using WBES and national survey and census data.

*Note:* The figure uses OECD1 and Birch1 measures of high-growth firm (HGF) incidence (see the note to figure 1.1). For both national surveys and enterprise surveys, firms are excluded in all years in which they have fewer than 10 employees. OECD = Organisation for Economic Co-operation and Development.

The results suggest that HGF incidence is highly correlated across the two data sources when using the OECD definition (correlation coefficient 0.71) and somewhat correlated when using the Birch definition (excluding Brazil, the correlation coefficient is 0.73). Moreover, in most cases the share calculated using the WBES is higher than when using national-level data sets—and much more so for the Birch definition of HGFs (with the exception of Brazil). This may be because the WBES primarily target larger, registered firms, and as a result, may oversample HGFs with more than 10 employees (at least for the countries shown in the figure).

a. Table 1A.3 in annex 1A provides the relevant firm counts for the two data sources.

## FIGURE 1.2  HGF Incidence and Per Capita Income

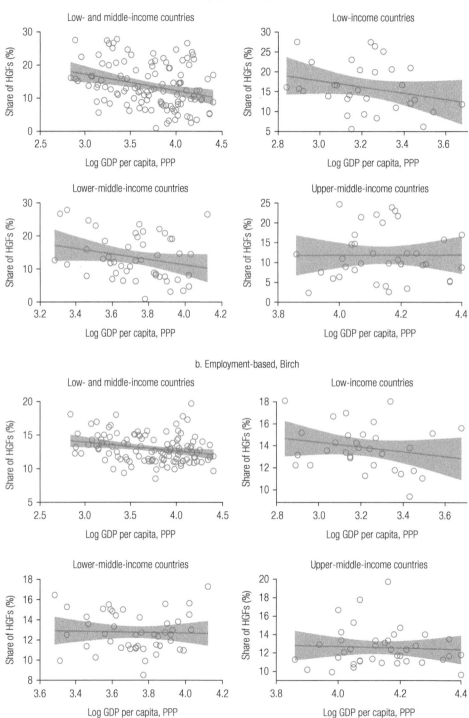

a. Employment-based, OECD

Low- and middle-income countries

Low-income countries

Lower-middle-income countries

Upper-middle-income countries

b. Employment-based, Birch

Low- and middle-income countries

Low-income countries

Lower-middle-income countries

Upper-middle-income countries

*Source:* Elaboration using World Bank Enterprise Survey data.

*Note:* HGF = high-growth firm; OECD = Organisation for Economic Co-operation and Development; PPP = purchasing power parity.

increase in the share of HGFs. Another channel for increased incidence of HGFs could be the variation in sectoral rates of growth; to the extent that HGF prevalence varies substantially across sectors (see the discussion in the following chapter), heterogeneity in sectoral composition and growth rates may drive overall differences in the share of HGFs across countries.

Empirical support for these channels in the countries analyzed for this book is, at best, limited. Estimates using employment data in Brazil, Côte d'Ivoire, Ethiopia, and Indonesia, and sales in India, show that higher industry concentration is generally positively associated with HGF incidence—except in Côte d'Ivoire and Brazil, where the relationship is negative (figure 1.3; all regressions include industry and year fixed effects so that the estimates are driven by changes in concentration across sectors rather than the initial values). Sectoral growth patterns also do not appear to have a significant association with HGF shares, except in Indonesia where the relationship is strongly positive.[16]

### FIGURE 1.3 HGF Incidence and Industry Concentration or Growth

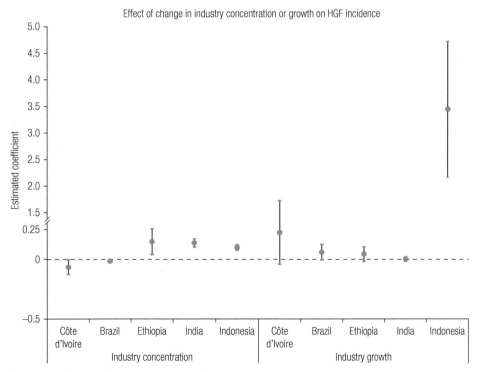

*Source:* Elaboration using national survey and census data.

*Note:* The figure is a rope-ladder representation of estimated coefficients and 95 percent confidence bands from regressions of high-growth firm (HGF) incidence (OECD, employment-based except for India where it is sales-based) on variables on the X-axis. Industry concentration is measured with normalized Herfindahl indexes. Regressions are estimated separately for each country at a 4-digit industry level, using national data sets (see annex 1A for data details). All regressions are estimated by ordinary least squares and include industry and year fixed effects. Results are robust to including both types of sectoral characteristics in the same model as well as their interactions. OECD = Organisation for Economic Co-operation and Development.

## Job and Output Creation: The "80/20" Rule

The academic and policy interest in HGFs stems primarily from their disproportionate contribution to job and output creation. In the United Kingdom, 6 percent of all firms with 10 or more employees created 54 percent of jobs between 2005 and 2008 (Anyadike-Danes et al. 2009).[17] Likewise, in Sweden, 6 percent of the firms created 42 percent of jobs over the same period (Daunfeldt et al. 2013),[18] while in Finland fewer than 5 percent of firms created 90 percent of jobs during 2003–06 (Deschryvere 2008). Defining HGFs as the set of firms expanding their employment by more than 25 percent per year, Decker et al. (2014) find that in the United States, HGFs constitute 10–15 percent of firms but create 50–60 percent of output and jobs (Decker et al. 2014; Haltiwanger et al. 2017).[19] Similar estimates on job gains for Canada (Quebec), France, Italy, the Netherlands, and Spain were produced by Schreyer (2000), although exact definitions of HGFs in this particular study varied by country.[20] For example, HGFs account for more than 50 percent of job creation in France, nearly 65 percent in the Netherlands and close to 90 percent in Spain. When it comes to output growth, Daunfeldt, Elert, and Johansson (2014) find that HGFs always contribute positively to sales growth in Sweden.

In quantifying the role of HGFs in job and output growth, it is important to distinguish between gross and net contributions (in the previous paragraph, Anyadike-Danes et al. (2009), Daunfeldt et al. (2013), and Deschryvere (2008) report net numbers, whereas Decker et al. (2014) and Schreyer (2000) report gross figures).[21] The gross contribution considers only firms that have added jobs or increased output during a (three-year) period and calculates the share of HGFs in total jobs or output created. By construction, this metric ranges between 0 and 100 percent and gives a sense of which firms create new jobs or sales in the economy. The net contribution is the difference between gross job or output creation and gross job or output destruction during the period. This concept gives a complete picture of changes in employment or sales over a given period but can be more difficult to interpret. When using absolute definitions of high growth such as the OECD's, HGFs by default only create jobs but do not destroy them—whereas other firms may either expand or contract. As a result, the net contribution of HGFs can be greater than 100 percent (if HGFs create 100,000 jobs and the rest of the firms destroy 50,000, for example) or even negative (if HGFs again create 100,000 jobs but the rest of the firms destroy 500,000). And with relative definitions of high growth, all firms could hypothetically destroy jobs, but HGFs could still make a positive net contribution.[22]

Figure 1.4 (panel a) shows the gross and net contributions of HGFs (OECD definition) to employment growth, focusing as before on firms with 10 or more workers in manufacturing and services sectors. In Côte d'Ivoire, Ethiopia, and Indonesia, HGFs make up less than 10 percent of the firm count, and yet they create more than one-half of all new jobs. In Hungary, HGFs account for 16 percent of firms but

## FIGURE 1.4 HGFs Contribute Disproportionately to Employment Growth

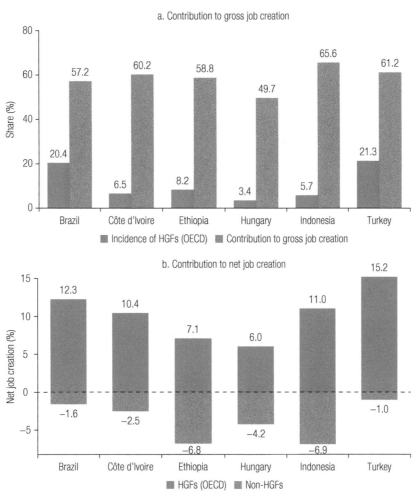

a. Contribution to gross job creation

b. Contribution to net job creation

*Source:* Elaboration using national survey and census data.

*Note:* High-growth firms (HGFs) are defined using employment-based metrics. HGF incidence is defined as OECD1 (see the note to figure 1.1). Contributions are calculated for each year and then an unweighted average is computed over the entire sample period. OECD = Organisation for Economic Co-operation and Development.

contribute to nearly half of gross job creation. In Brazil and Turkey, they represent about 20 percent of firm population and yet generate nearly 60 percent of new jobs. Moreover, panel b of figure 1.4 shows that, in all countries, firms other than HGFs experienced a net decline in employment, so that the only net jobs generated were those created by the HGFs.

Similar conclusions hold across firm cohorts and industries, as shown by data from Brazil and Mexico. Young Mexican non-HGFs experienced a decline in net employment across a range of cohorts and manufacturing industries, meaning that all job

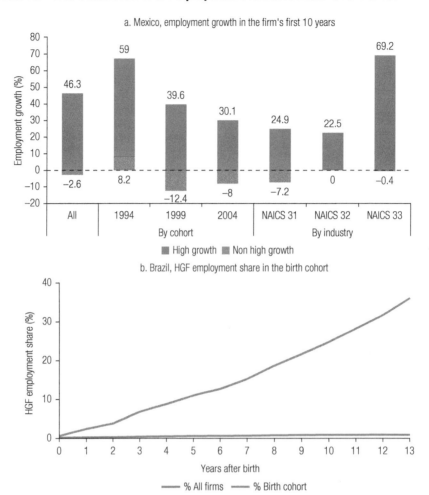

**FIGURE 1.5  HGF Contributions to Employment Growth in Brazil and Mexico**

a. Mexico, employment growth in the firm's first 10 years

b. Brazil, HGF employment share in the birth cohort

*Source:* Sanchez Bayardo and Iacovone (2018) for panel a; Bastos and Silva (2018) for panel b.

*Note:* NAICS code 31 includes food manufacturing, beverages and tobacco products, textile, apparel and leather and allied product manufacturing; NAICS code 32 includes wood, paper, printing, petroleum and coal, chemicals, plastics and rubber, non-metallic mineral products; NAICS code 33 includes primary metal manufacturing, fabricated metals, machinery, computer and electronics, electrical equipment, transport equipment, furniture and other manufacturing not included elsewhere. Together NAICS codes 31–33 constitute all manufacturing activities. HGF = high-growth firm; NAICS = North American Industry Classification System.

creation by young firms in manufacturing was done by HGFs (figure 1.5, panel a). In Brazil, HGFs and non-HGFs enter the market at approximately the same size, which means that at birth, future HGFs make up just 0.6 percent of employment of their birth cohort (figure 1.5, panel b). However, because of their rapid growth—and exit of some of the less dynamic firms—the share of HGFs in total cohort employment rises to more than 36 percent 13 years later.

Just as with employment, HGFs also make a disproportionate contribution to output growth. Using the OECD definition with sales-based metrics, figure 1.6 shows

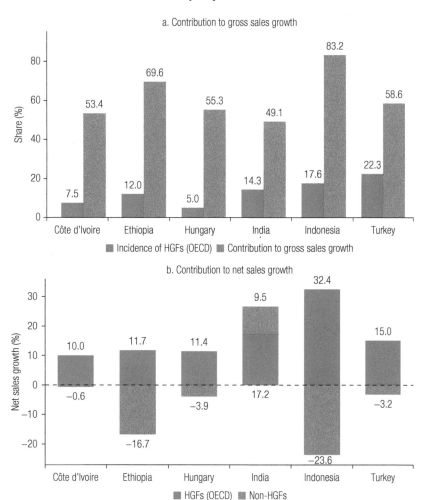

**FIGURE 1.6  HGFs Account for the Majority of Growth in Sales**

a. Contribution to gross sales growth

■ Incidence of HGFs (OECD)  ■ Contribution to gross sales growth

b. Contribution to net sales growth

■ HGFs (OECD)  ■ Non-HGFs

*Source:* Elaboration using national survey and census data.

*Note:* High-growth firms (HGFs) are defined using sales-based metrics. HGF incidence is defined as OECD1 (see the note to figure 1.1). Contributions are calculated for each year and then an unweighted average is computed over the entire sample period. OECD = Organisation for Economic Co-operation and Development.

that HGFs account for some 8–22 percent of the total number of firms in Côte d'Ivoire, Ethiopia, Hungary, India, Indonesia, and Turkey but contribute between 49 and 83 percent of the total change in output. And in five of the six cases—Côte d'Ivoire, Ethiopia, Hungary, Indonesia, and Turkey—HGFs are the only positive contributors to growth in output, with the rest of the firms in the economy experiencing a decline in sales.[23] Although that is not the case in India (perhaps because the data set is composed of the more successful and large firms that are registered on the stock exchange), HGFs there still account for nearly two-thirds of the net change in output.

## Linkages and Spillovers

Beyond the boundaries of the firm itself, HGFs have been documented to bring wider economic and social benefits, including facilitating the growth of other firms in the same locality (Mason, Bishop, and Robinson 2009) and particularly in industrial clusters (Stam et al. 2009; Brown 2011). Evidence from 43 industries in the Netherlands over 12 years shows that a higher ratio of HGFs in a particular sector has a positive impact on subsequent industry growth (Bos and Stam 2014). Their "pull factor" facilitates the convergence of less productive firms to the national frontier (Bartelsman, Haskel, and Martin 2008) and, when markets for production inputs are competitive, HGFs are able to increase overall efficiency by attracting resources away from less productive firms (Haltiwanger et al. 2017).

A large body of literature has studied the spillover effect from the entry of multinational enterprises (MNEs) (for surveys of this literature, see Görg and Strobl 2001; Görg and Greenaway 2004; Crespo and Fontoura 2007; Meyer and Sinani 2009; Havranek and Irsova 2011).[24] A key distinction in this literature is between within industry (horizontal) and across industry (vertical) spillovers, with several specific mechanisms for multinational entry to affect the performance of domestic firms. One such channel is the transfer of soft technologies such as management skills; for example, Javorcik (2004) finds that contacts between partially foreign owned firms and their local suppliers in Lithuania facilitate positive productivity spillovers.[25] Since similar logic and channels may apply to linkages with HGFs, this book follows the FDI literature by differentiating between three types of spillover: horizontal, backward vertical, and forward vertical.

The horizontal spillover (HS) measure for year $t$ is the share of firms that have become HGFs between year $t$ and $t + 3$ in the same industry and region:

$$HS_{jrt} = \frac{\sum_{i \in jr} HGF_{it}}{N_{jrt}}$$

where $N_{jrt}$ is the number of firms in industry $j$ in region $r$ and year $t$.

The forward and backward spillover (FS and BS, respectively) measures show the average share of HGFs in supplier and buyer industries in the region, weighted by the volume of intermediate goods flows across industries:

$$FS_{jrt} = \Sigma_m \alpha_{mj} HS_{jrt} \text{ and } BS_{jrt} = \Sigma_m \alpha_{jm} HS_{jrt}$$

where $\alpha_{mj}$ are the normalized coefficients from the input-output matrix representing (domestic) intermediate goods flows from industry $m$ to $j$. Because industries with many HGFs may also have high FDI shares, confounding HGF spillovers with those from MNEs, this book controls for backward and forward foreign presence by weighting the share of foreign-owned firms by the same weights as that obtained from input-output tables (following Javorcik 2004).

In Hungary, horizontal spillovers from the increased presence of HGFs tend to be either insignificant or negative, suggesting that the competition generated by HGFs may lead to lower revenues and profits for other firms (figure 1.7, panel a).[26] By comparison, vertical spillovers from HGFs tend to be positive and significant (figure 1.7, panel b). A higher share of HGFs in supplier industries (forward spillover) is associated with significantly faster growth in employment and revenue, likely due to improved access to inputs.[27] A higher share of HGFs in buyer industries (backward spillover) is associated with significantly larger increases in wages, productivity, and profitability (return on

**FIGURE 1.7    Buying from or Supplying to HGFs Improves Firm Performance in Hungary**

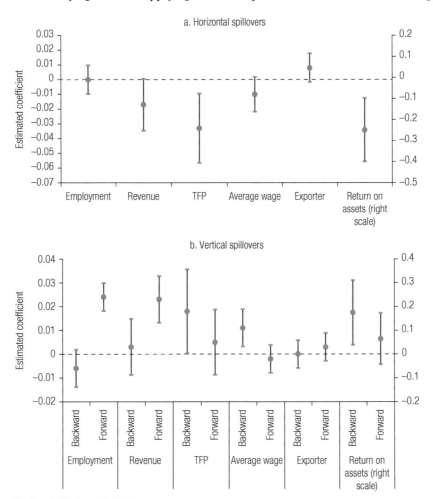

Source: Muraközy, de Nicola, and Tan 2018.

Note: The figures are rope-ladder representations of estimated coefficients and 95 percent confidence bands from a regression of the growth rate in the variables on the X-axis (log differences between years t and t+3) on the value of the horizontal or vertical spillovers in year t. Industry-year, region-year, and firm-level fixed effects are included in each estimate, and the regressions also control for initial total factor productivity (TFP) employment, and exporting status. The sample includes years 2000, 2003, 2006, and 2009, and observations exclude "singletons," that is, when an observation is "dummied out" by the fixed effects. Standard errors are clustered at both the industry-region-year and firm level.

assets), most likely through increases in demand that allow for greater markups. These results are robust to alternative specifications and controlling for growth and foreign share of vertically related industries. This suggests that the role of HGFs is different from that of MNEs: whereas the FDI spillover literature generally finds that backward linkages are more important than forward linkages, the results on Hungary show that firms can benefit from increased HGF presence at both ends of the value chain.

In the case of Turkey, the results are less encouraging.[28] As in Hungary, horizontal spillovers are insignificant or in some cases negative for variables such as sales, employment growth, total factor productivity, and average wages of non-HGFs, whereas forward spillovers of HGFs are positive and significant for employment growth. Unlike Hungary, however, forward spillovers are negative for revenue, whereas backward spillovers are small and insignificant.[29]

## Annex 1A

The data sets used in this book represent the majority of available high-quality, nationally representative longitudinal firm-level data sets in developing countries. They include the Relação Anual de Informações Socials (RAIS) in Brazil, Censo Economico (Industrial Census) in Mexico, Industrial Census in Côte d'Ivoire, Large and Medium Manufacturing Industry Survey (LMMIS) in Ethiopia, the South African Revenue Service and National Treasury Firm-Level Panel (SARSNT), India Human Development Survey (IHDS) and India Prowess firm database compiled by the Centre for Monitoring Indian Economy (CMIE), Thailand Department of Business Development tax return database, Indonesia Annual Manufacturing Survey, Tunisian Repertoire National des Enterprises (RNE), the Hungarian balance sheet and income statement panel collected by the National Tax Authority (NAV), the Annual Industry and Service Statistics (AISS) database by TurkStat, and the Entrepreneur Information System (EIS) by the General Directorate of Productivity at the Ministry of Science, Industry and Technology of Turkey. Table 1A.1 summarizes the main features of each of the data sets.

In Brazil, the Relação Annual de Informações Sociais (RAIS) is a labor census gathering longitudinal data on the universe of formal workers and firms in manufacturing and services sectors during 1994–2014. RAIS contains administrative social security records for employees and employers and is collected by the Ministry of Labor. It provides information on workers' demographics (age, gender, and schooling), job characteristics (occupation, wage, hours worked), as well as hiring and termination dates. It also includes information on a number of firm-level characteristics, notably number of employees, geographical location (municipality), and industry code (according to the 5-digit level of the Brazilian National Classification of Economic Activities). Unique identifiers (tax identification numbers) for workers and firms make it possible to follow them over time. The data also make it possible to separately identify the firm and the establishment. Although the RAIS data cover segments of the public sector, the analysis in this book is restricted to the private sector.

**TABLE 1A.1  Data Sources and Descriptions**

| Country | Period | Source | Source type | Type of firms covered | Firm size threshold | HGF definition metrics | Data coverage |
|---|---|---|---|---|---|---|---|
| Brazil | 1994–2014 | Relação Annual de Informaçoes Sociais (RAIS) | Labor census | Formal workers and firms | – | Employment | Manufacturing and services |
| Côte d'Ivoire | 2003–12 | Confidential registry of enterprises of the modern sector maintained by the National Statistics Institute (Institut National de la Statistique, INS) | Industrial census | Formal sector (all registered firms) | – | Employment and sales | Manufacturing and services |
| Ethiopia | 1996–2009 | Large and Medium Manufacturing Industry Survey (LMMIS) conducted by the Ethiopian Central Statistical Agency (CSA) | Industrial census | Firms that use power-driven machinery | 10 employees or more (in practice a few firms have fewer than 10 workers) | Employment and sales | Manufacturing |
| Hungary | 2000–15 | National Tax Authority (NAV) from corporate income tax statements | Census | All double entry bookkeeping enterprises | – | Employment and sales | Manufacturing and services |
| India | 1990–2013 | India Prowess firm database compiled by the Centre for Monitoring Indian Economy (CMIE) | Other: Publicly listed companies in manufacturing and services | Large, registered firms | Firms that have their annual statements publicly available (usually listed on stock exchange) | Sales | Manufacturing and services |
| Indonesia | 1990–2014 | Indonesia Annual Manufacturing Survey | Survey | Census of formal manufacturing plants | 20 or more employees | Employment and sales | Manufacturing |
| Mexico | 1993, 1998, 2003, 2008, 2013 | Censo Económico (Industrial Census, from the National Statistics Agency, INEGI) | Census (held every five years) | All firms (formal and informal) | – | Employment | Manufacturing |

*(Table continues on the following page.)*

**TABLE 1A.1  Data Sources and Descriptions** (*continued*)

| Country | Period | Source | Source type | Type of firms covered | Firm size threshold | HGF definition metrics | Data coverage |
|---|---|---|---|---|---|---|---|
| South Africa | 2008–15 (but we use only data from 2009 on because 2008 is not reliable) | South African Revenue Service and National Treasury Firm-Level Panel (SARS-NT) | Other: Administrative | Corporate income tax and value-added tax registered entities | — | Employment | Manufacturing and services |
| Thailand | 2004–15 | Department of Business Development tax return database | Census | All new registered firms since 1999 and any surviving registered firms before 1999 | — | Sales | Manufacturing and services |
| Tunisia | 1996–2015 | Repertoire National des Enterprises (RNE) | Census | All registered private firms | — | Employment | Manufacturing and services |
| Turkey | 2006–16 | The Entrepreneur Information System (EIS), provided by the General Directorate of Productivity at the Ministry of Science, Industry and Technology. | Census | Every establishment that employed more than one employee and operated more than a year during the period from 2006 to 2016 | — | Employment | Manufacturing and services |
| Turkey | 2005–14 | Annual Industry and Service Statistics (AISS) by TurkStat | Census | All firms (formal and informal) | 20 or more employees | Employment | All business sectors, except for agriculture and financial sector |
| United States | 1990–2013 | Longitudinal Business Database (LBD) by the U.S. Census Bureau | Census | All non-farm establishments with at least one paid employee | — | Employment | Manufacturing only (services excluded in the analysis for this book) |

In Côte d'Ivoire, the data come from the confidential registry of enterprises of the modern sector maintained by the Institut National de la Statistique (INS). It consists of yearly balance sheets and income statements reported to various government entities, including the tax administration (Direction Générale des Impôts) and the central bank system of West African countries (Banque Centrale des Etats Ouest-Africains) and covers all registered firms in Côte d'Ivoire. In addition to firms' characteristics such as location, year of establishment, legal form, and industry, it encompasses detailed information on revenue, employment, labor and intermediate input costs, and book value of assets. The data comprise 60,558 firm-year observations, corresponding to 24,573 unique firms for the period 2003–12.

In Ethiopia, the data are sourced from the Large and Medium Manufacturing Industries Survey (LMMIS) conducted by the Ethiopian Central Statistical Agency (CSA) on a yearly basis since 1976. Contrary to what the name suggests, the LMMIS is a census of all manufacturing establishments with 10 workers or more that use power-driven machinery. In practice, however, a number of firm-year observations have fewer than 10 workers, for once an establishment has been surveyed, it keeps being part of the census even though its size may shrink below the threshold. In addition to information on location, industry, legal form, and employment, the LMMIS includes relatively detailed balance sheet information regarding assets and inputs use. The sample used in this book is an unbalanced 12-year panel comprising 14,159 firm-year observations for 3,662 unique firms.

In Hungary, the data come from a balance sheet and income statement panel collected by the National Tax Authority (NAV) from corporate income tax statements. This census-type database includes balance sheet and income statement information for all double entry bookkeeping enterprises in Hungary between 2000 and 2014, although for the purposes of the analysis in this book data for agriculture or non-market service sectors are excluded. In addition to the standard balance sheet variables, the database also includes information on the number of employees; 4-digit industry (NACE code) of firms; the region of their headquarters; the share of foreign, private, and state or municipal ownership; as well as the date of foundation of the firm. The final sample consists of more than 700,000 observations with at least five employees.

For India, this book uses two data sets. For *large, registered* firms the data come from the Prowess database provided by the Centre for Monitoring Indian Economy (CMIE). The Prowess database contains information primarily from the income statements and balance sheets of publicly listed companies in manufacturing and services. It also contains detailed annual information on firms' product mix and, unlike the official Annual Survey of Industries, Prowess is a panel of firms rather than a repeated cross section. Data for these variables are available for 7,742 manufacturing firms (65,788 firm year observations) and 14,330 service sector firms (92,071 firm year observations) between 1990 and 2013. For *small household enterprises*, the data come from the India Human Development Survey (IHDS), conducted in 2004–05 and 2011–12. The IHDS is a nationally representative multitopic panel survey jointly administered by the University of Maryland and the National Council of Applied Economic Research. It includes a submodule on "non-farm businesses" owned and run by household members, including information on industry code, gross receipts, revenue, and labor cost. The surveys ask if the business has any hired workers but does not ask about the total employment level or enterprise age. As a result, revenue is the best available measure of size. The panel covers 34,643 households, of which 20 percent own at least one enterprise.

In Indonesia, the data set comprises 65,895 unique manufacturing firms in Indonesia from 1990 through 2014. The structure of the data is an unbalanced panel of about 550,000 firm-year observations, with a minimum threshold size of 20 employees. The variables of interest are information on sector classification at the 2-digit sector level and firm ownership, collected at the time of registration, and annual data on firm employment and output.

In Mexico, the economic census data collected by INEGI, the national Statistics Agency, cover most businesses in the country with detailed information on their organization, employment, wages, value of production, sales, exports, input expenditures, including imports of inputs, capital stock and accumulation, access to foreign investment, and research and development activities. Censuses are held every five years, and this book works with five of them: the censuses of 1993, 1998, 2003, 2008, and 2013. For the analysis in this book, firms in the manufacturing sector have been matched across census waves via an algorithm that relies on variables such as the name of the business, name of owner or parent company, address, city or town, municipality, state, sampling area and block numbers, and 6-digit economic activity sector.

In South Africa, the data source is the new South African Revenue Service and National Treasury Firm-Level Panel. Information in the panel is compiled from company income tax (CIT) data from all CIT-registered entities that submit CIT forms, employee tax data from the IRP5 and IT3 forms, customs records from traders and value-added tax (VAT) data from VAT-registered firms. The panel contains administrative records for manufacturing and services firms during 2008–14 and includes comprehensive financial and tax information, firm demographic characteristics such as the sector in which it operates, employment information, and trade data for registered entities. At the employee level the panel contains information regarding incomes, deductions, and payments made by firms related to their employees.

In Thailand, the data come from Banternghansa (2017), who compiled information from the Department of Business Development on all new registered firms since 1999 and any surviving registered firms before 1999. The data set includes total and main revenue, total cost of production, interest paid, administrative expense, tax, and profits as well as capital, current and noncurrent assets, current and noncurrent liabilities, and equity. It covers the period 2007 to 2015 and includes 1,292,322 firms, although firms in only the manufacturing and services sectors are included in the analysis for this book. A particular feature of this data set is the information on firm ownership: the names of the shareholders and their share amounts are provided, as well as the names of members of the board of directors. Since Thai family names are unique, this allows for identification of each family of entrepreneurs and how many firms they own.

In Tunisia, the data set is the Tunisian Statistical Business Register (the Répertoire National des Entreprises, RNE), collected by the National Institute of Statistics (Institut National de la Statistique). The RNE is an exhaustive data source, a result of a merge of different administrative folders coming from the social security fund (Caisse Nationale de la Sécurité Sociale, CNSS), which is the source for the employment data, as well as from Tunisian Customs, the Tunisian Ministry of Finance, and the Tunisian Investment Promotion Agency (l'Agence de Promotion de l'Industrie et de l'Innovation, APII). A major and unique advantage of the RNE is that it accounts for all enterprises and covers a relatively long period. It contains information on the number of employees, age, and main activity, as well as trade regime categorization (that is, offshore or onshore) of all registered private firms, and these data were merged with profit and turnover data from the Tunisian Ministry of Finance. The analysis in this book focuses on the period 1996–2015 and covers only private firms, yielding a sample of some 46,000–60,000 firms per year.

For Turkey, this book uses two sources of data. The first is the AISS, managed by the Turkish Statistical Office (TurkStat). The data set consists of a census of firms with at least 20 employees and a representative sample of firms with fewer than 20 employees in all business sectors, except for agriculture and the financial sector. The 20–sample is based on a survey stratified at the 4-digit industry (NACE classification), size groups, and 26 NUTS2 regions. The data are available for the period 2003–14; however, the information collected in 2003 and 2004 is generally regarded as less reliable, and the analysis for this book therefore focuses on the period 2005–14. The second source is the Entrepreneur Information System (EIS) provided by the General Directorate of Productivity at the Ministry of Science, Industry and Technology. This database consists of firms' balance sheets, income statements, and the business register for the period between 2006 and 2016. The descriptive on Turkey presented in this chapter (figures 1.1, 1.4, and 1.6; tables 1A.2 and 1A.3) is generated using the EIS data set. Although this data set does not impose any threshold on the firm size, we apply the standard 10 employee cutoff to make the statistics comparable with other countries studied in this book.

For the United States, descriptive statistics are computed using the U.S. Census Bureau's Longitudinal Business Database (LBD), which provides annual observations for every private sector establishment with payroll from 1976 onward. The only excluded sector is agriculture, forestry, and fishing. Sourced from U.S. tax records and Census Bureau surveys, the micro-records document the universe of establishments and firms rather than a stratified random sample or published aggregate tabulations. The comprehensive nature of the LBD also facilitates complete characterizations of entrepreneurial activity by industries. Although the data are available for the years before 1990, our descriptive statistics on overall incidence are constructed from

1990 onward, whereas the sectoral incidence is based on data from 2002 onward. For more information on the LBD, see, Jarmin and Miranda (2002).

In order to improve comparability across countries and for consistency with the majority of previous HGF studies, this book imposes a 10-employee minimum threshold for most of the data sets used in the analysis (except in Côte d'Ivoire, Indonesia, and Turkey). Table 1A.2 shows the drop in observations when imposing this threshold condition as well as the incidence of high growth prior to imposing a threshold.

**TABLE 1A.2  Firm-Year Observations for Constructing the Cross-Country Comparable Sample**

| Country | Observation count | Observation count after employee cutoff and sector restrictions | Share of observations dropped (%) | HGF incidence (OECD1) | | HGF incidence (Birch1) | |
|---|---|---|---|---|---|---|---|
| | | | | Before cutoff | After cutoff | Before cutoff | After cutoff |
| Brazil | 34,061,553 | 6,315,238 | 81.46 | 12.7 | 20.3 | 6.0 | 25.0 |
| Côte d'Ivoire | 53,828 | 30,078 | 44.12 | 4.4 | 6.5 | 3.1 | 5.1 |
| Ethiopia | 13,412 | 12,184 | 9.16 | 7.7 | 8.2 | 5.3 | 5.9 |
| Hungary | 5,168,144 | 456,355 | 91.17 | 9.0 | 16.0 | 6.0 | 29.2 |
| India | 256,430 | 256,430 | n.a. | 13.4 | 14.8 | 5.4 | 5.8 |
| Indonesia | 550,678 | 550,678 | n.a. | 5.7 | 5.7 | 7.6 | 7.6 |
| Mexico | 746,240 | 147,594 | 80.22 | 3.1 | 3.9 | 3.6 | 13.9 |
| South Africa | 6,426,931 | 318,546 | 95.04 | 6.2 | 17.3 | 3.5 | 12.8 |
| Thailand | 3,778,021 | 478,133 | 87.34 | 13.7 | 9.7 | 4.8 | 12.1 |
| Tunisia | 1,167,050 | 136,429 | 88.31 | 7.6 | 14.0 | 6.5 | 28.0 |
| Turkey | 11,530,421 | 1,446,805 | 87.45 | 12.1 | 21.3 | 5.7 | 20.8 |

*Note:* Côte d'Ivoire has a cutoff of five employees because of the limited number of observations. Ethiopia already has a cutoff of 10 employees, however, some firms still continue to be included in the census because at some point they had 10 or more employees. Indonesia's data set includes all manufacturing firms with more than 20 employees, whereas India's comprises large firms listed on the domestic stock market. For these two countries, the cutoff on employee count and sectoral restrictions are not binding. n.a. = not applicable.

For comparisons between national data and the World Bank Enterprise Surveys (WBES), table 1A.3 shows the WBES firm count and the mean firm size in both sources of data.

**TABLE 1A.3  World Bank Enterprise Surveys (WBES) Data Coverage**

| Country | WBES year | Firm count (10 workers or more) | Mean firm size (number of employees in firms with 10 workers or more) | |
|---|---|---|---|---|
| | | | National data | WBES data |
| Brazil | 2009 | 1519 | 57 | 175 |
| Côte d'Ivoire | 2009 | 394 | 70 | 56 |
| Hungary | 2013 | 192 | 15 | 96 |
| Indonesia | 2015 | 714 | 211 | 240 |
| Tunisia | 2013 | 481 | 90 | 119 |
| Turkey | 2013 | 1042 | 53 | 139 |

# Notes

1. This inference is drawn from analysis of longitudinal firm data sets, many of which limit observations to businesses with 10 or more employees in the manufacturing and, at times, in the services sectors. Thus, by definition, all firms in agriculture and small and informal firms in other sectors are excluded from this statement.

2. "Productivity isn't everything, but in the long run it is almost everything" (Krugman 1994, 11)

3. The Birch (1987) index is defined as the product of absolute and relative change in employment, therefore underweighting small firms that experience rapid growth (for example, a firm going from one to three employees) versus large firms that experience smaller relative changes but nonetheless increase the stock of their employees. If $L$ is employment at time $t$, then the Birch index $B_t = \left(L_t - L_{t-1}\right)\dfrac{L_t}{L_{t-1}}$.

4. Growth rates for the OECD definition are calculated as $g_{i,t} = \dfrac{L_{i,t} - L_{i,t-3}}{L_{t-3}}$, where L refers to either employment or revenue. This approach, by definition, means that firms that entered the market in the current period or either of the two previous ones (firms for which $L_{-3} = 0$) are never classified as HGFs. The book's qualitative findings, however, are robust to other measures that allow for more recent entrants to be classified as HGFs (such as Davis, Haltiwanger, and Schuh 1996).

5. If the employee count drops below 10 in a certain year, the firm is not counted in that specific year. This approach is costly in terms of observation count, consistent with findings of Li and Rama (2015) and Moreno and Coad (2015), who show that a large share of firms in developing countries (more than 85 percent in the former's sample and 95 percent in the latter's) have fewer than 10 employees. For data sets considered in this book, the 10-employee cutoff leads to a nearly 90 percent observation count loss in Hungary and an 80 percent loss in Mexico. However, as discussed later (for example, footnote 12 and Annex 1A), the qualitative findings on the incidence of HGFs hold irrespective of the cutoff.

6. Specifically, we exploit our limited access to the Manufacturing Survey of Thailand data set for the years 2003, 2007, and 2012, which has both employment and sales information, to arrive at a threshold on sales revenue. Keeping only the firms with employee counts of 8, 9, and 10 in the Manufacturing Survey, we compute the threshold separately for manufacturing and services sectors as average deflated sales, averaging over firms in the years 2003, 2007, and 2012, after accounting appropriately for the outliers. The descriptive statistics for Thailand are computed using only those firm-year observations with sales over this threshold. Moreover, given that the number of registered firms in some of the years before 2004 was volatile, the statistics computed for this book consider only years 2004 and onward.

7. Using $L$ to denote employment and $t$ time, a firm $i$ is classified as HGF in period $t$ if
$$\left(\frac{L_{i,t}}{L_{i,t-3}}\right)^{\frac{1}{3}} - 1 \geq 0.20.$$

8. Using $L$ to denote employment (or revenue) and $t$ time, define the Birch index for firm $i$ in period $t$ as $B_{i,t} = \left(L_{i,t} - L_{i,t-3}\right)\dfrac{L_{i,t}}{L_{i,t-3}}$. Then, rank all firms in period $t$ by values of $B_{i,t}$, from smallest to largest, and define $P^{90}(B_t)$ as the value of $B_{i,t}$ below which 90 percent of $B_{i,t}$ values fall. A firm $i$ is classified as HGF in period $t$ if $B_{i,t} > P^{90}(B_t)$.

9. In the case of the United States, Decker et al. (2014) define HGFs as those having annual growth rates above 25 percent, with no lower bound on initial size. Choi et al. (2017) use Clayton et al.'s (2013) definition, in which firms are recorded as high growth if they satisfy the OECD criterion when they have more than 10 employees, whereas firms with fewer than 10 workers are classified as high growth if they added 8 or more employees over a three-year period.

10. Davis, Haltiwanger, and Schuh (1996) propose an alternative measure of firm growth to address this issue. Their approach produces a growth distribution that is bounded as $g_{i,t} \in [-2,2]$, where $g_{i,t} = \dfrac{L_{i,t} - L_{i,t-3}}{\left(L_{i,t} + L_{i,t-3}\right)/2}$. To assign firms as HGFs or not, all firms are ranked in period $t$ by values of $g_{i,t}$, from smallest to largest, and $P^{90}(g_{i,t})$ is defined as the value of $g_{i,t}$ below which 90 percent of $g_{i,t}$ values fall. A firm $i$ is classified as HGF in period $t$ if $g_{i,t} > P^{90}(g_t)$. Other studies have used the firm count at the beginning of the reporting period (for example, Anyadike-Danes and Hart 2017), although this causes some problems, especially when computing incidence by sectors when a firm changes its sector by the end of the three-year window. Thus, for consistency with the sectoral incidence rates, the denominator should reflect the number of firms at the end of the reporting period (Peterson and Ahmad 2007).

11. The discussion that follows also illustrates the stability of high-growth incidence over time for these countries.

12. Although the HGF incidence in figure 1.1 is based on firms with 10 or more employees, the incidence is not very different when all firms are included. Applying the OECD1 HGF definition to the complete census of firms, the incidence ranges from 3.1 percent in Mexico to 12.7 percent in Brazil. Thus, despite the large drop in observation count mentioned earlier (see annex 1A), high-growth incidence remains relatively stable.

13. The next chapter explores the issue of volatility of firm growth in more detail.

14. A similar result is found in Aterido and Hallward-Driemeier (2018) using data from Vietnam, Moldova, and Morocco. Requiring sustained high performance greatly reduces the number of firms that meet the criteria—many "jump" to a new level in one year; many also zig zag, that is, over a three-year time frame they have growth but can also contract.

15. In a sensitivity analysis undertaken for Canada, Denmark, Finland, Italy, Latvia, Spain, Sweden, and the United States by Peterson and Ahmad (2007), the central thresholds of 10 employees and 20 percent per annum growth result in incidence of 3–5 percent for high-growth enterprises based on employment and 6–17 percent based on turnover.

16. The sign and significance of the results are sensitive to the level of aggregation (for example, whether they are estimated at the 4-digit or 2-digit industry level or whether industry growth is measured using employment or sales). For example, in the case of Ethiopia, the coefficient on industry concentration loses significance when estimated at a 2-digit level of significance, whereas in the case of Indonesia, the coefficient reverses signs and is significant. Likewise, if industry growth is measured using the sales metrics instead of employment, the coefficient loses significance in the case of Indonesia and is negative and significant in Ethiopia, even when estimations are run at a 4-digit level of industry classification.

17. The study covers two three-year periods, 2002–05 and 2005–08 using the data from the Office for National Statistics Business Structure Database.

18. Considering the Eurostat-OECD definition with a cutoff of 10 employees, Daunfeldt et al. (2015) note that only 1,891 firms would qualify as HGFs, creating 108,185 jobs, which is more than all new net jobs (80,247) created by surviving firms with more than 10 employees. However, firms with fewer than 10 initial employees created 172,010 jobs, or 39 percent of all new jobs, which is more than the number created by HGFs, while losing only 76,485 jobs, less than half as many as larger firms. Thus, one needs to be mindful of the contribution of firms with fewer than 10 employees; studies using the Eurostat-OECD definition of HGFs tend to exclude more than a third of new job creation and a majority of net job creation.

19. Haltiwanger et al. (2017) define HGFs as the top 10 percent of firms ranked by employment or output growth rates; Decker et al. (2014) define HGFs as firms expanding their employment by more than 25 percent per year.

20. For example, in France, HGFs were defined as the top 10 percent of all growing firms, whereas in Spain they were selected as the top 10 percent of all firms, whether growing or not.

21. For example, the "High-growth enterprise" section of OECD (2014, 70) argues that "High-growth enterprises are firms that by their extraordinary growth make the largest contribution to *net* job creation, despite typically representing a small proportion of the business population."

22. Kliesen and Maués (2011) note that during the 18-year period from 1992 to 2010, net job gains in the United States were significantly smaller than gross job gains even after excluding the recession period 2007–09. A more crucial difference between the two measures is that the importance of small enterprises as a source of job creation, emphasized since Birch (1979), fades away as one moves from gross to net measures. Since 1992, net job creation in the United States tends to be largest among the largest firms and accounts for about 38 percent of the total net jobs, while the contribution of small firms to net job creation is less dominant (Kliesen and Maués 2011).

23. As before, this statement refers only to firms with 10 employees or more in manufacturing and services sectors.

24. Note that the policy motivation of the two literatures is also very similar: facilitating MNE entry can create jobs, but such a policy is likely to be beneficial only if it also creates positive externalities for other firms (Blomström and Kokko 2003).

25. Similarly, Tan, Winkler, and Yde-Jensen (2018) find that hard and soft investments from abroad are highly correlated in Europe and Central Asia because countries with a higher share of foreign-owned firms also tend to have a high share of foreign managers.

26. The discussion in this paragraph uses the OECD definition of HGFs. Return on assets is defined as the ratio of net income (profit after taxes) to total assets of the firm. Competition from HGFs in the same industry can drive down the profits of the less efficient firms and thereby lower their returns. Likewise, because HGFs usually pay higher average wages, they attract more skilled workers, which also implies that when industry-specific talent supply is limited, declining firms will also lose human capital and thus their average wages could be negatively correlated with the presence of other HGFs in the same industry. One exception to the overall finding of no or negative effect is the case of employment growth, in which the horizontal spillovers are positive for firms in the bottom 90 percent of the growth distribution (that is, firms that are less likely to be direct HGF competitors).

27. These forward spillovers are about twice as large in services as in manufacturing.

28. It should be noted that there are no cross-country differences in the definition of a supplier and buyer industry, but the set of buyer and supplier industries for each country is determined by the input-output coefficients, which reflect their production technology and hence vary across countries.

29. In the case of Turkey, the underlying threshold firm size is different from that in Hungary. The data used for the analysis on spillovers in Turkey consist of censuses of firms with at least 20 employees and samples of firms with fewer than 20 employees. These data are sourced from the Annual Industry and Service Statistics, provided by the Turkish Statistical Office (TurkStat). This data source should not be confused with the descriptive statistics presented earlier in this chapter (figures 1.1, 1.4, and 1.6), which are derived from the Entrepreneur Information System (EIS), a firm-level data set provided by the General Directorate of Productivity at the Ministry of Science, Industry and Technology, covering every establishment that employed more than one employee and operated for more than one year during the period between 2006 and 2016 (although a cutoff of 10 employees was imposed to make it comparable with other countries).

## References

Anyadike-Danes, M., K. Bonner, M. Hart, and C. Mason. 2009. "Measuring Business Growth: High Growth Firms and Their Contribution to Employment in the UK." Research Report MBG/35, National Endowment for Science, Technology and the Arts, London.

Anyadike-Danes, M., and M. Hart. 2017. "The UK's High Growth Firms and Their Resilience over the Great Recession." ERC Research Paper 62, Enterprise Research Centre, Coventry and Birmingham, UK.

Autor, D., D. Dorn, L. F. Katz, C. Patterson, and J. Van Reenen. 2017. "The Fall of the Labor Share and the Rise of Superstar Firms." Working Paper 23396, National Bureau of Economic Research, Cambridge, MA.

Aterido, R., and M. Hallward-Driemeier. "The Elusive Search for Gazelles: Definitions Affect Firms Selected—But Not Their Potential for Long-Term Success." Unpublished manuscript, 2018, World Bank, Washington, DC.

Ayyagari, M., A. Demirgüç-Kunt, and V. Maksimovic. 2018. "Who Are America's Star Firms?" Policy Research Working Paper 8534, World Bank, Washington, DC.

Banternghansa, C. 2017. "Multi-Firm Entrepreneurship and Financial Frictions." PIER Discussion Paper 56, Puey Ungphakorn Institute for Economic Research, Bangkok.

Bartelsman, E. J., J. E. Haskel, and R. Martin. 2008. "Distance to Which Frontier? Evidence on Productivity Convergence from International Firm-Level Data." Discussion Paper 7032, Centre for Economic Policy Research, London.

Bastos, P., and J. Silva. 2018. "The Origins of High-Growth Firms: Evidence from Brazil." Background paper for *High-Growth Firms*, World Bank, Washington, DC.

Birch, D. 1979. "The Job Generation Process." MIT Program on Neighborhood and Regional Change, Cambridge, MA.

———. 1981. "Who Creates Jobs?" *Public Interest* 65 (Fall): 3–14.

———. 1987. *Job Creation in America: How Our Smallest Companies Put the Most People to Work.* New York: Free Press.

Blomstöm, M., and A. Kokko. 2003. "The Economics of Foreign Direct Investment Incentives." Working Paper 9489, National Bureau of Economic Research, Cambridge, MA.

Bos, J., and E. Stam. 2014. "Gazelles and Industry Growth: A Study of Young High-Growth Firms in the Netherlands." *Industrial and Corporate Change* 23 (1): 145–69.

Bravo-Biosca, A., C. Criscuolo, and C. Menon. 2016. "What Drives the Dynamics of Business Growth?" *Economic Policy* 31 (88):703–42.

Brown, W. 2011. "International Review: Industrial Relations in Britain under New Labour, 1997–2010: A Post Mortem." *Journal of Industrial Relations* 53 (3): 402–13.

Choi, T., A. Rupasingha, J. C. Robertson, and N. G. Leigh. 2017. "The Effects of High Growth on New Business Survival." *Review of Regional Studies* 47 (1): 1–23.

Clayton, R. L., A. Sadeghi, J. R. Spletzer, and D. M. Talan. 2013. "High-Employment-Growth Firms: Defining and Counting Them." *Monthly Labor Review* 136 (6): 3.

Crespo, N., and M. P. Fontoura. 2007. "Determinant Factors of FDI Spillovers—What Do We Really Know?" *World Development* 35 (3): 410–25.

Daunfeldt, S.-O., N. Elert, and D. Johansson. 2014. "Economic Contribution of High-Growth Firms: Do Policy Implications Depend on the Choice of Growth Indicator?" *Journal of Industry, Competition and Trade* 14 (3): 337–65.

Daunfeldt, S.-O., A. Lang, Z. Macuchova, and N. Rudholm. 2013. "Firm Growth in the Swedish Retail and Wholesale Industries." *Services Industries Journal* 33 (12): 1193–205.

Davis, S., J. Haltiwanger, and S. Schuh. 1996. *Job Creation and Destruction.* Cambridge, MA: MIT Press.

Decker, R., J. Haltiwanger, R. Jarmin, and J. Miranda. 2014. "The Role of Entrepreneurship in US Job Creation and Economic Dynamism." *Journal of Economic Perspectives* 28 (3): 3–24.

Deschryvere, Matthias. 2008. "High Growth Firms and Job Creation in Finland." ETLA Discussion Paper 1144, Research Institute of the Finnish Economy, Helsinki.

Du, J., and Y. Temouri. 2015. "High-Growth Firms and Productivity: Evidence from the United Kingdom." *Small Business Economics* 44 (1): 123–43.

Ferrantino, M. J., M. Mukim, A. Pearson, and N. Snow. 2012. "Gazelles and Gazillas in China and India." Working Paper 2012-10C, Office of Economics, U.S. International Trade Commission, Washington, DC.

Furman, J., and P. Orszag. 2018. "A Firm-Level Perspective on the Role of Rents in the Rise in Inequality." In *Toward a Just Society: Joseph Stiglitz and Twenty First-Century Economics*, edited by Martin Guzman, 19–47. New York: Columbia University Press.

Goedhuys, M., and L. Sleuwaegen. 2010. "High-Growth Entrepreneurial Firms in Africa: A Qauntile Regression Approach." *Small Business Economics* 34 (1): 31–51.

Görg, H., and E. Strobl. 2001. "Multinational Companies and Productivity Spillovers: A Meta-Analysis." *Economic Journal* 111 (475): 723–39.

Görg, H., and D. Greenaway. 2004 "Much Ado about Nothing? Do Domestic Firms Really Benefit from Foreign Direct Investment?" *World Bank Research Observer* 19 (2): 171–97.

Haltiwanger, J., R. S. Jarmin, R. Kulick, and J. Miranda. 2017. "High-Growth Firms: Contribution to Job, Output and Productivity Growth." In *Measuring Entrepreneurial Businesses: Current Knowledge and Challenges*, edited by John Haltiwanger, Erik Hurst, Javier Miranda, and Antoinette Schoar, 11–62. National Bureau of Economic Research Studies in Income and Wealth. Chicago: University of Chicago Press.

Halvarsson, D. 2013. "Identifying High-Growth Firms." Working Paper 215, Ratio Institute, Stockholm.

Havranek, T., and Z. Irsova. 2011. "Estimating Vertical Spillovers from FDI: Why Results Vary and What the True Effect Is." *Journal of International Economics* 85 (2): 234–44.

Hoffmann, A. N., and M. Junge. 2006. "Documenting Data on High-Growth Firms and Entrepreneurs across 17 Countries." Working Paper, FORA, Copenhagen.

Jarmin, Ron S., and Javier Miranda. 2002. "The Longitudinal Business Database." Discussion Paper CES 02–17, Center for Economic Studies, U.S. Census Bureau, Department of Commerce, Washington, DC.

Javorcik, B. S. 2004. "Does Foreign Direct Investment Increase the Productivity of Domestic Firms? In Search of Spillovers through Backward Linkages." *American Economic Review* 94 (3): 605–27.

Kliesen, K. L., and J. S. Maués. 2011. "Are Small Businesses the Biggest Producers of Jobs?" *Regional Economist* (Apr): 8–9.

Krugman, P. 1994. *The Age of Diminished Expectations*. Cambridge, MA: MIT Press.

Lee, A. 2013. "Welcome to The Unicorn Club: Learning from Billion-Dollar Startups." TechCrunch. https://techcrunch.com/2013/11/02/welcome-to-the-unicorn-club/.

Li, Y., and M. Rama. 2015. "Firm Dynamics, Productivity Growth, and Job Creation in Developing Countries: The Role of Micro- and Small Enterprises." *World Bank Research Observer* 30: 3–38.

Mason, G., K. Bishop, and C. Robinson. 2009. "Business Growth and Innovation: The Wider Impact of Rapidly-Growing Firms in UK City-Regions." NESTA research report, National Endowment for Science, Technology and the Arts, London.

Mamburu, M. 2017. "Defining High-Growth Firms in South Africa." WIDER Working Paper 2017/107, April, UNU-WIDER, Helsinki.

Meyer, K. E., and E. Sinani. 2009. "When and Where Does Foreign Direct Investment Generate Positive Spillovers? A Meta-Analysis." *Journal of International Business Studies* 40 (7): 1075–94.

Moreno, F., and A. Coad. 2015. "High-Growth Firms: Stylized Facts and Conflicting Results." In *Entrepreneurial Growth: Individual, Firm, and Region*, edited by A. C. Corbett, J. A. Katz, and A. Mckelvie, vol. 17, 187–230. Bingley, UK: Emerald Publishing.

Muraközy, B., F. de Nicola, and S. W. Tan. 2018. "High-Growth Firms in Hungary." Background paper for *High-Growth Firms*, World Bank, Washington, DC.

Nightingale, P., and A. Coad. 2014. "Muppets and Gazelles: Political and Methodological Biases in Entrepreneurship Research." *Industrial and Corporate Change* 23 (1): 113–43.

OECD (Organisation for Economic Co-operation and Development). 2007. *Eurostat-OECD Manual on Business Demography Statistics*. Paris: OECD.

———. 2014. *Entrepreneurship at a Glance 2014*. Paris: OECD Publishing.

Petersen, D. R., and N. Ahmad. 2007. "High-Growth Enterprises and Gazelles: Preliminary and Summary Sensitivity Analysis." OECD-FORA, Paris. http://www.oecd.org/industry/business -stats/39639605.pdf. Retrieved November 21, 2018.

Sanchez Bayardo, L. F., and L. Iacovone. 2018. "High-Growth Firms and Spillovers in Mexico." Background paper for *High-Growth Firms*, World Bank, Washington, DC.

SBA Office of Advocacy. 2008. "High-Impact Firms: Gazelles Revisited," by Z. J. Acs, W. Parsons, and S. Tracy. Small Business Research Summary 328, Washington, DC.

Schreyer, Paul. 2000. "High-Growth Firms and Employment." OECD Science, Technology, and Industry Working Paper 2000/03, OECD Publishing, Paris.

Shepherd, D., and J. Wiklund. 2009. "Are We Comparing Apples with Apples or Apples with Oranges? Appropriateness of Knowledge Accumulation across Growth Studies." *Entrepreneurship Theory and Practice* 33 (1): 105–23.

Stam, E., K. Suddle, J. Hessels, and A. van Stel. 2009. "High-Growth Entrepreneurs, Public Policies, and Economic Growth." In *Public Policies for Fostering Entrepreneurship,* edited by Rui Baptista and João Leitão, 91–110. New York: Springer.

Tan, S. W., H. Winkler, and T. Yde-Jensen. 2018. "Connectivity and Firms." In *Critical Connections: Why Europe and Central Asia's Connections Matter for Growth and Stability*. Washington, DC: World Bank.

United Kingdom, Department of Business Innovation and Skills. 2014. "Innovative Firms and Growth," by A. Coad, M. Cowling, P. Nightingale, G. Pellegrino, M. Savona, and J. Siepel. UK Innovation Survey, London.

World Bank. 2019. *World Development Report 2019: The Changing Nature of Work*. Washington, DC: World Bank.

# 2. Facets of High-Growth Events

The previous chapter explores the main reasons why researchers and policy makers care about high-growth firms (HGFs), focusing on their extraordinary ability to create jobs and linkages. This chapter examines some of the key characteristics of HGFs, starting with the stylized facts that have been established in the literature on high-income countries. Beyond the evidence on the incidence and the disproportionate impact of HGFs—which the previous chapter documents and confirms is similar to high-income economies—the three most important stylized facts about these firms from studies of high-income countries are the following:

1. HGFs are young but not necessarily small
2. HGFs are found in all types of sectors and locations
3. High firm growth is short-lived and episodic

The evidence collected and analyzed for this book confirms that these stylized facts also largely hold for developing countries. Regardless of the definition used, HGFs tend to be younger than an average firm, although for many of them the high-growth episode begins only after the start-up phase. HGFs in developing countries also are not necessarily small, and larger HGFs contribute much more to overall job creation than smaller HGFs. HGFs are found across various sectors of economic activity and do not tend to be more numerous or particularly concentrated in high-tech industries. They also operate across a range of geographies and locations, although the discussion in the following chapter points to the special role of agglomeration economies and densely populated environments in facilitating high growth. Finally, and most important, high firm growth is difficult to sustain and the likelihood of a repeated episode, either immediately or later in the firm's life cycle, is low. Some firms move from high growth to low growth or vice versa, while many others exit the market altogether following an episode of high growth. Given this fragility of high growth, this book suggests distinguishing between the concept of a "high-growth episode" and a "high-growth firm" since all of the previously documented benefits of HGFs take place only within this narrow window and do not appear to be a permanent attribute of the firm.

The importance of properly capturing and understanding these features goes well beyond descriptive statistics: when it comes to any readily identifiable characteristic of a potential HGF, one must be cautious that positive distinctions do not become normative. Policy makers have directed substantial resources into small and medium enterprise (SME) support programs, partly under the assumption that these firms generate the bulk of new jobs in the economy. However, studies beginning with Davis, Haltiwanger, and Schuh (1996) have identified the fallacy of such conclusions because they are often based on misleading interpretations of the data.[1] Similarly, "many policies for promoting HGFs [have been] directed towards high-technology industries" (United Kingdom, Department of Business Innovation and Skills 2014, citing OECD 2010), despite evidence that HGFs are not more common in high-tech sectors. This has prompted some recent studies to call for reorienting policies to encourage HGFs that are sector-neutral, and therefore allow for broader sectoral coverage (Mason and Brown 2013; Brown, Mason, and Mawson 2014). And, despite the evidence that high-growth episodes are often transient, the focus thus far has been on identifying potential beneficiary firms, leading to strategies that are more akin to "picking winners" rather than creating the conditions to enable a wide range of firms to experience faster growth. The following discussion explores these issues in more detail.

## Size and Age

Most of the early approaches to linking firm size and growth focused on some version of Gibrat's Law, namely, that the expected growth rate of a firm is independent of its initial size (Gibrat 1931). Subsequently, however, the focus of many academic and policy efforts to identify firms with the greatest growth potential shifted to small firms. This was based on empirical results such as those in Birch (1979, 1981), who argued that small firms in the United States were responsible for the majority of job creation in the early 1970s. Since then, other studies—for example, Evans (1987) and Hall (1987) for the United States; Dunne and Hughes (1994) for the United Kingdom; Picot, Baldwin, and Dupuy (1995) for Canada; and Fagiolo and Luzzi (2006) for Italy—have documented a negative relationship between firm size and growth. This focus has been reinforced by studies showing that SMEs account for some two-thirds of permanent, full-time employment in Organisation for Economic Co-operation and Development (OECD) economies and in developing countries alike (for example, OECD 1997; IFC 2013)—discounting the critical distinction between the stock of jobs and their flow (creation and destruction).

Some of the more recent work has suggested that the contribution of small firms has been significantly overestimated because of methodological flaws and data inadequacy (for example, Davis, Haltiwanger, and Schuh 1996).[2] In particular, the results reported in earlier studies did not always fully reflect the relationship between firm size and age since firms generally tend to start small *relative to incumbents*. This may happen because firms have to pay some fixed cost to enter and remain in the market (Hopenhayn 1992) or they face uncertainty regarding their productivity levels (Jovanovic 1982).[3] As a result, less efficient entrants will exit while more efficient ones will grow rapidly—perhaps at a decelerating pace as they become older and larger.[4] Indeed, most studies find that younger firms face "up or out" dynamics: they tend to grow more rapidly than older firms but also face lower survival probabilities (Davis, Haltiwanger, and Schuh 1996; Haltiwanger 2012). Other reasons why young firms are more likely to grow faster could be due to the possibility that older firms use older capital vintages, making them less productive than younger firms that invest in more advanced technology (Hopenhayn 2007; Luttmer 2011).[5] Similarly, Arkolakis, Doxiadis, and Galenianos (2017) argue that younger firms revise their beliefs more frequently than older firms do, enabling surviving young firms to grow more rapidly than older firms.

For these reasons, much of the academic and policy efforts to identify HGFs have looked for these firms among start-ups and young businesses.[6] In the United States, Haltiwanger, Jarmin, and Miranda (2013) and Haltiwanger et al. (2017) show that HGFs are disproportionately young, and evidence from Colombia shows that young firms (aged 0–4 years) grow two to three times more rapidly than the rest (Eslava and Haltiwanger 2013). The latter is not an artifact of micro firms experiencing fast growth by adding one or two workers; in fact, large young firms (those with more than 200 employees) have by far the fastest rate of growth among all Colombian firms that survived between 1993 and 2009. Moreover, Haltiwanger, Jarmin, and Miranda (2013) argue that the negative relationship between firm size and subsequent growth is driven entirely by the fact that most young firms start small and that size has no significant relationship with growth once age is taken into account.

The evidence collected for this book shows that firms are more likely to experience a high-growth episode during the early part of their life cycles. To make this point, figure 2.1 compares the age distribution of employment-based HGFs with that of all firms in Brazil, Côte d'Ivoire, Ethiopia, Hungary, and Indonesia (age in these calculations reflects the age of the firm at the beginning of a three-year window used to calculate HGF status). The figure shows that, when using the OECD definition, HGFs are indeed younger than an average firm; firms 0–5 years old are overrepresented among HGFs relative to the general firm population, while older firms are underrepresented. The pattern is less clear for the larger HGFs captured by the Birch definition: the results are consistent with the OECD definition for Brazil, but HGFs are overrepresented among older firms in Côte d'Ivoire and Ethiopia.

The negative relationship between firm age and the likelihood of a high-growth event remains robust for most countries studied for this book even when introducing additional controls. In Côte d'Ivoire, older firms are less likely to experience a high-growth episode when controlling for firm size, location, industry, and year effects, although the relationship is not always statistically significant.[7] In Turkey, older firms are significantly less likely to attain HGF status when controlling for demand shocks, ownership structure, and year, industry, and region fixed effects. Similarly, in Hungary, older firms have a significant, progressively lower likelihood of experiencing a high-growth event when controlling for total factor productivity (TFP), return on assets, exporting status, wages, sector, and firm size.[8] In Tunisia, age is negatively associated with HGF status, after controlling for trade activities and foreign ownership as well as sector, region, and year fixed effects: each additional year of age reduces the likelihood of becoming an HGF (OECD, employment-based) by 0.9 percent.[9] In India, the results are more nuanced: firm age is not a significant determinant of attaining HGF status according to the OECD definition in manufacturing, but it is in services. However, when using a more continuous measure of growth across quantiles, estimates

## FIGURE 2.1  HGFs Are More Likely to Be Young

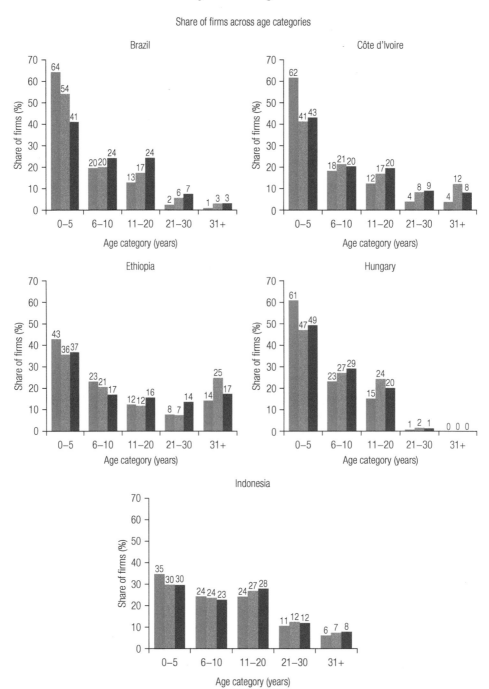

Share of firms across age categories

**Brazil**

**Côte d'Ivoire**

**Ethiopia**

**Hungary**

**Indonesia**

■ HGF (OECD)   ■ HGF (Birch)   ■ All firms

*Source:* Elaboration using national survey and census data.

*Note:* Shares are calculated for each year and then an unweighted average is computed over the entire sample period for each country. HGF = high-growth firm; OECD = Organisation for Economic Co-operation and Development.

suggest that age has a negative and significant association with firm growth in the top quantiles even in the manufacturing sector.[10] On the other hand, Ethiopia offers a counterexample: older manufacturing firms are more likely to achieve high growth in a specification that controls for TFP, exporting status, wages, sector, firm size, and agglomeration effects.[11]

Although many HGFs are young, they are not exactly start-ups. Splitting the 0–5 HGF age category into two groups—firms that begin a high-growth episode within two years of birth (start-ups) and those that first experience high growth three to five years after entering the market (young but not start-ups)—reveals that start-ups account for about 40 percent of all OECD-defined HGFs in Brazil, Côte d'Ivoire, Ethiopia, and Hungary and about 30 percent in Indonesia. For Birch-defined HGFs, the share of start-ups is even lower: it ranges from 13 percent in Indonesia to 26 percent in Hungary, with Brazil a lone outlier at 35 percent.

If young firms are generally more likely to undergo a high-growth episode, does it also mean that most HGFs are small? The evidence collected for this book suggests that this is not necessarily the case, and HGFs are found across all size categories. Among micro firms, there is indeed a negative relationship between firm size and HGF status; in a nationally representative survey of Indian household enterprises, the average share of HGFs is about 18 percent, whereas the incidence of HGFs at the 80th percentile of the distribution of household firms is just 3 percent.[12] However, once one moves beyond the domain of microenterprises, small HGFs become much less prominent. For example, nearly half of HGFs in Indonesia employed more than 50 workers at the beginning of the high-growth spell, and this share rises to nearly 80 percent when HGFs are defined according to the Birch index (figure 2.2, panels a and b).

If many HGFs are already relatively large at the beginning of the high-growth episode, it is not surprising that HGFs end up larger than an average firm at the conclusion of the high-growth episode. This is true in the case of Indonesia, where 80–90

## FIGURE 2.2 Most HGFs in Indonesia Are Medium-to-Large Firms

a. Share of HGFs (employment-based, OECD) by initial size

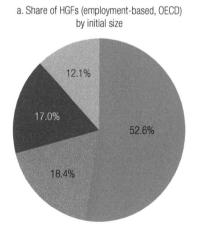

b. Share of HGFs (employment-based, Birch) by initial size

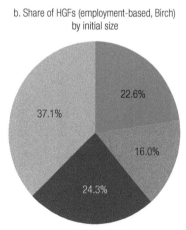

*(Figure continues on the following page.)*

FIGURE 2.2    **Most HGFs in Indonesia Are Medium-to-Large Firms *(continued)***

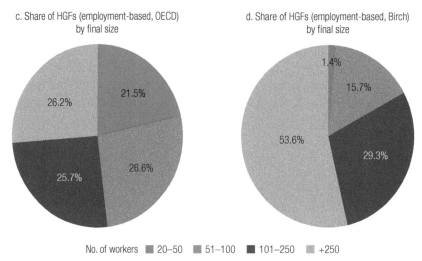

c. Share of HGFs (employment-based, OECD) by final size

d. Share of HGFs (employment-based, Birch) by final size

No. of workers  ■ 20–50  ■ 51–100  ■ 101–250  ■ +250

*Source:* Ferro and Kuriakose 2018.

*Note:* Size is defined as the number of workers employed by high-growth firms (HGFs) either at the beginning of the growth episode (initial size) or at the end of the growth episode (final size). OECD = Organisation for Economic Co-operation and Development.

percent of HGFs employed more than 50 workers by the end of the high-growth episode (figure 2.2, panels c and d). Panel a of figure 2.3 shows that, in all cases except Hungary, OECD-defined HGFs are at least 4 percent larger than an average firm, whereas Birch-defined HGFs are anywhere from 42 percent to six times bigger than an average firm. Consequently, HGFs tend to account for a larger share of total jobs than their share in the firm count; this is illustrated in panels b and c of figure 2.3, which show that OECD-defined HGFs contribute disproportionately to the stock of jobs in all countries except Hungary and South Africa, whereas Birch-defined HGFs account for close to or more than half of all jobs in Brazil, Mexico, Tunisia, and Turkey and at least 18 percent of all jobs in the other countries studied in this book (figure 2.3, panel c).

FIGURE 2.3    **HGFs Tend to Be Larger than Other Firms**

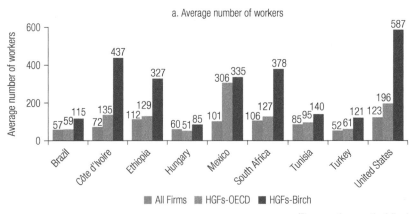

a. Average number of workers

■ All Firms  ■ HGFs-OECD  ■ HGFs-Birch

*(Figure continues on the following page.)*

FIGURE 2.3 **HGFs Tend to Be Larger than Other Firms** *(continued)*

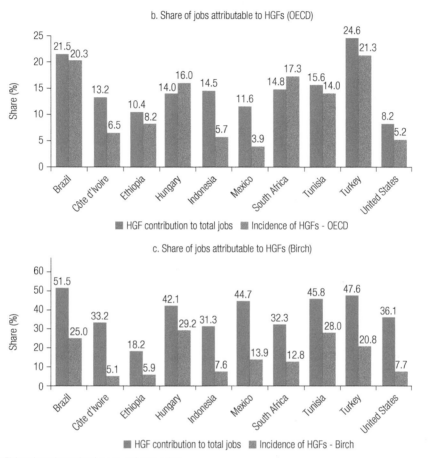

b. Share of jobs attributable to HGFs (OECD)

c. Share of jobs attributable to HGFs (Birch)

*Source:* Elaboration using national survey and census data.

*Note:* Indonesia is omitted from panel a to make the figure readable for other countries because the average high-growth firm (HGF) size (using the employment-based OECD definition) is 500 employees relative to 192 for all firms. In panels b and c, HGF incidence is calculated as employment-based OECD1 and Birch1 (see note to figure 1.1). OECD = Organisation for Economic Co-operation and Development.

In Turkey, size differences between HGFs and non-HGFs become more pronounced as firm size increases. Although HGFs are underrepresented in the 20–49 worker size category, their share is much higher than the economywide average in the larger size categories (figure 2.4).[13]

A review of the literature finds that smaller firms tend to be at a disadvantage when it comes to high-growth experience. For example, SBA Office of Advocacy (2008) shows that small HGFs have a lower survival probability, a lower likelihood of repeating fast growth, and a lower probability of being a growing firm in the next four-year period than do large fast-growing firms. Analysis carried out for this book also shows that larger HGFs create more jobs than smaller HGFs. In Indonesia, for example, chapter 1 showed that HGFs

## FIGURE 2.4 HGFs in Turkey Are More Likely to Be Larger than Other Firms

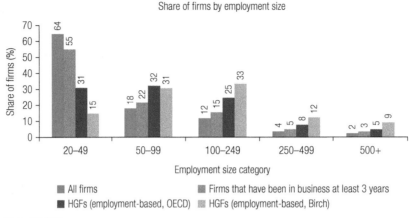

Share of firms by employment size

Source: Atiyas et al. 2018.

Note: HGF = high-growth firm; OECD = Organisation for Economic Co-operation and Development.

## FIGURE 2.5 Large HGFs in Indonesia Create a Disproportionately Greater Number of Jobs

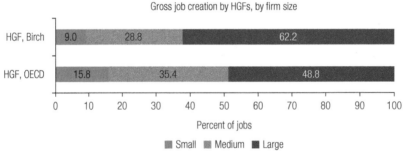

Gross job creation by HGFs, by firm size

Source: Ferro and Kuriakose 2018.

Note: HGF status calculated based on employment. Small firms are those with 20 to 50 employees; medium firms have 51–250 employees; large firms are those with more than 250 employees.

account for 66 percent of all jobs created. Most of this employment, 49–62 percent, takes place within HGFs that started out as large firms (figure 2.5). HGFs that start out small, on the other hand, contribute just 9–16 percent to that total employment created by HGFs.

Unlike the evidence on high-growth status and age, the relationship between firm size and the likelihood of experiencing a high-growth event becomes mixed when other firm characteristics that may be correlated with size are taken into account. In Turkey, firm size (measured by the number of employees) is a positive and significant determinant of attaining high-growth status (using the employment-based OECD definition) when controlling for demand shocks, ownership structure, and year, industry, and region fixed effects. Similarly, in Mexico, a 1 percent increase in the number of employees is associated with a 0.9–1.4 percentage point increase in the likelihood of attaining high-growth status in the next 5–10 years, and similar results are obtained when using value added or the wage bill as a proxy for firm size. Evidence from Côte d'Ivoire is mixed, with the sign of the relationship changing from positive to negative depending on the definition (OECD versus Birch), broad sectoral affiliation (manufacturing versus services), and specific set of controls (for example, whether industry and location effects are included).

By comparison, the relationship between firm size and the probability of achieving high growth is significant and negative for employment-based definitions in Brazil and sales-based definitions in India. Similarly, in Hungary, firms with five to nine employees have the highest odds of experiencing high growth (defined by the OECD measure) when controlling for TFP, return on assets, exporting status, wages, sector, and firm size. In Ethiopia, the relationship between initial size and OECD-defined HGF status (using employment as the growth metric) is negative and significant after controlling for a similar set of firm traits as well as agglomeration variables, implying that larger-sized plants are less likely to attain HGF status.[14] In Tunisia as well, larger firms are less likely to attain HGF status after controlling for trade, foreign ownership, and sector, region, and year fixed effects.

## Sector and Location

It is a common misunderstanding that HGFs are found in high-tech sectors. Although the bulk of the evidence goes against this perception, there is a reason why it has lived for so long. Given that entrepreneurial ability matters for high growth, highly talented entrepreneurs are more likely to self-select into certain sectors based on their potential growth opportunities and entry conditions (Hurst and Pugsley 2011). Thus, if low-tech sectors have fewer growth opportunities and lower entry costs, this is where one would observe large shares of "subsistence" entrepreneurs. These sectors may show high rates of dispersion in growth (due to high rates of turnover) but lower skewness given that such firms have little prospect of or aspirations for growth.

The narrative behind this relationship between high-performing firms and high-potential sectors draws on evidence from earlier research that purported to find a link between technology and firm growth (Storey 1991, 1994; Kirchhoff 1994), and a few recent studies that show a positive correlation between high-tech status or research and development (R&D) intensity and HGFs (Schreyer 2000; Delmar, Davidsson, and Gartner 2003; Hölzl 2009; Stam and Wennberg 2009). For example, a study of six European countries finds evidence that HGFs are more technology intensive than the average firm (Schreyer 2000) and have a higher R&D intensity than non-HGFs (Hölzl 2009). Although it may be true that high-ability entrepreneurs self-select into potentially high-growth activities, high growth does not necessarily coincide with technological sophistication. Hence, the perception that HGFs are found in technology-intensive sectors is not entirely borne out in empirical analysis (Hölzl 2009; Brännback et al. 2010). Many studies fail to find any link, or find a negative link, between high-tech intensity or R&D and the presence of HGFs (Birch and Medoff 1994; Birch, Haggerty, and Parsons 1995; Almus 2002; SBA Office of Advocacy 2008; NESTA 2009; Wyrwich 2010).

On the contrary, evidence from developed countries suggest that HGFs are found in all sectors and in expanding industries with low mobility costs (Hölzl 2010; Deschryvere 2008; Anyadike-Danes et al. 2009; López-Garcia and Puente 2009; NESTA 2009). The literature survey by Henrekson and Johansson (2010) finds no evidence that HGFs are overrepresented in high-technology industries; if anything, these firms are overrepresented in services, especially the ones with high human capital and knowledge content (Autio, Sapienza, and Almeida 2000; Schreyer 2000; Halabisky, Dreessen, and Parsley 2006; Delmar, Davidsson, and Gartner 2003; Davidsson and Delmar 2006; Deschryvere 2008; Daunfeldt, Johansson, and Halvarsson 2015). In the United States, the relationship between sectors with large incidence of HGFs and sectors that are generally perceived as more dynamic is not fully intuitive; for example, the construction sector has a particularly high output share accounted for by HGFs, whereas in biotech industries the shares of employment and output attributable to HGFs are no different from the average for the United States (Haltiwanger et al. 2017). Likewise, small business–intensive sectors do not have significantly higher or lower high-growth activity in terms of output or employment (Haltiwanger et al. 2017). NESTA (2009) finds that HGFs are nearly equally present in high-tech and low-tech sectors in the United Kingdom. Similarly, a study of Finnish gazelles—firms that experienced sales growth of at least 50 percent during three consecutive years—finds that high-technology firms were not overrepresented in the gazelle population during 1994–97 (Autio, Sapienza, and Almeida 2000). And in Sweden, Daunfeldt, Johansson, and Halvarsson (2015) suggest that higher R&D intensity may even imply a smaller share of HGFs in the industry. In the United States (state of Georgia), Choi et al. (2017) find relatively higher prevalence of high-growth start-ups in manufacturing and management consulting firms, although wholesale trade; professional, scientific, and technical services; and construction have higher absolute numbers of HGFs.

Evidence collected for this book shows that sectors that are more knowledge- or technology-intensive often exhibit higher-than-average prevalence of HGFs, but so do other sectors that are substantially less high-tech such that there is no clear cross-country pattern indicative of a set of "target" sectors with a greater chance of observing HGFs. For example, in Hungary, figure 2.6 shows that HGFs (following the employment-based OECD definition) are more prevalent in knowledge-intensive services (the vertical green line on the figure shows economywide average prevalence).[15] In Mexico, however, the incidence of HGFs, following the same definition, is particularly high in computers, electronics, electric appliances, and communications, measurement, and transportation equipment—but also in in textiles.

**FIGURE 2.6    HGFs in Hungary Are More Common in Knowledge-Intensive Sectors**

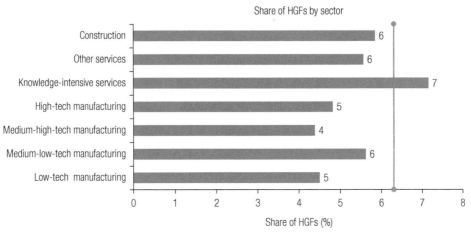

Source: Muraközy, de Nicola, and Tan 2018.

Note: Vertical green line represents economywide average share of high-growth firms (HGFs) (employment-based, OECD). The data include all enterprises with more than five employees between 2010 and 2014. OECD = Organisation for Economic Co-operation and Development.

More generally, when considering the sectoral distribution of HGFs, there are two sets of measures that one may wish to compute:

1. The absolute prevalence of HGFs, which answers the question "which sectors are home to the majority of HGFs?" Said differently, it is essentially a measure of the contribution of a sector to the total count of HGFs. This measure of prevalence is termed "absolute" because sectors are ordered by the absolute count of the HGFs that they house. For a given sector $i$, this is calculated as

$$s_i^a = \frac{\sum_{n \in i} HGF_n}{\sum_i \sum_{n \in i} HGF_n} .$$

2. The relative prevalence of HGFs, which answers the question "which sectors are more likely to be home to an HGF (relative to the economywide average)?" For a given sector $i$, this is calculated as $s_i^r = \dfrac{\sum_{n \in i} HGF_n / \sum_{n \in i} F_n}{\sum_i \sum_{n \in i} HGF_n / \sum_i \sum_{n \in i} F_n} - 1,$

where $F$ is any firm (HGF or not). The share $s_i^r$ may be called the "relative prevalence quotient" (RPQ), akin to the revealed comparative advantage index used in trade analysis. An RPQ greater than 0 means that a given sector is more likely to be home to an HGF than the economywide average.

Figure 2.7 shows the top five manufacturing sectors under each of the measures, using employment-based OECD definitions of HGFs.[16] Three main insights emerge

## FIGURE 2.7  HGFs Are Found in High-Tech and Low-Tech Industries Alike

a. Sectors with the largest number of HGFs, absolute prevalence, $s_i^a$ (%)

Brazil

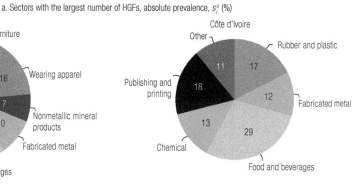

Côte d'Ivoire

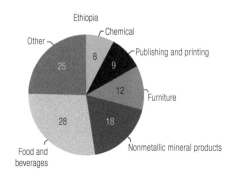

Ethiopia

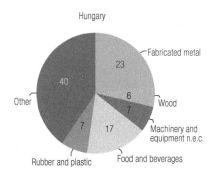

Hungary

Indonesia

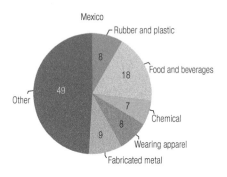

Mexico

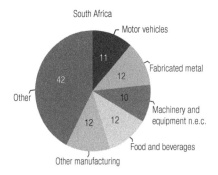

South Africa

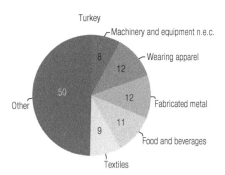

Turkey

*(Figure continues on the following page.)*

b. Sectors with the highest incidence of HGFs, relative prevalence, $s_i^a$ (RPQ)

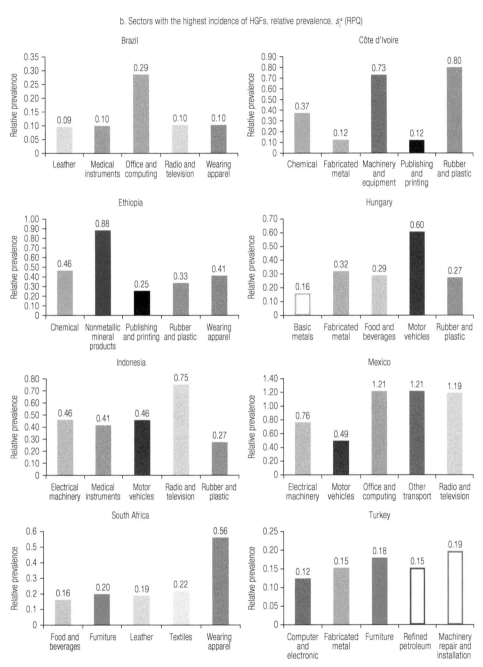

*Source:* Elaboration using national survey and census data.

*Note:* High-growth firm (HGF) status calculated according to the OECD employment-based definition. The figure shows only the top five sectors by each of the prevalence measures, dropping sectors with less than 20 firms. Prevalence is calculated for each year and averaged across the entire sample period for every country. n.e.c. = not elsewhere counted; OECD = Organisation for Economic Co-operation and Development; RPQ = relative preference quotient.

from this analysis. First, no single sector stands out as hosting the largest share of HGFs across all countries studied in this book. Second, the top five industries identified using absolute prevalence of HGFs typically do not completely overlap with the top five sectors identified using relative prevalence.[17] Said differently, the sectors that host most of the HGFs in absolute count are not usually the ones that generate more HGFs relative to the countrywide average. For example, in Indonesia, Mexico, and South Africa, there is no overlap in sectors identified by the two measures, whereas in Brazil, the only industry that hosts both the largest number of HGFs and a disproportionately large share of HGFs is the wearing and apparel sector. Third, HGFs are present across a diverse range of sectors and are not necessarily concentrated in high-tech industries. For example, Hungary's top five manufacturing sectors for HGFs include not only motor vehicles but also food and beverages.[18]

These findings also hold for the contribution of HGFs to job and output creation. Figure 2.8 shows that in Indonesia, HGFs (using either the OECD or the Birch definition, with employment as the growth indicator) are more common in high-tech and medium-high-tech sectors (for example, electrical equipment) but also in low-tech manufacturing (for example, tobacco and wood products).[19] Shifting the focus from HGF incidence to sectors in which HGFs contribute disproportionately to job creation or output growth yields the same set of relatively high-tech sectors but also some low-tech sectors, such as food products, apparel and leather, and furniture.

Moving from sector to physical location, fewer studies focus on the geography of firm growth. Audretsch and Dohse (2004), for instance, find that firms grow more rapidly when located in an agglomeration abundant in knowledge resources. Consistent with these findings, Anyadike-Danes, Bonner, and Hart (2013) document that Greater London has an above-average share of HGFs and, in absolute terms, accounts for almost one-fifth of all HGFs in the United Kingdom. However, they also show that there are a number of relatively remote, sparsely populated, largely rural places that record impressively high shares of HGFs. Similarly, Stam (2005) shows that in the Netherlands, HGFs were likely to emerge in both highly urbanized areas as well as in accessible rural areas, although they were slightly underrepresented in remote rural areas. Likewise, in the United States, SBA Office of Advocacy (2008) finds that high-impact firms can be found in virtually every region, state, and county, with nearly one-quarter of high-impact firms located in rural areas outside of a metropolitan agglomeration.

Similar to these results, evidence from Brazil supports the view that there is no clear regional pattern in the distribution of HGFs. Richer Brazilian states have a higher incidence of HGFs (figure 2.9, panel a), but this relationship is driven by greater rates of new firm formation in states with higher per capita incomes (figure 2.9, panel b). Indeed, the proportion of new firms that become HGFs does not appear to be systematically higher in richer states (figure 2.9, panel c).

FIGURE 2.8 **HGFs in Indonesia Are More Common in High-Tech Manufacturing...
but also in Some Low-Tech**

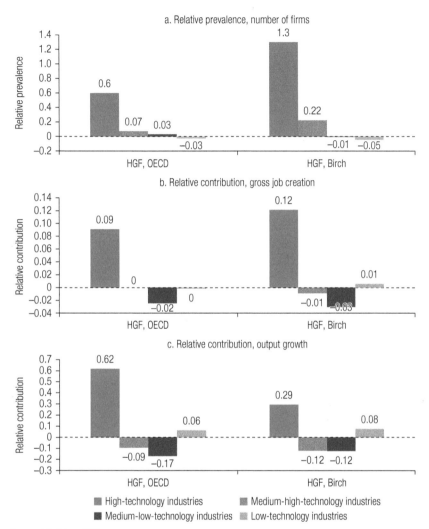

*Source:* Ferro and Kuriakose 2018.

*Note:* The relative prevalence and relative contribution of HGFs is calculated as the RPQ for a given group of industries. RPQ greater than 0 means that the prevalence of HGFs in that group (or their contribution to job creation or output growth) is greater than the economywide average. OECD = Organisation for Economic Co-operation and Development; RPQ = relative preference quotient.

In Mexico, evidence suggests that the northern states, the Mexico City megalopolis, and Jalisco-Guanajuato are not only home to the majority of HGFs, but these states also have higher concentrations of HGFs as measured by the share of HGFs in the total number of firms in each state (figure 2.10, panel a). However, when it comes to other urban agglomerations, the picture is somewhat different; although more than a third of

## FIGURE 2.9   More Entrepreneurship Translates into More HGFs across Brazilian States

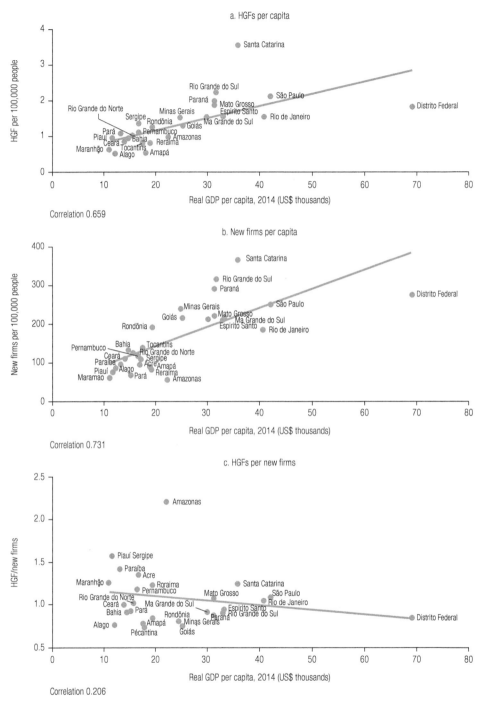

a. HGFs per capita

Correlation 0.659

b. New firms per capita

Correlation 0.731

c. HGFs per new firms

Correlation 0.206

*Source:* Bastos and Silva 2018.

*Note:* GDP per capita is expressed in thousands of 2014 US$. Panel c plots high-growth firms (HGFs) as a share of all new firms against state GDP per capita.

FIGURE 2.10 **HGFs Are More Common in the North of Mexico and in Large Cities**

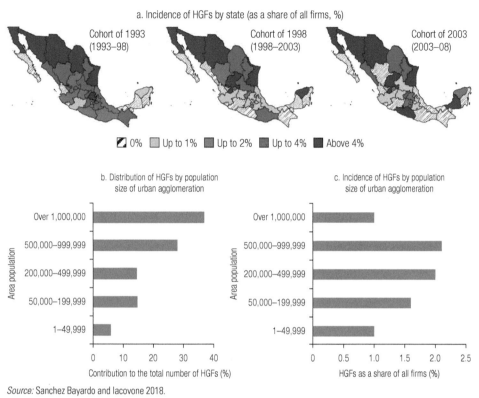

a. Incidence of HGFs by state (as a share of all firms, %)

Cohort of 1993
(1993–98)

Cohort of 1998
(1998–2003)

Cohort of 2003
(2003–08)

⬚ 0%  ⬚ Up to 1%  ⬛ Up to 2%  ⬛ Up to 4%  ⬛ Above 4%

b. Distribution of HGFs by population
size of urban agglomeration

c. Incidence of HGFs by population
size of urban agglomeration

*Source:* Sanchez Bayardo and Iacovone 2018.
*Note:* HGF = high-growth firm.

HGFs are located in megalopolises with 1 million inhabitants or more (figure 2.10, panel b), these localities have a lower incidence of HGFs as compared with less densely populated areas (figure 2.10, panel c).

The literature on agglomeration economies emphasizes that the reason certain locations, such as cities, may exhibit a higher incidence of HGFs is because these areas may offer thicker markets for customers, capital, labor and material inputs, and knowledge spillovers, as well as reduced transaction costs (see, for example, Lechner and Dowling 2003; Fujita, Krugman, and Venables 1999; Audretsch and Feldman 1996; Jaffe, Trajtenberg, and Henderson 1993; Saxenian 1990). Clustering of economic activity can also yield dynamic benefits, such as increased innovation, and may reduce the scope for opportunistic behavior (Matsuyama 1991; Collier and Venables 2008; Audretsch and Dohse 2004). For example, in Ethiopia, 50–60 percent of all OECD-defined HGFs are located in Addis Ababa, the capital city. However, the relative importance of Addis Ababa as a home to HGFs has varied substantially over time. After declining in the early 2000s, the relative prevalence of HGFs in the capital rose rapidly following the implementation of trade and industrial reforms in 2004 (figure 2.11) and surpassed all other major Ethiopian cities.

Location can be particularly critical if it offers improved connectivity in terms of physical infrastructure. Previous studies have noted that firms in areas close to national highways that were upgraded during the late 1990s and early 2000s as part of India's large-scale Golden Quadrilateral project optimized their input structure toward more efficient suppliers and reduced average input costs (Datta 2011) and also experienced higher entry rates, larger increases in plant productivity (Ghani, Grover Goswami, and Kerr 2015), and faster growth of formal manufacturing (Ghani, Grover Goswami, and Kerr 2016).[20] Analysis carried out for this book similarly confirms the positive impact of improved access to infrastructure due to highway construction – and the likely increase in competition that followed – on firm growth among Indian micro-enterprises, although the effect is heterogeneous by firm size. Thanks to better infrastructure, larger firms grew more rapidly, while the incidence of high growth among the smallest firms fell.[21] This is illustrated in figure 2.12, which shows that all firms closer to the GQ highways have a higher likelihood of achieving high-growth status, and the relationship between firm size and the likelihood of high growth is positive for rural districts closer to the GQ. Similar results hold for another major highway network (North-South-East-West, or

**FIGURE 2.11   Reforms Increased the Concentration of HGFs in Ethiopia's Capital City**

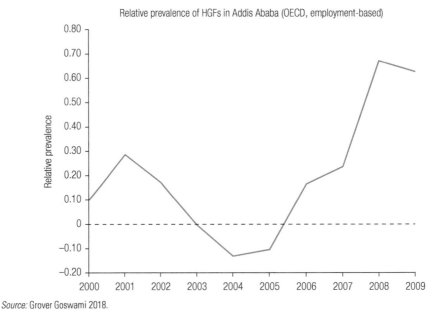

Relative prevalence of HGFs in Addis Ababa (OECD, employment-based)

*Source:* Grover Goswami 2018.

*Note:* The relative prevalence of HGFs in location *i* is computed as $RPQ = \dfrac{Share\ of\ HGFs\ in\ location\ i}{Share\ of\ firms\ in\ location\ i} - 1$, thus, RPQ greater than 0 means that the share of HGFs in Addis Ababa is greater than the share of all firms in that location. HGF = high-growth firm; OECD = Organisation for Economic Co-operation and Development; RFQ = relative prevalence quotient.

High-Growth Firms

## FIGURE 2.12    Larger Micro-Enterprises in India Benefit More from Improved Connectivity

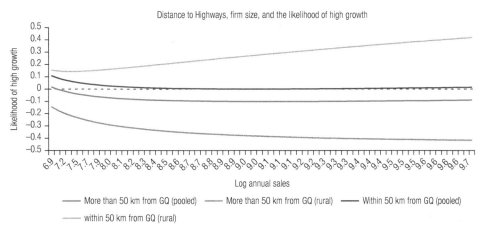

Distance to Highways, firm size, and the likelihood of high growth

——— More than 50 km from GQ (pooled)    ——— More than 50 km from GQ (rural)    ——— Within 50 km from GQ (pooled)

——— within 50 km from GQ (rural)

*Source:* Kim and Sharma 2018.

*Note:* The figure plots the fitted value from the second stage of a two-stage regression. In the first stage, residuals are obtained from a linear regression of high-growth status on household level controls, such as size, age, education, assets, land, and distance from the North-South and East-West highways. Using residuals obtained from the first stage as the dependent variable, the second stage runs a cubic regression on logged size in which size is defined as the household enterprise's annual sales. High-growth firm is defined using the OECD definition, with sales as the growth indicator. OECD = Organisation for Economic Co-operation and Development.

NS-EW), where household enterprises benefit from proximity to the highway relative to those located more than 50 kilometers away.[22]

## Firms and Episodes

Firm growth has been widely documented to be volatile and episodic (for example, Brown, Mason, and Mawson 2014). To an extent, this volatility is driven by overall economic conditions; for example, Sedlácek and Sterk (2017) find that the number of U.S. start-ups in 2009 was 30 percent below its precrisis level in 2006, whereas Moreira (2017) documents that U.S. businesses born during economic downturns start smaller and remain smaller up to 10 years or more into the future, compared with businesses that start during economic upswings. And in the United Kingdom, Anyadike-Danes and Hart (2017) find that the onset of the great recession instigated a fall in the incidence of HGFs, which was followed by a reduction in the repeat high-growth episodes (induced by the fall in firm births).

Even in the absence of external shocks, periods of rapid growth are usually difficult to sustain because they require continued investments in building the customer base, adopting new technologies, and strengthening firm capabilities. Thus, evidence shows that the likelihood of firms experiencing repeated high-growth episodes is low (United Kingdom, Department of Business Innovation and Skills 2014; Daunfeldt and Halvarsson 2015; Hölzl 2014; Parker, Storey, and van Witteloostuijn 2010). For example, in Australia, more than half of HGFs end their high-growth episode within four years and nearly 90 percent within seven years, and a quarter of HGFs lose jobs four years after the conclusion of a high-growth episode (Commonwealth of Australia 2017). Using several definitions of high-performing firms, recent analysis of job destruction in Vietnam illustrates that relative to all firms, high-performing firms are responsible for substantial job destruction before, during, and after the high-performance episode (Aterido and Hallward-Driemeier 2018). This negative effect of high growth on subsequent performance—the so-called "curse of fast growth"—has also been documented by SBA Office of Advocacy (2008) for the United States, Parker, Storey, and van Witteloostuijn (2010) for the United Kingdom (albeit in a small sample), and Hölzl (2014) for Austria. Studies explain that the rapid scaling experienced by an HGF may require a transition to new managerial and organizational practices; to the extent such transitions are not automatic and the firm lacks the capability to organize managerial resources, implement organizational changes, and dynamically adapt strategic focus, its future performance may be compromised (Hambrick and Crozier 1985; Covin and Slevin 1997; see also box 2.1).

The challenges in sustaining high growth and the differences in subsequent growth trajectories of firms that have previously undergone a high-growth episode suggest that

---

**BOX 2.1**

### Firm Organization and High Growth

Firms that expand (or contract) significantly are usually involved in a reorganization process. Firms are hierarchical, with a large base of production workers, who are paid less, and layers of higher management with employees who are more knowledgeable and better paid (Garicano 2000; Caliendo and Rossi-Hansberg 2012). As they expand, thriving firms add more specialized employees in a well-organized hierarchical structure. Caliendo, Monte, and Rossi-Hansberg (2015) identify a number of robust empirical patterns in the organization of firms as well as the changes in this organization as firms grow, based on firm-level data from France. They also show that firms that do not reorganize typically change very little.

The larger the firm, the higher the likelihood that it will reorganize its production by adding a layer (Caliendo, Monte, and Rossi-Hansberg 2015; Caliendo et al. 2015). Firms can respond to a given increase in the demand for their product with or without a reorganization. Firms expanding without reorganization must have more employees at each layer and must pay them more, which would lead to an increase in the average wages at all layers. As firms get larger it makes sense to add one layer in the organization of knowledge, occupied by more specialized workers, usually managers, dealing with nonroutine problems. This reduces the need for knowledge of everyone below. In this case, firms grow by reorganizing.

Evidence suggests that when firms expand by reorganizing they have a larger number of employees than they used to in all layers, but the average wage at preexisting layers tends to fall (Caliendo, Monte, and Rossi-Hansberg 2015; Caliendo et al. 2015; Cruz, Bussolo, and Iacovone 2018). Following the logic above, this drop in average wages has a very clear economic rationale. The objective of the reorganization is exactly to economize on the knowledge of all preexisting layers. Moreover, changes in firms' organization are positively correlated with export performance, which reinforces the mechanism of expansion (Caliendo, Monte, and Rossi-Hansberg 2017; Cruz, Bussolo, and Iacovone 2018).

"HGFs do not appear to be a type of firm, but rather a phase that some firms go through during their life cycle" (Commonwealth of Australia 2017, vi).[23] Evidence from the United States bears this out: only 1.2 percent of U.S. HGFs are able to repeat a high-growth episode in the three years following the event, and the fraction falls to 0.1 percent 10 years after the conclusion of the initial high-growth episode. Likewise, evidence for developing countries in this book strongly supports and reinforces this insight. For example, in Tunisia, more than one-third of firms that were in business during the entire 1996–2009 sample period achieved HGF status (according to the employment-based OECD definition) at least once.[24] However, just 0.01 percent of firms experienced high growth continuously throughout the entire period. Similarly, in Indonesia, the likelihood of a repeated high-growth episode is low despite a significant positive correlation in firm growth rates over time. This is illustrated in figure 2.13 (panel a), which

**FIGURE 2.13   HGFs in Indonesia Are Volatile and Lack Persistence**

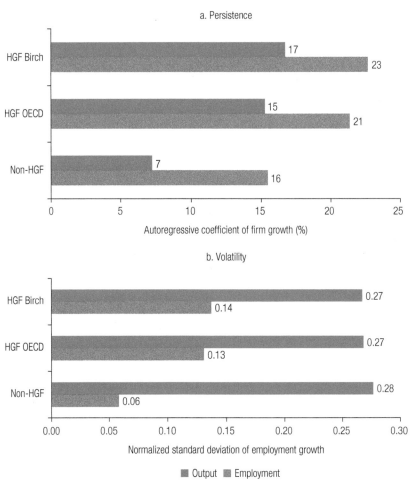

*Source:* Ferro and Kuriakose 2018.

*Note:* Persistence is defined as the autoregressive coefficient of firm growth, expressed in percentage points. Volatility is defined as the normalized standard deviation of growth. HGF = high-growth firm; OECD = Organisation for Economic Co-operation and Development.

plots the autoregressive coefficient of firm growth from one period to the next (in percentage points).[25] The figure shows that the persistence of growth is nearly twice as high for HGFs relative to non-HGFs, but that even for the HGFs it is relatively low in absolute terms. Moreover, once firms have completed a high-growth episode, they add jobs at a slower pace than firms that have never experienced a high-growth event—suggesting that their disproportionate contribution to employment creation is limited to just the high-growth phase.

Volatility is another important aspect in the growth path of HGFs. Fast growth in one period is weakly correlated with rapid growth in the next, and a high-growth episode may well be a function of rapid growth in one year and little to no growth—or even contraction—during other years. This is shown in panel b of figure 2.13 for Indonesia, where the normalized standard deviation of employment growth for firms that have never experienced a high-growth episode is lower than the standard deviation of employment growth for firms that have had at least one high-growth event during their life cycle.[26] Such dynamics raise an important concern about the contribution of HGFs to employment or output generation: a given high-growth firm's contribution to job or output growth over its entire life cycle may be lower than during just the high-growth event.

Transition matrices present a more complete picture of just how difficult it is for firms to sustain high growth, or even remain in the market at all. Table 2.1 shows these matrices for HGFs (employment-based, OECD) in Brazil, Côte d'Ivoire, Ethiopia, Hungary, Indonesia, and Turkey averaged over the maximum number of periods available in the data sets deployed for these countries. Using the full set of possible three- or six-year periods reduces the impact of volatility associated with good and bad times. Within each of the matrices, the numbers in each cell represent the probability that a firm in one of three possible states during an initial three-year period—having just entered the market (*birth*), having grown at an average rate of less than 20 percent per year (*survival*), or having grown at an average of 20 percent per year or more (*high growth*)—either continues growing or exits the market in the next three-year period or six-year period.

The matrices in table 2.1 provide three main insights. First, as was shown before, high growth is difficult to sustain. For example, in Côte d'Ivoire, the likelihood of a repeated high-growth event in the next three-year period is 7.5 percent and about half that (3.4 percent) over the next six-year period (the share is lower in the latter calculation because as time passes more HGFs exit the market). Second, the probability of attaining high growth in the next period is only slightly larger for HGFs as compared with firms that did not experience high growth in the previous period. Continuing with the example of Côte d'Ivoire, the likelihood that a firm that was previously a non-HGF experiences a high-growth event is 6.0 percent in the next

**TABLE 2.1  High Growth Improves Survival Odds, but Only Slightly**

### Brazil

| | 3-year transition probability for firms observed in 1994, 1997, 2000, 2003, 2006, and 2009 (%) | | | 6-year transition probability for firms observed in 1994, 1997, 2000, 2003, and 2006 (%) | | |
|---|---|---|---|---|---|---|
| | Exit | Survival | High growth | Exit | Survival | High growth |
| Birth | 25.6 | 64.3 | 10.2 | 40.0 | 54.7 | 5.2 |
| Survival | 13.0 | 80.0 | 7.1 | 24.6 | 69.6 | 5.8 |
| High growth | 11.7 | 77.4 | 10.9 | 23.8 | 67.9 | 8.4 |

### Côte d'Ivoire

| | 3-year transition probability for firms observed in 2003, 2006, and 2009 (%) | | | 6-year transition probability for firms observed in 2003 and 2006 (%) | | |
|---|---|---|---|---|---|---|
| | Exit | Survival | High growth | Exit | Survival | High growth |
| Birth | 50.1 | 43.9 | 5.9 | 65.0 | 31.6 | 3.4 |
| Survival | 39.4 | 54.6 | 6.0 | 59.7 | 36.7 | 3.7 |
| High growth | 38.4 | 54.1 | 7.5 | 54.4 | 42.3 | 3.4 |

### Ethiopia

| | 3-year transition probability for firms observed in 1997, 2000, 2003, and 2006 (%) | | | 6-year transition probability for firms observed in 1997, 2000, and 2003 (%) | | |
|---|---|---|---|---|---|---|
| | Exit | Survival | High growth | Exit | Survival | High growth |
| Birth | 44.1 | 49.9 | 6.1 | 49.0 | 47.0 | 4.0 |
| Survival | 28.3 | 63.8 | 7.9 | 37.8 | 56.6 | 5.6 |
| High growth | 22.2 | 69.7 | 8.1 | 31.7 | 57.0 | 11.4 |

### Hungary

| | 3-year transition probability for firms observed in 2000, 2003, 2006, 2009, and 2012 (%) | | | 6-year transition probability for firms observed in 2000, 2003, 2006, and 2009 (%) | | |
|---|---|---|---|---|---|---|
| | Exit | Survival | High growth | Exit | Survival | High growth |
| Birth | 75.5 | 24.1 | 0.5 | 75.3 | 21.8 | 2.9 |
| Survival | 38.3 | 59.4 | 2.3 | 46.0 | 51.1 | 2.9 |
| High growth | 17.8 | 74.1 | 8.1 | 32.1 | 63.0 | 5.0 |

### Indonesia

| | 3-year transition probability for firms observed in 1996, 1999, 2002, 2005, 2008, and 2011 (%) | | | 6-year transition probability for firms observed in 1996, 1999, 2002, 2005, and 2008 (%) | | |
|---|---|---|---|---|---|---|
| | Exit | Survival | High growth | Exit | Survival | High growth |
| Birth | 29.5 | 62.7 | 7.8 | 43.2 | 53.1 | 3.8 |
| Survival | 19.8 | 74.7 | 5.5 | 34.4 | 61.9 | 3.8 |
| High growth | 10.8 | 84.5 | 4.7 | 21.1 | 72.7 | 6.2 |

### Turkey

| | 3-year transition probability for firms observed in 2006, 2009, and 2012 (%) | | | 6-year transition probability for firms observed in 2006 and 2009 (%) | | |
|---|---|---|---|---|---|---|
| | Exit | Survival | High growth | Exit | Survival | High growth |
| Birth | 21.6 | 68.5 | 9.9 | 32.3 | 57.7 | 10.0 |
| Survival | 17.2 | 72.6 | 10.2 | 29.2 | 63.9 | 6.9 |
| High growth | 15.4 | 71.4 | 13.1 | 28.0 | 63.0 | 9.0 |

*Note:* HGF status calculated according to the OECD employment-based definition. Birth refers to the first year that a firm is observed in the sample rather than that firm's actual start date. Rows do not always sum to 100 because of rounding. HGF = high-growth firm; OECD = Organisation for Economic Co-operation and Development.

three years and 3.7 percent in the next six years. Annex table 2A.1 further empha-sizes this point by breaking up the "survival" category into three components—negative growth, low (0–5 percent) growth, and moderate (between 5 and 20 percent) growth—showing that firms with negative growth in the previous three-year period are just as, and sometimes even more likely to experience a high-growth event in the next three years as previous HGFs. Third, high growth does not lend much assurance of survival. More than 38 percent of Ivorian firms that expe-rienced a high-growth event are likely to exit the market altogether in the next three years, and the figure rises to above 54 percent over a six-year horizon—both comparable to the exit probabilities of firms that did not experience a high-growth event. HGFs in other countries face lower but still double-digit probabilities of exiting the market in the three years immediately following the high-growth event, and survival probabilities are similarly comparable for HGFs and non-HGFs in most cases.

Evidence from Indonesia shows that survival probabilities are higher when a firm experiences a high-growth event earlier in its life cycle. Figure 2.14 plots Kaplan-Meier survival estimates for a subset of HGFs that experienced rapid employment growth *and* doubled their sales over a three-year period versus firms of the same age that did not go through a high-growth event. The figure shows that, when a high-growth event occurs during a firm's first five years in the market (panel a), it tends to have a lasting impact on that firm's survival probability over the long run (20 or more years). However, these differences diminish for firms that experience a high-growth event later in their life cycle and in some cases—for example, for firms that experience a high-growth episode 6–10 years after birth (panel b)—the survival probability of firms that have never gone through a high-growth phase can actually be higher. Panels c and d of figure 2.14 repeat the same for 11–15 years after birth and 16–20 years after birth.

Finally, evidence from Mexico further reinforces the difficulty of sustaining high growth but also reveals an additional insight: high growth is truly episodic, with some firms attaining it early and others late in their life cycle, whereas others move in and out of high-growth phases. Figure 2.15 provides a visual representa-tion of these transitions, tracing the growth trajectories of Mexican firms over a 20-year period. The challenge of maintaining high growth is illustrated by follow-ing the green arrows at the top of the figure: among a group of firms that experi-enced a high-growth episode during 1994–99, just under 10 percent went through a repeated high-growth episode in the next period (1999–2004). Within this group, only 7 percent (0.7 percent of the original number of HGFs) continued in high-growth status for a third time, and no firm managed to maintain high-growth performance for the entire 20-year period. The episodic nature of high growth is illustrated in the rest of the figure: among firms that survive for the entire 20-year

**FIGURE 2.14** **Survival Probability Is Higher When High Growth Occurs during a Firm's Early Years**

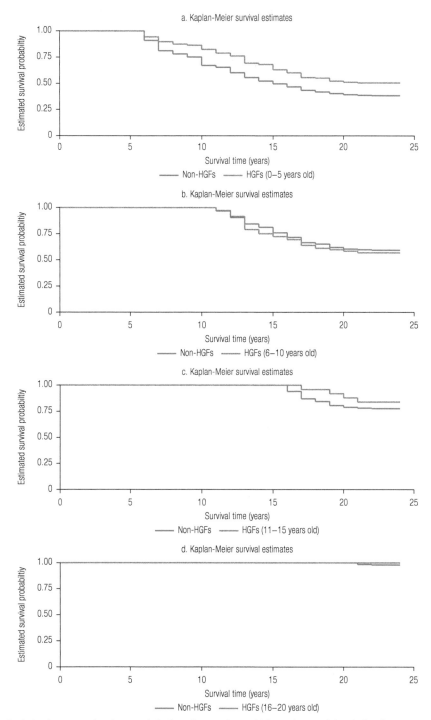

*Note:* Survival estimates are plotted separately for firms that experience a high-growth event during the first five years post-birth [HGF (0–5)], years 6–10 [HGF(6-10)], years 11–15 [HGF(11–15)], and years 16–20 [HGF(16–20)]. HGF = high-growth firm.

## FIGURE 2.15 Firms Move In and Out of HGF Status in Mexico

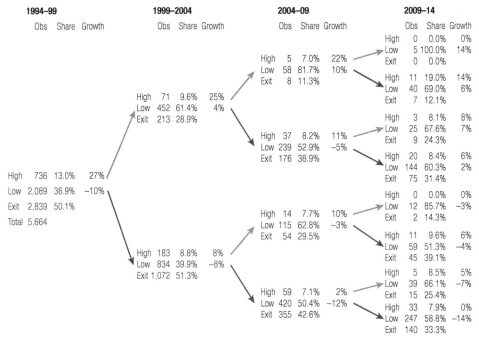

*Source:* Sanchez Bayardo and Iacovone 2018.

*Note:* The figure tracks firms born in 1991–93 for the next 20 years. Because the data are available only every five years, high-growth firms (HGFs) are defined as firms with an average annual growth of 12 percent or more (equivalent to 20 percent per year for three years, the OECD definition). Sample is restricted to firms with a minimum of 10 employees at birth. Obs = observations; OECD = Organisation for Economic Co-operation and Development.

period, there are those that first experience a high-growth episode following 5, 10, and even 15 years of low- to moderate-growth, whereas others go from high to moderate, back to high, and back to moderate growth.

These results suggest that high-growth episodes are much more common than high-growth firms; that is, many more firms experience a high-growth episode at some point in their life cycle than maintain high-growth performance throughout. In addition, high growth—special as it may be in terms of contributing to employment and output creation as well as stimulating other firms—does not offer much protection against exiting the market and provides little assurance of sustaining that performance in the next period. Therefore, searching for high-potential firms may prompt policy makers to undertake the arduous task of trying to target the right firm at the right time (just before the beginning of what is likely to be a short-lived growth episode)—at the cost of pursuing policies that may be firm-agnostic but growth-episode-friendly. To shape our understanding of what such policies may look like, the next chapter explores the potential drivers of high-growth episodes.

# Annex 2A

## FIGURE 2A.1   HGFs in Services Sectors

a. Sectors with the largest number of HGFs, absolute prevalence, $s_i^a$ (%)

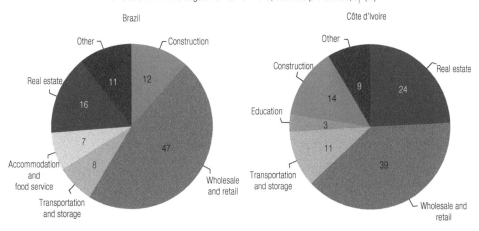

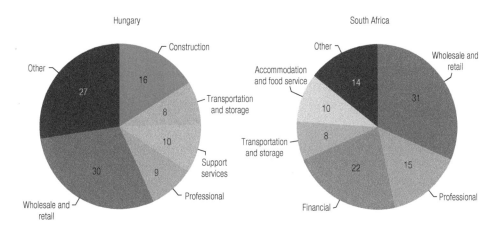

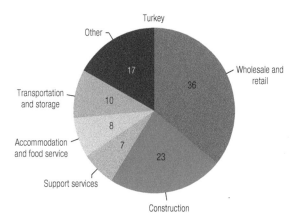

*(Figure continues on the following page.)*

b. Sectors with the highest incidence of HGFs, relative prevalence, $s_j^r$ (RPQ)

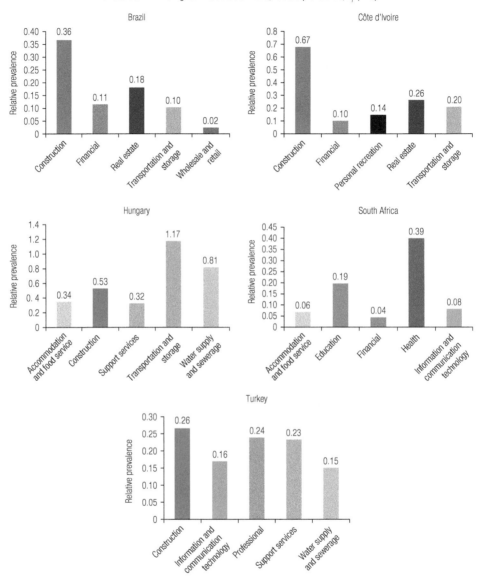

*Source:* Elaboration using national survey and census data.

*Notes:* The figure uses the employment-based OECD definition for HGFs, showing only the top three sectors by each of the prevalence measures, dropping sectors with less than 20 firms. Prevalence is calculated for each year and averaged across the entire sample period for every country. HGF = high-growth firm; RFQ = relative prevalence quotient.

## Côte d' Ivoire

| 3-year transition probability for firms observed in 2003, 2006, and 2009 (%) | | | | | 6-year transition probability for firms observed in 2003 and 2006 (%) | | | | | |
|---|---|---|---|---|---|---|---|---|---|---|
| | Exit | Survival (growth<0) | Survival (low growth) | Survival (moderate growth) | High growth | | Exit | Survival (growth<0) | Survival (low growth) | Survival (moderate growth) | High growth |
| Birth | 50.1 | 23.1 | 9.8 | 11.1 | 5.9 | Birth | 65.0 | 14.1 | 9.1 | 8.5 | 3.4 |
| Survival (growth<0) | 31.2 | 26.7 | 19.0 | 16.5 | 6.6 | Survival (growth<0) | 52.5 | 18.7 | 14.8 | 10.6 | 3.3 |
| Survival (low growth 0-5%) | 36.7 | 25.8 | 19.2 | 13.5 | 4.8 | Survival (low growth 0-5%) | 54.0 | 19.1 | 12.6 | 9.8 | 4.7 |
| Survival (moderate growth >5% & <20%) | 43.9 | 22.9 | 13.3 | 13.8 | 6.1 | Survival (moderate growth >5% & <20%) | 66.2 | 14.2 | 9.4 | 6.6 | 3.6 |
| High growth | 38.4 | 27.2 | 13.6 | 13.3 | 7.5 | High growth | 54.4 | 17.5 | 12.8 | 12.1 | 3.4 |

## Ethiopia

| 3-year transition probability for firms observed in 1997, 2000, 2003, and 2006 (%) | | | | | 6-year transition probability for firms observed in 1997, 2000, and 2003 (%) | | | | | |
|---|---|---|---|---|---|---|---|---|---|---|
| | Exit | Survival (growth<0) | Survival (low growth) | Survival (moderate growth) | High growth | | Exit | Survival (growth<0) | Survival (low growth) | Survival (moderate growth) | High growth |
| Birth | 44.1 | 30.1 | 9.3 | 10.5 | 6.1 | Birth | 49.0 | 24.6 | 7.6 | 14.8 | 4.0 |
| Survival (growth<0) | 22.2 | 38.7 | 16.8 | 15.0 | 7.4 | Survival (growth<0) | 32.1 | 28.4 | 14.9 | 19.4 | 5.2 |
| Survival (low growth 0-5%) | 21.8 | 40.6 | 16.2 | 16.6 | 4.8 | Survival (low growth 0-5%) | 42.0 | 32.0 | 25.0 | 24.0 | 9.0 |
| Survival (moderate growth >5% & <20%) | 35.4 | 26.3 | 13.7 | 15.2 | 9.4 | Survival (moderate growth >5% & <20%) | 44.7 | 18.9 | 8.3 | 22.5 | 5.6 |
| High growth | 22.2 | 46.0 | 13.0 | 10.8 | 8.1 | High growth | 31.7 | 24.1 | 8.9 | 24.1 | 11.4 |

## Indonesia

| 3-year transition probability for firms observed in 1996, 1999, 2002, 2005, 2008, and 2011 (%) | | | | | 6-year transition probability for firms observed in 1996, 1999, 2002, 2005, and 2008 (%) | | | | | |
|---|---|---|---|---|---|---|---|---|---|---|
| | Exit | Survival (growth<0) | Survival (low growth) | Survival (moderate growth) | High growth | | Exit | Survival (growth<0) | Survival (low growth) | Survival (moderate growth) | High growth |
| Birth | 29.5 | 25.2 | 22.4 | 15.2 | 7.8 | Birth | 43.2 | 23.7 | 18.8 | 10.6 | 3.8 |
| Survival (growth<0) | 19.7 | 33.0 | 29.6 | 12.1 | 5.6 | Survival (growth<0) | 34.6 | 29.0 | 24.1 | 8.6 | 3.7 |
| Survival (low growth 0-5%) | 18.6 | 31.3 | 36.5 | 9.0 | 4.8 | Survival (low growth 0-5%) | 32.9 | 26.4 | 28.8 | 8.2 | 3.7 |
| Survival (moderate growth >5% & <20%) | 21.0 | 34.8 | 25.4 | 12.7 | 6.0 | Survival (moderate growth >5% & <20%) | 35.2 | 26.7 | 24.8 | 9.4 | 3.9 |
| High growth | 10.8 | 45.0 | 27.3 | 12.2 | 4.7 | High growth | 21.1 | 36.9 | 24.8 | 10.9 | 6.2 |

## Notes

1. Davis, Haltiwanger, and Schuh (1996) point out that the widely espoused claims about small business's contribution to job creation rests on two common fallacies—the size distribution fallacy and the regression fallacy—and confusion between net and gross job creation.

2. One weakness of many studies has been that they have relied on the analysis of cross-sectional data, in which the movements of firms between size classes may substantially undermine the suitability of such data for the analysis of the job-creation ability of small firms.

3. Because firms face uncertainty regarding market conditions and their own productivity levels, the risk-averse strategy is to start smaller than optimal.

4. For instance, Luttmer (2007) combines independent replication of blueprints with heterogeneity in blueprint quality to explain the decline in firm growth rate after a certain period following entry. Although the quality of the blueprint follows the frontier, nonetheless a given firm and all its blueprints may experience a one-time reduction in quality at some random time. When this occurs, incentives to replicate and maintain blueprints are reduced, and this slows down the growth rate of the firm.

5. In comparison with the Luttmer (2011) model in which firms face a one-time reduction in quality from using older technology, the technology used by firms in the Hopenhayn (2007) model stop tracking the frontier altogether after an exponentially distributed waiting time, which slows down firm growth with age.

6. Atkeson and Kehoe (2005) offer a counterpoint, arguing that plants are more likely to invest in new technologies, develop new markets, and produce a wider array of higher quality products as they age and hence are more likely to experience higher growth.

7. Specifically, OECD-defined HGFs tend to be (unconditionally) younger and smaller than the average firm. However, the evidence on size is less clear-cut when using average size to correct for regression-to-the-mean bias (as proposed by Davis, Haltiwanger, and Schuh 1996), whereas Birch-defined HGFs (top 5 percentile of the distribution) are both older and bigger than the average firm at the beginning of their high-growth spell. This is arguably an artifact of the Birch index because it is more sensitive to absolute changes than to relative ones (Hölzl 2014).

8. In the context of both Turkey and Hungary, these results are based on the OECD definition with growth computed over a three-year window, although the minimum size threshold in Hungary is five employees, whereas in Turkey it is 20 employees.

9. An average firm in the Tunisia data is 14 years old.

10. These results are consistent with prior research on India using census data (Coad and Tamvada 2008) that finds a negative impact of age and size on firm growth in most specifications.

11. This result holds for both OECD and Birch definitions that use employment as the growth indicator.

12. In this data set, which contains information on household enterprises at just two points in time (2004–05 and 2011–12), a firm is defined as an HGF if its average annual sales growth was 25 log points or higher (approximately a 25 percent rate of growth). The 80th percentile of household enterprises in India earn annual revenue of US$5,796 in urban and US$2,576 in rural areas.

13. The data underpinning figure 2.4 are drawn from the Annual Industry and Service Statistics, a census of firms with at least 20 employees. However, Turkish data in figures 2.3, 2.7, and A2.1 and table 2.1 showing cross-country comparisons are drawn from the Entrepreneur Information System data set without a minimum employment threshold (the 10-employee cut-off is imposed on these data for comparability with other country data sets).

14. This relationship is, however, not significant when using the Birch definition.

15. The categories are defined by combining firms' disaggregate industry codes into six industry types—high-tech, medium-high-tech, medium-low-tech, and low-tech manufacturing, as well as knowledge-intensive services (KIS) and other services (NKIS)—based on Eurostat's high-tech classification: http://ec.europa.eu/eurostat/cache/metadata/Annexes/htec_esms_an3.pdf.

16. The corresponding figures for services shown in figure 2A.1.

17. Similar conclusions hold for the services sector and across HGF definitions (OECD versus Birch).

18. Within services, sectors with a higher prevalence of HGFs include knowledge-intensive services (for example, information and communication technology and financial services) in South Africa but also less knowledge-intensive ones (for example, transportation and storage) in Hungary and Côte d'Ivoire.

19. High-technology industries include 2-digit ISIC Revision 3.1 industries 30 (Office, accounting and computing machinery), 32 (Electronics, radio, television, and communication apparatus), and 33 (Medical precision, optical instruments, watches and clocks). Medium-high-technology industries include 2-digit ISIC Revision 3.1 industries 24 (Chemical and chemical products), 29 (Machinery and equipment n.e.c.), 31 (Electrical equipment), 34 (Motor vehicles, trailers, and semi-trailers), and 35 (Other transportation equipment). Medium-low-technology industries include 2-digit ISIC Revision 3.1 industries 23 (Oil processing), 25 (Rubber and plastic products), 26 (Other nonmetal mineral products), and 27 (Basic metal). Low-technology industries include 2-digit ISIC Revision 3.1 industries 15 (Food products and beverages), 16 (Tobacco), 17 (Textiles), 18 (Wearing apparel), 19 (Tanning and dressing of leather), 20 (Wood products except furniture and plaiting materials), 21 (Paper and paper products), 22 (Publishing, printing, and reproduction of recorded media), 36 (Furniture and Manufacturing n.e.c.), and 37 (Recycling products).

20. The project, called the "Golden Quadrilateral," upgraded a network of national highways connecting major metropolitan areas located in the north, west, south, and east nodes of the country (Delhi, Mumbai, Chennai, and Kolkata). Studies for other countries have found positive economic effects in nonnodal locations due to transportation infrastructure in China (for example, Banerjee, Duflo, and Qian 2012; Roberts et al. 2012; Baum-Snow et al. 2017), the United States (for example, Fernald 1999; Chandra and Thompson 2000; Michaels 2008; Duranton and Turner 2012; Baum-Snow 2007; Lahr, Duran, and Varughese 2005), Spain (Holl and Viladecans-Marsal 2011), and Japan (Hsu et al. 2011). A related literature considers nontransportation infrastructure investments in developing economies (for example, Duflo and Pande 2007; Dinkelman 2011).

21. See note 13 for the specific HGF definition used in this example.

22. The NS-EW and the GQ were both part of the National Highways Development Project. The NS-EW network, with an aggregate span of 7,300 kilometers, connects Srinagar in the North to Kanyakumari in the South and Silchar in the East to Porbandar in the West.

23. Despite the difficulty of sustaining or repeating high-growth episodes, however, they may not always be "one-hit wonders." The likelihood of repeating high growth is sensitive to overall economic conditions: Anyadike-Danes and Hart (2017) show that U.K. firms that had experienced a high-growth episode recorded an unusually large number of repeat episodes during the upswing following the Great Recession. There is also some persistence in the overall growth path: using Austrian data, Hölzl (2014) shows that, relative to firms that have never attained HGF status, firms that have experienced a high-growth episode grow on average 2–2.5 percentage points faster following the episode. And in the United States, Haltiwanger et al. (2017) find that the likelihood of suffering the "curse of high growth" diminishes with the number of high-growth episodes that a firm experiences.

24. Only 34 percent of the 44,000 firms that were in business in 1996 survived throughout the sample period.

25. The autoregressive coefficient $\beta$ is calculated as follows:

$$Growth\ Rate_{i,t} = \beta * Growth\ Rate_{i,t-1} + \alpha_t + \gamma_i + \varepsilon_{it}$$

where the growth rate is defined as the first difference in logs for both output and employees, $\alpha_t$ is a vector of time effects, $\gamma_i$ is a vector of firm specific effects, and $\varepsilon_{it}$ is an idiosyncratic error term. The model is estimated using system generalized method of moments following Blundell and Bond (1998).

26. The normalized standard deviations are similar for output growth.

# References

Almus, M. 2002. "What Characterizes a Fast-Growing Firm?" *Applied Economics* 34 (12): 1497–508.

Anyadike-Danes, M., K. Bonner, and M. Hart. 2013. "Exploring the Incidence and Spatial Distribution of High Growth Firms in the UK and Their Contribution to Job Creation." Working Paper 13/05, National Endowment for Science, Technology and the Arts, London.

Anyadike-Danes, M., K. Bonner, M. Hart, and C. Mason. 2009. "Measuring Business Growth: High Growth Firms and Their Contribution to Employment in the U.K." Research Report MBG/35, National Endowment for Science, Technology and the Arts, London.

Anyadike-Danes, M., and M. Hart. 2017. "The UK's High-Growth Firms and Their Resilience over the Great Recession." ERC Research Paper 62, Enterprise Research Centre, Birmingham, UK.

Arkolakis, C., A. Doxiadis, and M. Galenianos. 2017. "The Challenge of Trade Adjustment in Greece." In *Beyond Austerity: Reforming the Greek Economy*, edited by Costas Meghir, Christopher A. Pissarides, Dimitri Vayanos, and Nikolaos Vettas. 103. Cambridge, MA: MIT Press.

Aterido, R., and M. Hallward-Driemeier. "The Elusive Search for Gazelles: Definitions Affect Firms elected—But Not Their Potential for Long-Term Success." Unpublished manuscript, World Bank, Washington, DC.

Atiyas, I., O. Bakis, F. de Nicola, and S. W. Tan. 2018. "High-Growth Firms in Turkey." Background paper for *High-Growth Firms*, World Bank, Washington, DC.

Atkeson, A., and P. J. Kehoe. 2005. "Modeling and Measuring Organization Capital." *Journal of Political Economy* 113 (5): 1026–53.

Audretsch, D. B., and D. Dohse. 2004. "The Impact of Location on Firm Growth." CEPR Discussion Paper 4332, Centre for Economic Policy Research, London.

Audretsch, D. B., and M. P. Feldman. 1996. "Innovative Clusters and the Industry Life Cycle." *Review of Industrial Organization* 11 (2): 253–73.

Autio, E., H. J. Sapienza, and J. G. Almeida. 2000. "Effects of Age of Entry, Knowledge Intensity, and Imitability on International Growth." *Academy of Management Journal* 45 (5): 909–24.

Banerjee, A., E. Duflo, and N. Qian. 2012. "On the Road: Access to Transportation Infrastructure and Economic Growth in China." Working Paper 17897, National Bureau of Economic Research, Cambridge, MA.

Bastos, P., and J. Silva. 2018. "The Origins of High-Growth Firms: Evidence from Brazil." Background paper for *High-Growth Firms*, World Bank, Washington, DC.

Baum-Snow, N. 2007. "Did Highways Cause Suburbanization?" *Quarterly Journal of Economics* 122 (2): 775–805.

———, L. Brandt, J. V. Henderson, M. A. Turner, and Q. Zhang. 2017. "Roads, Railroads and Decentralization in Chinese Cities." *Review of Economics and Statistics* 99 (3): 435–48.

Birch, D. L. 1979. *The Job Generation Process*. MIT Program on Neighborhood and Regional Change, Cambridge, MA.

———. 1981. "Who Creates Jobs?" *Public Interest* 65 (Fall): 3–14.

———, A. Haggerty, and W. Parsons. 1995. *Who's Creating Jobs?* Cambridge, MA: Cognetics, Inc.

Birch, D., and J. Medoff. 1994. "Gazelles." In *Labor Markets, Employment Policy, and Job Creation*, edited by L. C. Solomon and A. R. Levenson, 159–67. Boulder, CO: Westview Press.

Blundell, R., and S. Bond. 1998. "Initial Conditions and Moment Restrictions in Dynamic Panel Data Models." *Journal of Econometrics* 87 (1): 115–43.

Brännback, M., N. Kiviluoto, A. Carsrud, and R. Östermark. 2010. "Much Ado about Nearly Nothing? An Exploratory Study on the Myth of High Growth Technology Start-up Entrepreneurship." *Frontiers of Entrepreneurship Research* 30 (12): 1.

Brown, R., C. Mason, and S. Mawson. 2014. "Increasing 'The Vital 6 Percent': Designing Effective Public Policy to Support High Growth Firms." Working Paper 14/01, National Endowment for Science, Technology and the Arts, London.

Caliendo, L., G. Mion, L. Opromolla, and E. Rossi-Hansberg. 2015. "Productivity and Organization in Portuguese Firms." Working Paper 21811, National Bureau of Economic Research, Cambridge, MA.

Caliendo, L., F. Monte, and E. Rossi-Hansberg. 2015. "The Anatomy of French Production Hierarchies." *Journal of Political Economy* 123 (4): 809–52.

———. 2017. "Exporting and Organizational Change." Working Paper 23630, National Bureau of Economic Research, Cambridge, MA.

Caliendo, L., and E. Rossi-Hansberg. 2012. "The Impact of Trade on Organization and Productivity." *Quarterly Journal of Economics* 127 (3): 1393–467.

Chandra, A., and E. Thompson. 2000. "Does Public Infrastructure Affect Economic Activity? Evidence from the Rural Interstate Highway System." *Regional Science and Urban Economics* 30 (4): 457–90.

Choi, T., A. Rupasingha, J. C. Robertson, and N. G. Leigh. 2017. "The Effects of High Growth on New Business Survival." *Review of Regional Studies* 47 (1): 1–23.

Coad, A., and J. P. Tamvada. 2008. "The Growth and Decline of Small Firms in Developing Countries." Papers on Economics and Evolution 0808, Phillips-Universität Marburg, Marburg, Germany.

Collier, P., and A. J. Venables. 2008. "Managing the Exploitation of Natural Assets: Lessons for Low Income Countries." OxCarre Working Paper 011, Oxford Centre for the Analysis of Resource Rich Economies, University of Oxford, Oxford.

Commonwealth of Australia. 2017. "Australian Innovation System Report 2017." Office of the Chief Economist, Department of Industry, Innovation and Science, Canberra. https://www.industry .gov.au/data-and-publications/australian-innovation-system-report/australian -innovation-system-report-2017.

Cruz, M., M. Bussolo, and L. Iacovone. 2018. "Organizing Knowledge to Compete: Impacts of Capacity Building Programs on Firm Organization." *Journal of International Economics* 111 (March): 1–20.

Datta, A. 2011. "Information Technology Capability, Knowledge Assets and Firm Innovation: A Theoretical Framework for Conceptualizing the Role of Information Technology in Firm Innovation." *International Journal of Strategic Information Technology and Applications* (IJSITA) 2 (3): 9–26.

Daunfeldt, S.-O., and D. Halvarsson. 2015. "Are High-Growth Firms One-Hit Wonders? Evidence from Sweden." *Small Business Economics* 44 (2): 361–83.

Daunfeldt, S.-O., D. Johansson, and D. Halvarsson. 2015. "Using the Eurostat-OECD Definition of High-Growth Firms: A Cautionary Note." *Journal of Entrepreneurship and Public Policy* 4 (1): 50–56.

Davis, S., J. Haltiwanger, and S. Schuh. 1996. *Job Creation and Destruction*. Cambridge, MA: MIT Press.

Davidsson, P., and F. Delmar. 2006. "High-Growth Firms and Their Contribution to Employment: The Case of Sweden 1987–96." In *Entrepreneurship and the Growth of Firms*, edited by Per Davidsson, Frederic Delmar, and Johan Wiklund, 156–78. Cheltenham, UK.: Edward Elgar.

Delmar, F., P. Davidsson, and W. B. Gartner. 2003. "Arriving at the High-Growth Firm." *Journal of Business Venturing* 18 (2): 189–216.

Deschryvere, Matthias. 2008. "High Growth Firms and Job Creation in Finland." Discussion Paper 1144, Research Institute of the Finnish Economy, Helsinki.

Dinkelman, T. 2011. "The Effects of Rural Electrification on Employment: New Evidence from South Africa. *American Economic Review* 101 (7): 3078–108.

Duflo, E., and R. Pande. 2007. "Dams." *Quarterly Journal of Economics* 122 (2): 601–46.

Dunne, P., and A. Hughes. 1994. "Age, Size, Growth and Survival: UK Companies in the 1980s." *Journal of Industrial Economics* 42 (2): 115–40.

Duranton, G., and M. A. Turner. 2012. "Urban Growth and Transportation." *Review of Economic Studies* 79 (4): 1407–40.

Eslava, M., and J. Haltiwanger. 2013. "Young Businesses, Entrepreneurship, and the Dynamics of Employment and Output in Colombia's Manufacturing Industry." Working paper, CAF, Caracas.

European Commission. 2008. "Integrated Guidelines for Growth and Jobs (2008–2010)." Council of the European Union, Brussels.

Evans, D. 1987. "The Relation between Firm Growth, Size, and Age: Estimates for 100 Manufacturing Industries." *Journal of Industrial Economics* 35 (4): 567–81.

Fagiolo, G., and A. Luzzi. 2006. "Do Liquidity Constraints Matter in Explaining Firm Size and Growth? Some Evidence from the Italian Manufacturing Industry." *Industrial and Corporate Change* 15 (1): 1–39.

Fernald J. G. 1999. "Roads to Prosperity? Assessing the Link Between Public Capital and Productivity." *American Economic Review* 89 (3): 619–38.

Ferro, E., and S. Kuriakose. 2018. "Indonesia: High-Growth Firms." Background paper for *High-Growth Firms,* World Bank, Washington, DC.

Fujita, M., P. Krugman, and A. J. Venables. 1999. *The Spatial Economy: Cities, Regions and International Trade.* Cambridge, MA: MIT Press.

Garicano, L. 2000. "Hierarchies and the Organization of Knowledge in Production." *Journal of Political Economy* 108 (5): 874–904.

Ghani, E., A. Grover Goswami, and W. R. Kerr. 2015. "Highway to Success: The Impact of the Golden Quadrilateral Project for the Location and Performance of Indian Manufacturing." *Economic Journal* 126 (591): 317–57.

———. 2016. "Highways and Spatial Location within Cities: Evidence from India." *World Bank Economic Review* 30 (Supplement 1): S97–S108.

Gibrat, R. 1931. *Les Inégalités Économiques.* Paris: Recueil Sirey.

Grover Goswami, A. 2018. "Firms Far Up! Productivity, Agglomeration, and Growth Entrepreneurship in Ethiopia." Background paper for *High-Growth Firms,* World Bank, Washington, DC.

Halabisky, D., E. Dreessen, and C. Parsley. 2006. "Growth in Firms in Canada, 1985–1999." *Journal of Small Business and Entrepreneurship* 19 (3): 255–68.

Hall, B. 1987. "The Relationship between Firm Size and Firm Growth in the U.S. Manufacturing Sector." *Journal of Industrial Economics* 35 (4): 583–606.

Haltiwanger, J. 2012. "Job Creation and Firm Dynamics in the United States." In *Innovation Policy and the Economy,* edited by Josh Lerner and Scott Stern, vol. 12, 17–38. Cambridge, MA: NBER.

———, R. S. Jarmin, R. Kulick, and J. Miranda. 2017. "High-Growth Firms: Contribution to Job, Output, and Productivity Growth." In *Measuring Entrepreneurial Businesses: Current Knowledge and Challenges,* edited by John Haltiwanger, Erik Hurst, Javier Miranda, and Antoinette Schoar, 11–62. Chicago: University of Chicago Press.

Haltiwanger, J., R. S. Jarmin, and J. Miranda. 2013. "Who Creates Jobs? Small versus Large versus Young." *Review of Economics and Statistics* 95 (2): 347–61.

Hambrick, D. C., and L. M. Crozier. 1985. "Stumblers and Stars in the Management of Rapid Growth." *Journal of Business Venturing* 1 (1): 31–45.

Henrekson, M., and D. Johansson. 2010. "Gazelles as Job Creators: A Survey and Interpretation of the Evidence." *Small Business Economics* 35 (2): 227–44.

Henrekson, M., and T. Sanandaji. 2014. "Small Business Activity Does Not Measure Entrepreneurship." *Proceedings of the National Academy of Sciences* 111 (5): 1760–65.

Holl, A., and E. Viladecans-Marsal. 2011. "Infrastructure and Cities: The Impact of New Highways on Urban Growth." Working Paper, Universitat de Barcelona-Institut d'Economia de Barcelona.

Hölzl, W. 2009. "Is the R&D Behaviour of Fast-Growing SMEs Different? Evidence from CIS III Data for 16 Countries." *Small Business Economics* 33 (1): 59–75.

———. 2010. "The Economics of Entrepreneurship Policy: Introduction to the Special Issue." *Journal of Industry, Competition and Trade* 10 (3): 187–97.

———. 2014. "Persistence, Survival and Growth: A Closer Look at 20 Years of Fast-Growing Firms in Austria." *Industrial and Corporate Change* 12 (1): 199–231.

Hopenhayn, H. A. 1992. "Entry, Exit, and Firm Dynamics in Long Run Equilibrium." *Econometrica* 60 (5): 1127–50.

———. 2007. "Knowledge, Diffusion and Reallocation." Unpublished manuscript, University of California, Los Angeles.

Hsu, W. C., X. Gao, J. Zhang, and H. Mei Lin. 2011. "The Effects of Outward FDI on Home-Country Productivity: Do Location of Investment and Market Orientation Matter?" *Journal of Chinese Economic and Foreign Trade Studies* 4 (2): 99–116.

Hurst, E., and B. W. Pugsley. 2011. "What Do Small Businesses Do?" Working Paper 17041, National Bureau of Economic Research, Cambridge, MA.

IFC (International Finance Corporation). 2013. "IFC Jobs Study: Assessing Private Sector Contributions to Job Creation and Poverty Reduction." Washington, DC.

Jaffe, A. B., M. Trajtenberg, and R. Henderson. 1993. "Geographic Localization of Knowledge Spillovers as Evidenced by Patent Citations." *Quarterly Journal of Economics* 108 (3): 577–98.

Jovanovic, B. 1982. "Selection and the Evolution of Industry." *Econometrica* 50 (3): 649–70.

Kim, K., and S. Sharma. 2018. "Microenterprise Growth Dynamics: Evidence from India." Background paper for *High-Growth Firms*, World Bank, Washington, DC.

Kirchhoff, B. A. 1994. *Entrepreneurship and Dynamic Capitalism: The Economics of Business Firm Formation and Growth*. Westport, CT: Praeger.

Lahr, M., R. Duran, and A. Varughese. 2005. "Estimating the Impact of Highways on Average Travel Velocities and Market Size." Center for Urban Policy Research, Rutgers University, New Brunswick, NJ.

Lechner, C., and M. Dowling. 2003. "Firm Networks: External Relationships as Sources for the Growth and Competitiveness of Entrepreneurial Firms." *Entrepreneurship and Regional Development* 15 (1): 1–26.

López-García, P., and S. Puente. 2009. "What Makes a High-Growth Firm? A Probit Analysis Using Spanish Firm-Level Data." Documentos de Trabajo 0920, Bank of Spain.

Luttmer, E. G. 2007. "Selection, Growth, and the Size Distribution of Firms." *Quarterly Journal of Economics* 122 (3): 1103–44.

———. 2011. "On the Mechanics of Firm Growth." *Review of Economic Studies* 78 (3): 1042–68.

Mason, C., and R. Brown. 2013. "Entrepreneurial Ecosystems and Growth-Oriented Entrepreneurship." Background Paper for OECD LEED Program and the Dutch Ministry of Foreign Affairs.

Matsuyama, K. 1991. "Increasing Returns, Industrialization, and Indeterminacy of Equilibrium." *Quarterly Journal of Economics* 106 (2): 617–50.

Michaels, G. 2008. "The Effect of Trade on the Demand for Skill: Evidence from the Interstate Highway System." *Review of Economics and Statistics* 90 (4): 683–701.

Moreira, S. 2017. "Firm Dynamics, Persistent Effects of Entry Conditions, and Business Cycles." Working Paper CES 17–29, Center for Economic Studies, U.S. Census Bureau, Department of Commerce, Washington, DC.

Muraközy, B., F. de Nicola, and S. W. Tan. 2018. "High-Growth Firms in Hungary." Background paper for *High-Growth Firms*, World Bank, Washington, DC.

NESTA (National Endowment for Science, Technology and the Arts). 2009. "The Vital 6 Percent: How High-Growth Innovative Businesses Generate Prosperity and Jobs." NESTA, London.

OECD (Organisation for Economic Co-operation and Development). 1997. *Small Business, Job Creation and Growth: Facts, Obstacles and Best Practices*. Paris: OECD.

———. 2010. *High-Growth Enterprises: What Governments Can Do to Make a Difference*. Paris: OECD.

Parker, S. C., D. J. Storey, and A. van Witteloostuijn. 2010. "What Happens to Gazelles? The Importance of Dynamic Management Strategy." *Small Business Economics* 35 (2): 203–26.

Picot, G., J. R. Baldwin, and R. Dupuy. 1995. "Small Firms and Job Creation—A Reassessment." *Canadian Economic Observer* 3: 1–318.

Roberts, M., U. Deichmann, B. Fingleton, and T. Shi. 2012. "Evaluating China's Road to Prosperity: A New Economic Geography Approach." *Regional Science and Urban Economics* 42 (4): 580–94.

Sanchez Bayardo, L. F., and L. Iacovone. 2018. "High-Growth Firms and Spillovers in Mexico." Background paper for *High-Growth Firms*, World Bank, Washington, DC.

Saxenian, A. 1990. "Regional Networks and the Resurgence of Silicon Valley." *California Management Review* 33 (1): 89–112.

SBA Office of Advocacy. 2008. "High-Impact Firms: Gazelles Revisited," by Z. J. Acs, W. Parsons, and S. Tracy. Small Business Research Summary 328, Washington, DC.

Schreyer, Paul. 2000. "High-Growth Firms and Employment." OECD Science, Technology, and Industry Working Paper 2000/03, Organisation for Economic Co-operation and Development, Paris.

Sedláček, P., and V. Sterk. 2017. "The Growth Potential of Startups over the Business Cycle." *American Economic Review* 107 (10): 3182–210.

Slevin, D. P., and J. G. Covin. 1997. "Strategy Formation Patterns, Performance, and the Significance of Context." *Journal of Management* 23 (2): 189–209.

Stam, E. 2005. "The Geography of Gazelles in the Netherlands." *Tijdschrift voor Economische en Sociale Geografie* 96 (1): 121–27.

———, and K. Wennberg. 2009. "The Roles of R&D in New Firm Growth." *Small Business Economics* 33 (1): 77–89.

Storey, D. J. 1991. "The Birth of New Firms—Does Unemployment Matter? A Review of the Evidence." *Small Business Economics* 3 (3): 167–78.

———. 1994. *Understanding the Small Business Sector*. London: Routledge.

United Kingdom, Department of Business Innovation and Skills. 2014. "Innovative Firms and Growth," by A. Coad, M. Cowling, P. Nightingale, G. Pellegrino, M. Savona, and J. Siepel. UK Innovation Survey, London.

Wyrwich, M. 2010. "Assessing the Role of Strategy and Socioeconomic Heritage for Rapidly Growing Firms: Evidence from Germany." *International Journal of Entrepreneurial Venturing* 1 (3): 245–63.

# 3. What Makes for High Growth?

The previous chapters explore the main reasons why researchers and policy makers care about high-growth firms (HGFs) as well as their basic characteristics, focusing particularly on features that have been mentioned in discussions on targeting firms. This chapter examines some of the potential drivers of the success of HGFs, noting the key distinction between firm and episode introduced in chapter 2. It begins with a brief review of how economic thinking on firm growth has evolved, identifying some of the potential determinants of productivity and growth that may be particularly relevant for HGFs. Then, leveraging the particular features of each of the data sets analyzed for this book—for example, the ability to link firms and workers in Brazil, to zoom in on product details in India, or to trace firm networks in Thailand—the chapter considers how each of the specific channels—innovation, agglomeration and networks, skills and managerial experience, global linkages, and financial development—may contribute to the likelihood of a firm experiencing a high-growth event. To illustrate the ability of these channels to facilitate high growth, this chapter also offers specific examples of HGFs across countries and sectors.

Although the results in this chapter stop short of identifying the relative importance of these channels, they confirm the significant contribution that each makes to increasing the probability of a high-growth episode (see table 3.1 for a summary of the evidence across various channels). The role of productivity is difficult to pinpoint because firm growth and survival depend first and foremost on profitability, which is related to productivity but also to markups (prices) and demand shocks. Hence, results show that productivity is positively related to the likelihood of high growth in Ethiopia and Hungary, whereas the relationship in Côte d'Ivoire and Turkey is mixed. Indeed, given the multiple factors at play in determining firm growth, data from Côte d'Ivoire show limited overlap between a set of "efficient" HGFs (those firms that would attain HGF status if resources across the economy were allocated according to firms' productivity) and the observed HGFs. Productivity-limiting distortions may not only reduce the number of firms that could attain high growth but are also likely to misallocate resources in a way that allows less efficient firms to achieve high growth—obscuring the relationship between high growth and productivity.

The relationship between various measures of innovation and the probability of experiencing a high-growth event is generally positive, and evidence from India shows that it is much stronger for top performers (firms in the top quantiles of the growth rate distribution). Network economies and agglomeration similarly play an important role; for example, in Thailand, firms that are more connected with others via direct

TABLE 3.1  **Correlates of High Firm Growth: Summary of Chapter Results**

| | Productivity | Innovation | Agglomeration and networks | Skills and managerial capabilities | Global linkages Exports | FDI |
|---|---|---|---|---|---|---|
| Côte d'Ivoire | (+) (−)          (−) | | | | | |
| Brazil | | | | (+) | | |
| Ethiopia | (+) | | (+) | (+) | (+) | (+) (−) |
| Hungary | (+) | | | (+) | (+) | |
| India | | (+) | | | (+) | |
| Indonesia | | | | | (+) | |
| Mexico | | (+) | | (+) | (+) | (+) |
| Thailand | | | (+) | | | |
| Turkey | (+)          (−) | | | | (+) (−) | (−) |
| Tunisia | | | | | (+) | (+) |

Legend

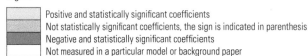

Positive and statistically significant coefficients
Not statistically significant coefficients, the sign is indicated in parenthesis
Negative and statistically significant coefficients
Not measured in a particular model or background paper

*Note:* Côte d'Ivoire productivity: Statistically insignificant for TFPQ (sign varies depending on whether a dummy variable for Abidjan is included), negative and significant for TFPR. Turkey productivity: Positive premium with only year and industry controls, negative premium with controls for demand, capital intensity, ownership, industry, and region. India innovation: Significance driven primarily by firms in services. Indonesia exports: Driven by firms that experience a high-growth event in the first 10 years. Skills: Proxied by wages in all countries except Brazil, where both wages and previous experience are taken into account. FDI = foreign direct investment; TFPQ = quantity total factor productivity; TFPR = revenue total factor productivity.

ownership, holding companies, or subsidiaries are more likely to experience high growth, whereas Ethiopian plants located in or close to large urban centers have a greater probability of attaining high growth than more distantly located firms. The latter is reminiscent of the evidence from India presented in the previous chapter, which showed that policies aimed at improving physical connectivity can facilitate high growth while also weeding out some of the smallest and least efficient producers. Global linkages—measured by a firm's own exporting status, share of exporters, foreign direct investment (FDI) recipients in a given location or sector, or imports of technology—significantly increase the probability of a high-growth event for firms in Hungary, India, Mexico, and Tunisia. When it comes to employees and managers, firms that pay higher wages and attract better workers have a greater likelihood of subsequently attaining high growth—reflecting the key role that the human capital of founding managers and employees (for example, previous experience in the formal sector, in a larger firm, and in management) plays in determining future firm growth trajectories. Finally, the likelihood of attaining high growth also depends on firms' ability to access finance, although given the large number of other potential distortions in the business environment, the link can be robustly identified in only upper-middle-income countries.

Together these results underscore the importance of firm capabilities (for example, innovation, managerial practices, and quality of human capital), cross-firms linkages (for example, agglomeration and networks), and an enabling policy environment (for example, external openness, financial development) in stimulating firm growth and encouraging high-growth episodes. But in addition to these, as the first part of this chapter explains, a large part of firm growth is also driven by demand forces. Although difficult to disentangle empirically, the distinction is crucial from a policy perspective: the arguments in support of targeted public policy for HGFs normally envision giving a further boost to better-managed, more innovative firms rather than supporting firms that may already be benefiting from lack of competition or political connections or just happen to be in the right place at the right time. Because one cannot rule out the likelihood of these forces driving firm growth—indeed, as the evidence for Côte d'Ivoire in this chapter shows, an "efficient" distribution of HGFs could look very different from the observed distribution—policy makers should exercise great caution in pursuing targeted firm policies.

## Productivity

A fundamental point of departure when thinking about firm growth is a firm's production function: a relationship expressed as a quantity of output produced by a certain combination of quantities of inputs—for example, intermediate materials, labor, capital, and so on—and a technical efficiency term (productivity). It is well known that variations in productivity trump any other source of heterogeneity in firm performance: in the United States, firms in the 90th percentile of the productivity distribution produce twice as much with the same set of inputs as firms in the 10th percentile (Syverson 2011), whereas in China and India the gap is 5:1 (Hsieh and Klenow 2009).

Although potentially simple in concept, estimating even a basic Cobb-Douglas production function with firm-level data can be a major challenge. In addition to a host of endogeneity issues that may prevent an analyst from accurately estimating the contributions from various inputs and therefore correctly backing out the unobserved productivity term (see Ackerberg, Caves, and Frazer [2015] and Gandhi, Navarro, and Rivers [2017] for a review of challenges and recent advances in this area), the production function is fundamentally a relationship of quantities rather than values. However, with a few exceptions and even then primarily for narrowly defined sectors (for example, see an application to the cement industry in Syverson [2004]), the analyst usually observes the values (price × quantity) of inputs and outputs. This means that, when a firm grows, it is often difficult to tell whether it does so by producing more units or charging higher prices, possibly as a result of better quality but also potentially due to positive demand shocks or market power (see box 3.1 for an overview of theoretical frameworks of firm growth).[1]

## Theories of Firm Growth

One of the more well-known approaches to conceptualizing firm growth in economics is Gibrat's Law, which states that growth is independent of firm size (Gibrat 1931). Most applications of Gibrat's Law parameterize firm growth as a series of random shocks, with a firm's current size being the realization of the sum of past shocks. This produces a lognormal distribution of firm size that closely resembles observed patterns, but the lack of a theoretical foundation explaining why some firms may grow more rapidly than others has encouraged economists to pursue more structural explanations.[a] Within the neoclassical literature, such efforts have been primarily motivated by two concepts: the idea that each firm has an "optimal" size given market conditions, transaction costs, and management capabilities (Viner 1932; Coase 1937; Lucas 1978), and a concept of "evolutionary" competition in which inefficient incumbents are forced out of the market and their resources are absorbed by more efficient firms (Alchian 1950; Friedman 1953).

If there is some sort of optimal size for firms, why do firms not enter the market at the "right" size? One reason could be that firms face some uncertainty about their productivity levels and therefore start smaller than optimal—but once the most efficient producers realize their actual productivity levels, they scale rapidly (Nelson 1981; Jovanovic 1982; Hopenhayn 1992; Luttmer 2007; Decker et al. 2016).[b] Alternatively, firms need to make investments in accumulation of intangible capital that determines their productivity, and some firms are able to make these investments easier than others (for example, Luttmer 2011). This cost advantage can disappear over time, or firms can take a productivity draw each period, aided by investments in intangible assets to influence this draw (for example, Ericson and Pakes 1989).

A separate set of explanations focuses on demand-side dynamics. It takes time and effort for firms to learn and accumulate demand by building a customer base through offering bundled services, investing in advertising, and pursuing other strategies that create relationship capital along buyer-supplier links (Foster, Haltiwanger, and Syverson 2016). As a result, young firms are likely to be smaller than incumbents with more developed demand relationships, but those that are able to leverage active demand accumulation will grow rapidly compared with other entrants or existing firms.[c] For example, Eaton, Kortum, and Sotelo (2012) build a model in which firms actively learn their product appeal by forming new matches with buyers, whereas Arkolakis (2015) makes firm growth dependent on accumulating demand at the firm level. The predictions of these models are broadly consistent with empirical findings in the United States (for example, Davis et al. 2009), suggesting that aspects such as marketing costs and continuing customer relationships (for example, Eaton, Kortum, and Sotelo 2012), and investments in quality certifications and adjustment frictions (Itskhoki and Helpman 2014; Cosar, Guner, and Tybout 2010) may be important channels for firms to achieve more rapid growth through active demand accumulation.

Distortions in allocation of resources can inhibit the competition channel from distributing resources to the most efficient firms (Hsieh and Klenow 2009) and can have additional dynamic effects by adversely affecting firm decisions to make productivity-enhancing investments (Bento and Restuccia 2017). When such distortions are disproportionately binding on some firms versus others, they generate differences in observed growth rates. For example, models such as Evans and Jovanovic (1989) focus on liquidity constraints, whereas Hsieh and Klenow (2014) link firm growth to investments in organization capital, with constraints on accumulation of such capital varying by firm size (being particularly binding on larger firms) and country. These constraints can be linked to

*(Box continues on the following page.)*

institutional factors such as trust environment, resulting in poor managerial delegation efficiency, lack of firm selection, and "local market satisficing" (Akcigit, Grigsby, and Nicholas 2017).

A number of other approaches to explain firm growth have received less attention in the mainstream economic literature. These include Penrose's theory of managerial attention span, in which managers face the trade-off of diverting attention from running existing projects efficiently or developing new growth projects (Penrose 1959); the "managerial theory" approach in which managers derive utility from the size of their firm (for example, Marris 1963, 1964; Mueller 1969); and the "organizational ecology" approach which conditions growth on the availability of new niches with rich resource pools (Hannan and Freeman 1977; Hannan 2005).

a. The Pareto distribution is a closer empirical approximation (see, for example, Luttmer 2007), although in practice the two distributions are quite similar (de Wit 2005).
b. In Nelson (1981) firms make technological bets with inherent uncertainties and end up with different productivities, whereas Jovanovic (1982) models firms with a time-invariant efficiency parameter, implying that a firm's productivity varies initially but converges over time to a constant value. Melitz (2003) and Asplund and Nocke (2006) introduce assumptions regarding sunk costs, learning, and the stability of productivity. These models imply that over time more productive firms expand at the expense of less productive ones, suggesting a positive correlation between productivity and firm size.
c. This also means that demand is likely to become a more important determinant of firm growth later in the firm's life cycle—see the discussion in box 3.2.

The empirical literature has struggled to pin down a strong relationship between productivity and firm growth. Although some studies document a positive association (for example, Pavcnik [2002] for Chile, Sleuwaegen and Goedhuys [2002] for Côte d'Ivoire, and Liu, Tsou, and Hammit [1999] for Taiwan, China), others find only a weak effect (for example, Foster et al. [1998] for the United States, Bottazzi, Cefis, and Dosi [2002] and Bottazzi, Secchi, and Tamagni [2006] for Italy), and yet others establish a negative relationship (for example, Haltiwanger [1997] and Disney, Haskel, and Heden [2003] for the United Kingdom and the United States).[2] One reason could be due to measurement issues: because data on firm-level prices are rarely available, total factor productivity (TFP) is often measured in revenue (known as TFPR) rather than quantity terms (known as TFPQ). As mentioned earlier, firms may charge higher prices—and therefore appear to be more productive in TFPR terms—for reasons that are unrelated to technical efficiency, which could conflate and bias the true relationship between efficiency and growth.[3] Another reason could be market structure, such as lack of competition, given that competition is what forces inefficient firms to exit and allows more efficient ones to grow by absorbing the available resources (see for example, Baily and Farrell 2006; Cabral 2007).[4] Finally, some firms may become more productive through downsizing (Coad 2007) or may choose to exploit higher productivity by spending less on inputs, including workers, rather than expanding output (Daunfeldt, Elert, and Johansson 2010).

Focusing specifically on HGFs, SBA Office of Advocacy (2008) shows that revenue-based labor productivity (output per worker) in the United States is higher for HGFs and this difference has increased over time.[5] Mason, Robinson, and Rosazza-Bondibene (2012) find that HGFs in the United Kingdom are on average more productive, although they make a limited overall contribution to productivity growth. Similarly, Du and Temouri (2015) show that faster TFP growth in a prior period significantly increases the likelihood that manufacturing and services firms in the United Kingdom experience a high-growth event in the subsequent period.

Data from Ethiopia and Hungary confirm a positive and statistically significant association between productivity and subsequent episodes of high firm growth. In Ethiopia, a 1 percentage point increase in a firm's initial period revenue-based TFP raises the likelihood of subsequently experiencing a high-growth event by an average of 0.17–0.27 percentage point. The strength of the relationship rises rapidly with the plant's initial period TFP level, and the estimates are larger for the Birch definition, implying a greater advantage for larger firms (figure 3.1).[6]

**FIGURE 3.1 Higher Initial TFP Is Associated with Subsequent High Growth among Ethiopian Plants**

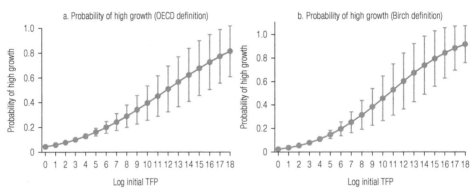

a. Probability of high growth (OECD definition)

b. Probability of high growth (Birch definition)

*Source:* Grover Goswami 2018.

*Note:* The figure shows the probability of experiencing a high-growth event at different values of three-year lagged plant-level TFP (estimated using the Levinsohn and Petrin [2003] approach) and controlling for three-year lagged values of firm size, age, interaction of age and size, average wage, ownership, foreign direct investment, and export status, as well as location, industry, and time effects. Robust standard errors are clustered at the plant level. All variables other than TFP are held at their means. Estimates are performed with a dynamic probit model and robust standard errors are clustered at the plant level. Height of vertical lines corresponds to the 95 percent confidence interval. Data cover the period from 1996 to 2009. OECD = Organisation for Economic Co-operation and Development; TFP = total factor productivity.

For Hungary, figure 3.2 shows that firms that go on to experience a high-growth episode outperform their peers on multiple dimensions of productivity, including TFP, return on assets (ROA), and output per worker. This link from higher TFP to the probability of a high-growth event remains robust even when controlling for a prior high-growth episode, suggesting that a high-growth experience requires prior investment or improvement in productivity, that is, the relationship is more than just a level difference in productivity between firms that experience a high-growth event and those that do not.

FIGURE 3.2

**FIGURE 3.2    Future HGFs Outperform Other Hungarian Firms on Multiple Dimensions of Productivity**

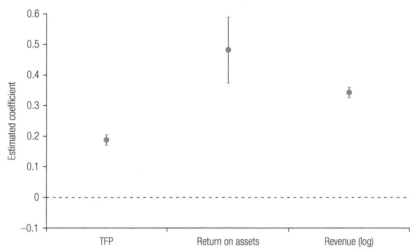

*Source:* Muraközy, de Nicola, and Tan 2018.

*Note:* The figure is a rope-ladder representation of estimated coefficients and 95 percent confidence bands from regressions of variables on the X-axis in year *t* on a firm's high-growth status (employment-based, OECD definition) from *t* to (*t* + *3*). All regressions control for firm age, exporting status, and average wages and include firm size, category, industry, and year fixed effects. Regressions are estimated by ordinary least squares, and standard errors are clustered at the firm level. HGF = high-growth firm; OECD = Organisation for Economic Co-operation and Development.

Consistent with this argument, HGFs also outperform other Hungarian firms during the high-growth episode. Employment and revenue of HGFs grow more rapidly than those of non-HGFs during the high-growth event by definition; furthermore, their TFP growth is also significantly higher, and the difference increases with the length of the high-growth episode (figure 3.3 panel a). By comparison, the rate of increase in ROA is lower, possibly because high growth may require large investments in fixed capital that may turn profitable only with time. The change in the ROA coefficient from negative to insignificantly different from zero with the change from a three-year time window over which high growth is computed to a five-year window is consistent with this hypothesis.

These findings are robust to sectoral composition—they hold in aggregate as well as for manufacturing versus services and high-tech versus low-tech industries—as well as heterogeneity between the group of HGFs versus non-HGFs. One may be concerned that the group of firms that are more likely to experience high growth could differ from other firms for a host of reasons (for example, unobservable differences in managerial quality, customer base, and so on), and that these reasons rather than high-growth status per se could be driving the results. To mitigate these concerns, panel b of figure 3.3 shows the results from a 1-nearest neighbor matching exercise, which uses the lagged values of the variable of interest as well as the levels of TFP, ROA, exporter status, industry concentration (the Herfindahl index), the share of foreign-owned firms in the 4-digit industry, as well as age, size, industry, and year

## FIGURE 3.3 Firm Performance in Hungary Improves during High-Growth Episodes

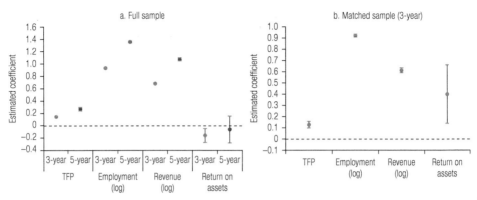

Source: Muraközy, de Nicola, and Tan 2018.

Note: The figure is a rope-ladder representation of estimated coefficients and 95 percent confidence bands from regressions of changes in the variables on the X-axis following year t, on a firm's high-growth status (employment-based, OECD definition) beginning from year t. All regressions include firm size, category, industry, and year fixed effects. The regression is estimated by ordinary least squares, and standard errors are clustered at the firm level. The matched sample is created by one nearest neighbor matching within the industry-year categories based on the lagged value of the left-hand-side variables (their changes during the previous three years) and the level of total factor productivity (TFP), return on assets, exporter status (the Herfindahl index), and the share of foreign-owned firms in the 4-digit industry as well as age and size category. OECD = Organisation for Economic Co-operation and Development.

categories to identify the best comparators to the set of HGFs. Encouragingly, all estimated coefficients are similar in magnitude and significance to the earlier results, with the exception of ROA. Using the matched sample, ROA of HGFs grows faster during the high-growth episode; since the comparator firms are similar, this may be because both HGFs and non-HGFs in this sample make certain investments in the hope of generating high growth, but the investments pay off only for the HGF group (versus the sample of all firms, in which non-HGFs may have a lower likelihood of making these investments in the first place).

Just as firms experience rising productivity during or prior to a high-growth event, high growth can also generate feedback effects on productivity. Some channels are almost mechanical: when productivity is defined as output per worker, rapid expansion in employment during a high-growth event may appear as a reduction in productivity growth (see, for example, Daunfeldt, Elert, and Johansson [2010] for an application to Sweden during 1997–2005). Others may reflect the selection of HGFs on productivity; for example, Du and Temouri (2015) and Du, Gong, and Temouri (2013) show that U.K. firms that have experienced a high-growth episode are more likely to exhibit faster TFP growth later on—suggesting that the process of high growth may be self-reinforcing. Evidence from Ethiopia confirms the presence of this feedback channel; as shown in figure 3.4, a high-growth event in the past is positively associated with faster TFP growth in the future, and the magnitude of the effect increases consistently along the quantiles of the TFP distribution.[7]

## FIGURE 3.4  High-Growth Experience Boosts TFP Growth in Ethiopia, Particularly So for Top Performers

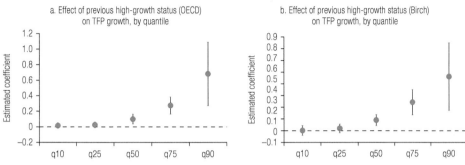

a. Effect of previous high-growth status (OECD) on TFP growth, by quantile

b. Effect of previous high-growth status (Birch) on TFP growth, by quantile

*Source:* Grover Goswami 2018.

*Note:* The figure is a rope-ladder representation of estimated coefficients and 95 percent confidence bands from quantile regressions of (reve-nue) total factor productivity (TFP) growth over a three-year period on employment-based high-growth status, controlling for age, size, interaction of age and size, agglomeration dummy, export status, ownership, bank ties, average wage, industry concentration, and time and location fixed effects. Robust standard errors are clustered at the plant level. OECD = Organisation for Economic Co-operation and Development; q = quantile.

Unlike the results from Ethiopia and Hungary, the evidence on the relationship between high growth and productivity in Turkey and Côte d'Ivoire is mixed. Controlling for industry and year effects, Turkish HGFs have significantly higher TFP than firms that have not experienced a high-growth event, with differences robust to different HGF definitions as well as both ordinary least squares and Levinsohn and Petrin (2003) approaches to calculating TFP. However, the estimated relationship between the likelihood of experiencing high growth and previous period TFP is statistically significant and negative in a fully specified model that also controls for demand shocks, employment, share of knowledge-based investments, capital intensity, public ownership, age, and region.[8] Similarly in Côte d'Ivoire, estimates of revenue-based TFP suggest a significant negative association between TFP and high growth in a model that also controls for firm age, size, sector, year, and location, whereas estimates of quantity-based TFP suggest that the relationship is not significantly different from zero.[9]

What could be the reasons for these diverse findings across countries? As discussed earlier, it is often difficult to tell whether a firm grows because of higher technical efficiency or because of higher mark-ups—but the distinction is critical because the underlying causes for the two modes of growth may be completely different. Recent advances in the literature that have enabled researchers to distinguish between changes in technical efficiency and producer-specific demand show that demand forces play a major role in determining firm survival and growth. For example, Foster, Haltiwanger, and Syverson (2008, 2016) document that demand is more important than efficiency for the survival of large manufacturing plants in the United States. Likewise, in Colombia, Eslava and Haltiwanger (2017) show that demand is the dominant factor explaining high growth among manufacturing firms, especially during the later stages of the firm's life cycle (see box 3.2). Although active demand accumulation requires investments in firm capabilities as mentioned in box 3.1, demand shocks can also be idiosyncratic or related to market power.

**BOX 3.2**

### Productivity and Demand over the Firm's Life Cycle

Using data for Colombian manufacturing establishments, Eslava and Haltiwanger (2017) decompose growth over a plant's life cycle into four components: (1) physical productivity, (2) demand shocks, (3) input prices, and (4) firm-specific distortions that eventually weaken the link between fundamentals and observed growth. On average, fundamentals explain about 70 percent of the variation in firm output relative to its initial level, with the remainder explained by distortions and other unobserved factors. More importantly, however, the relative prominence of the components varies by firm age.

During the early period of firm growth, physical productivity is much more important than demand and input prices. However, if a firm manages to survive until age 15, the contribution of changes in demand surpasses the contribution of physical productivity and unobserved factors in explaining long-run growth, in part because other firms can catch up with technical improvements through imitation more easily than accumulate relationship and demand capital. Likewise, distortions explain more than 50 percent of growth up to age seven, but their contribution falls to less than 25 percent by about age 20.

*Source:* Eslava and Haltiwanger 2017.

Recognizing that high growth may be driven by forces other than productivity gives rise to a policy maker's dilemma: those enterprises that are observed to be more successful may not actually have the highest levels of technical efficiency, and supporting them may not help improve the allocation of resources or economywide productivity. Moreover, the appropriate kind of support is likely to vary across different types of shocks; for example, studies show that adjusting to a decline in demand often involves simply reducing the scale of production with unchanged technology (Bloom and Van Reenen 2010; Bloom, Sadun, and Van Reenen 2012; Dranove et al. 2014), whereas adjusting to a decline in productivity may require more complex business process reorganization (for example, change in the skill mix of the employees, use of different types of capital inputs, and so on; see Pozzi and Schivard [2016] for an application to manufacturing firms in Italy).[10]

Evidence from Côte d'Ivoire provides an empirical illustration of this dilemma for a policy maker. Panels a–c of figure 3.5 plot the distribution of observed HGFs for three indicative periods versus the distribution of "efficient" HGFs, that is, those firms that would attain HGF status if resources across the economy were efficiently allocated according to firms' productivity so that the most productive ones would attract the largest shares of labor and capital. The figure highlights two insights: first, under an efficient allocation of resources, many more firms would experience high growth (compare the wider distribution of counterfactual "efficient" HGFs with a narrower distribution of observed HGFs, or the column sum of "efficient" HGFs in the table shown in panel d, 23.5 percent, with the "observed" row sum, 10.7 percent). And second, the overlap between the observed and "efficient" HGFs is very limited: among the

**FIGURE 3.5  The Overlap between Observed and "Efficient" HGFs Is Limited**

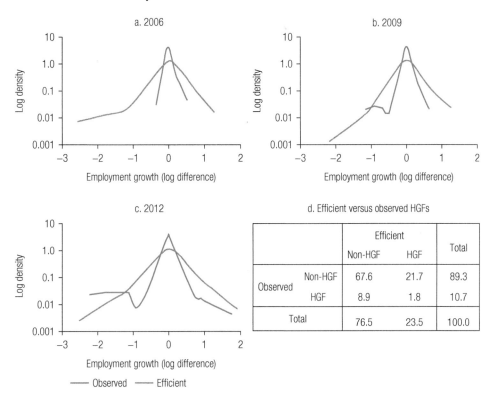

Source: Cirera, Fattal Jaef, and Gonne 2018.

Note: The figures plot the kernel density of employment growth rates in Côte d'Ivoire, as observed in the data, and in an "efficient" coun-terfactual that allocates labor and capital across firms to reduce distortions (disparities in marginal products) to levels observed in the United States (the "efficient" benchmark, following Hsieh and Klenow (2009). Because more productive firms have higher marginal prod-ucts, they attract more resources and grow more rapidly, giving rise to "efficient" high-growth firms (HGFs). See Cirera, Fattal Jaef, and Gonne (2018) for more details on the approach.

23.5 percent of Ivorian firms that would be HGFs under an efficient allocation of resources, only 1.8 percent are observed as HGFs. Alternatively, out of the 10.7 percent of Ivorian firms that attained HGF status, 8.9 percent would not have been able to do so if resources were allocated according to firm productivity (that is, in a hypothetical economy relatively free of distortions).

These results highlight the complexity of the relationship between firm growth and productivity. Given the limited overlap between observed and "efficient" HGFs—due to a range of potential distortions in factor and output markets—it is perhaps not surpris-ing that the empirical relationship is difficult to pin down. Even in instances when productivity emerges as a positive contributor to the likelihood of experiencing high growth, firm-level TFP may embed a host of factors capturing firm competencies, such as the quality of managerial capacity and workers' ability, use of information technology, knowledge spillovers, and extent of research and development (R&D) and product innovation, making the exact causal link somewhat difficult.[11] In addition to their contribution to productivity, and therefore indirectly to high growth, many of these channels have also been explored in the literature as potential direct drivers of high growth. The following sections therefore examine the role of these factors in stimulating high-growth events in more detail.

## Innovation

Much of the literature on firm dynamics associates innovation with higher firm growth.[12] However, the standard empirical approach of focusing on the "average effect for the average firm" has not always identified a significant relationship between the two variables. This is because the impact of innovation on firm growth is sensitive to (1) the choice of growth metrics (employment versus sales), (2) the indicators for measuring innovation (such as patents, R&D investments) and the type of innovation (new products or processes),[13] (3) the interplay between internal dynamics of the firm and the external environment,[14] and (4) the time horizon of the analysis.[15] Although the available evidence on the link between firm growth and innovation has been accumulated primarily in high-income country settings with more developed national innovation systems, studies show that even in this rather "homogeneous" set of countries, the technological and economic position of a country substantially affects the success rate and the choice of innovation and R&D-based firm growth strategy (Hölzl 2009).

Evidence of a positive relationship between innovation and firm growth tends to be stronger for firms in the top quantiles of the growth rate distribution (Goedhuys and Sleuwaegen 2010; Hölzl 2009; Falk 2012; Czarnitzki and Delanote 2013; Mazzucato and Parris 2015). The top 10 percent of most rapidly growing firms in Austria are more innovative than other firms, as measured by the share of innovative products (Hölzl 2007).[16] Likewise, more innovative firms tend to grow faster than other firms in the United Kingdom, Scotland, and United States (NESTA 2009; Mason, Bishop, and Robinson 2009; Mason and Brown 2010; Jorgenson, Ho, and Stiroh 2005; Oliner, Sichel, and Stiroh 2008). Mason and Brown (2010) find that most HGFs in Scotland are knowledge-based and innovative, and the same factors were an important driver of output and productivity growth in the United States during 1995–2006 (Jorgenson, Ho, and Stiroh 2008).[17] Coad and Rao (2011) and Stam and Wennberg (2009) also find a positive association between innovation in high-tech industries, as measured by patenting and R&D activities, and firm growth in the United States and the Netherlands. Boxes 3.3 and 3.4 provide examples of Bangladeshi and Colombian firms that were able to achieve high growth to a large extent through technology and marketing innovations.

Consistent with these studies, this book finds that in India, the link between innovation and firm growth strengthens along the firm growth distribution. Figure 3.6 shows this by plotting the results from a quantile regression of firm revenue growth on a range of firm characteristics and two alternative measures of innovation: whether a firm has introduced a new product or service that it was not producing or supplying previously (panels a and b)

### Firms in Focus: Chaldal, Bangladesh

Founded by Waseem Alim, Tejas Viswanath, and Zia Ashraf in 2013, Chaldal is the leading online grocery supplier in Bangladesh. The company sells fresh fruits and vegetables, meat and dairy, groceries, and personal care and household items via its website and mobile apps, and it is now expanding into adjacent services in the underdeveloped e-commerce space, starting with logistics and e-commerce platform services. It uses software for monitoring wastage, predicting the sale of time-sensitive items, such as vegetables, and tracking deliveries. The company is currently serving Dhaka city, delivering more than 1,500 orders per day and serving more than 20,000 households.

As a young but fast-growing company, Chaldal began its operations with a team of five people. In three years it grew to about 300 employees.[a] In its first year of establishment, it earned revenues of 1.3 million takas, which increased to 17 million takas the following year and to 77 million in 2015. In the years 2016 and 2017, revenues skyrocketed to 180 million takas and 380 million takas.[b] In the online grocery space, Chaldal has an estimated market share of more than 90 percent.

a. https://futurestartup.com/2016/06/07/waseem-alim-of-chaldal-part-one/.
b. https://www.thedailystar.net/city/profiles-ict-awards-winners-1511428.

### Firms in Focus: Rappi, Colombia

Rappi is a three-year old Colombian marketplace start-up that will deliver nearly any product or service to its customers. It began as a four-person venture, using freelance couriers to deliver liquor and soft drinks from local shops to residential customers. Today, the company has expanded to all major cities in Colombia as well as Mexico City and has plans to reach every country in Latin America. It has more than 400 full-time workers, employs a network of more than 10,000 couriers, and has seen its sales grow by some 40–50 percent per month.

Rappi's success story can be traced back in large part to its decision to include a blank box in the app for unlisted items (the app works like a virtual supermarket in which users add products to their cart). Soon, customers began requesting all kinds of products and services beyond what the founders had envisioned: food from restaurants that did not deliver, cash from ATMs, income tax payments to be sent to banks, dog walking, and any other request that could be fulfilled by a courier on a bicycle or motorcycle. Regular customers average more than four orders per week, paying about US$1 per order or a flat monthly fee of about US$7.

Rappi's business model addresses some of the key challenges facing consumers in Latin America: neighborhood bike couriers compensate for traffic congestion and poor logistics; ability to deliver cash or payments mitigates security issues; and accepting cash as a payment method opens the service to the unbanked. Using technology to solve these issues enabled the company to grow extremely rapidly. After securing its initial seed funding in early 2015, Rappi became the first Latin American company to enter the well-known accelerator program Y Combinator, graduating in March 2016. In subsequent rounds, Rappi has raised close to US$400 million in series A-D venture financing, reaching a valuation of more than US$1 billion in the most recent round.

## FIGURE 3.6   The Fastest-Growing Firms in India Are Significantly More Innovative

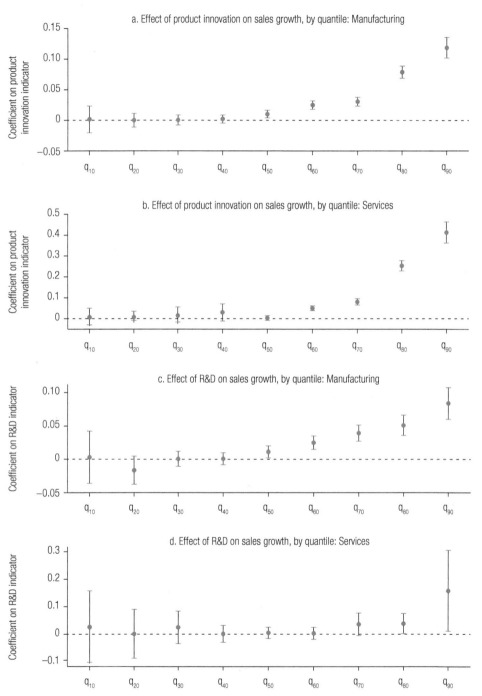

a. Effect of product innovation on sales growth, by quantile: Manufacturing

b. Effect of product innovation on sales growth, by quantile: Services

c. Effect of R&D on sales growth, by quantile: Manufacturing

d. Effect of R&D on sales growth, by quantile: Services

*Source:* Manghnani 2018.

*Note:* The figure is a rope-ladder representation of estimated coefficients and 95 percent confidence bands from quantile regressions of sales growth in manufacturing and services sectors over a three-year period on alternative measures of innovation, including product innovation and research and development (R&D) expenditure. These regressions control for size, age, age squared, product scope (measured by the natural log of number of products and services produced by the firm), firm export status, and firm and year fixed effects. Robust standard errors are clustered at the firm level. q = quantile.

and whether a firm engages in R&D (panels c and d).[18] The results indicate that the effect of product innovation for growth of manufacturing and services firms in the 90th percentile of the firm growth distribution is more than 10 times that of the effect for the median firm. The results for innovation measured through firms' R&D investments are not as strong, especially for the services sector; however, they similarly show a rising importance of innovation for firm growth throughout the distribution.

Figure 3.7 illustrates the results of alternative specifications that further explore the impact of innovation on the likelihood that a firm experiences a high-growth event. Panel a shows that the overall relationship between product innovation and the probability of high growth is insignificant for manufacturing and significant for services at only the 10 percent level. However, a more detailed examination reveals that the relevant driver is the interplay between innovating and exporting. Consistent with the recent theoretical literature that emphasizes complementarity between exporting and innovation through learning spillovers, Indian services firms that introduce new products *and* export are significantly more likely to experience a high-growth episode than firms that introduce new products only in the domestic market.[19] Panel b of figure 3.7 similarly breaks down the effect of R&D by showing that high-growth events in manufacturing and services are driven by persistent rather than occasional R&D and by firms that conduct R&D to reach external rather than exclusively domestic markets.

Likewise, in Mexico, firms that have specific personnel dedicated to R&D activities or engage in R&D more broadly are significantly more likely to experience a high-growth episode in the next five to ten years (figure 3.8). And in Turkey, a recent

## FIGURE 3.7  Innovation Increases the Likelihood of High Growth in India

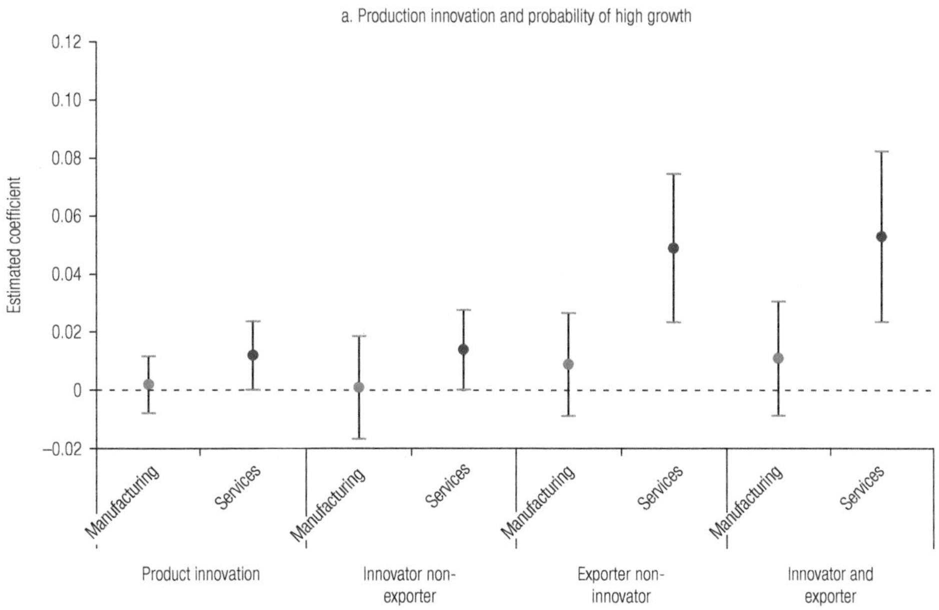

a. Production innovation and probability of high growth

*(Figure continues on the following page.)*

## FIGURE 3.7   Innovation Increases the Likelihood of High Growth in India *(continued)*

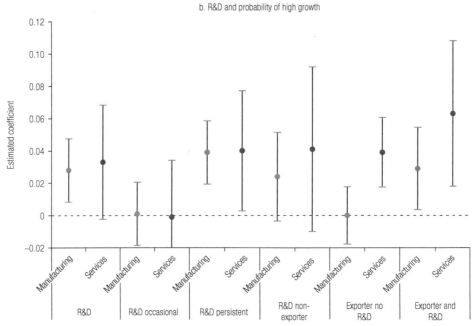

b. R&D and probability of high growth

*Source:* Manghnani 2018.

*Note:* The figure is a rope-ladder representation of estimated coefficients and 95 percent confidence bands from linear regressions of firm's high-growth status (sales-based, OECD definition), on three-period lagged firm traits, including size, age, age squared, product scope (measured by the natural log of number of products and services produced by the firm), firm export status, firm and year fixed effects, and industry-year interactions. Regressions were estimated separately for manufacturing and services. Product innovation is a dummy variable indicating that the firm has introduced a new product or service that it is was not producing or supplying previously, Research and development (R&D) activity is a dummy variable indicating that the firm has engaged in R&D. Persistent R&D is defined as engaging in R&D for two consecutive years or longer (following Lööf et al. 2012). OECD = Organisation for Economic Co-operation and Development.

## FIGURE 3.8   R&D Activity in Mexico Correlates Positively with High Growth

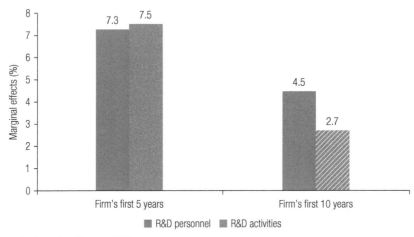

*Source:* Sanchez Bayardo and Iacovone 2018.

*Note:* The figure shows the marginal effect of hiring research and development (R&D) personnel and engaging in R&D activities on the probability of attaining high-growth status (employment-based, OECD definition), in percentage points. Estimates are obtained from a probit regression that includes cohort, industry, and region fixed effects. Solid bars indicate statistical significance at 10 percent level or higher; shaded bars are not statistically significant. OECD = Organisation for Economic Co-operation and Development.

study using firms' applications to the national patent institute as a proxy for product innovation similarly finds a positive and significant impact of product innovation on firm employment growth in manufacturing and services during 2006–16 (Kılınç 2018).[20]

## Agglomeration and Firm Networks

A range of studies have found that agglomeration economies—arising from firms in the same location sharing inputs, pooling workers, accessing a diverse range of suppliers and customers, and benefiting from knowledge spillovers—are positively associated with firm performance (Rosenthal and Strange 2004; Glaeser and Kerr 2009; Ghani, Kerr, and O'Connell 2011; Lechner and Dowling 2003; Mukim 2011).[21] In particular, the literature suggests that industry clustering contributes to higher rates of firm growth because of enhanced product demand and greater ability to harness reputational advantage (Gilbert, McDougall, and Audretsch 2006, 2008).

Evidence collected for this book confirms that agglomeration networks play an important role in facilitating high-growth episodes. For example, figure 3.9 shows that Ethiopian HGFs are more likely to be located in an agglomeration center—defined as one of the country's top five cities (Addis Ababa, Hawassa, Bahir Dar, Dire Dawa, and Mekelle)—or areas closer to one than an average firm.[22] Moving away from the top five agglomeration centers, the share of economic activity consistently declines, and the pace of decline is sharper for HGFs, suggesting that HGFs may be benefiting disproportionately from the externalities offered by agglomeration centers.

**FIGURE 3.9**  **HGFs in Ethiopia Are More Common In or Close to Agglomeration Centers**

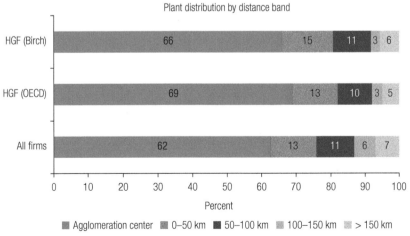

*Source:* Grover Goswami 2018.

*Note:* Distance bands are defined as the distance to the nearest of the top five agglomeration centers in Ethiopia: Addis Ababa, Hawassa, Bahir Dar, Dire Dawa, and Mekelle. Shares are averaged over the 1999–2009 period. HGF = high-growth firm; OECD = Organisation for Economic Co-operation and Development.

Figure 3.10 presents a more formal test of this hypothesis by plotting the change in probability of experiencing a high-growth episode as a function of being located in an agglomeration center as well as a measure of industry spatial concentration (the Ellison-Glaeser index). The figure shows that, controlling for an extensive range of establishment-level traits, plants located in agglomeration centers are significantly more likely to experience a high-growth event relative to plants located more than 150 kilometers from the nearest center.[23]

However, there is a point at which congestion forces come into play. Figure 3.10 also shows that the advantage conferred by locating in an agglomeration center diminishes as industry concentration increases, and all benefits disappear for large values of the concentration index. This is likely due to congestion externalities and competition for similar resources, which discourage a high-growth spell. These results are consistent with the findings of Siba et al. (2012), who use the same Ethiopian manufacturing data set to find that agglomeration generates positive externalities but also increases competitive pressure, as well as the work of Lall, Henderson, and Venables (2017), who find that cities in Africa are costly, crowded, and disconnected such that agglomeration benefits are often inadequately realized.

**FIGURE 3.10**  **Agglomeration Increases the Likelihood of High Growth in Ethiopia, while Industry Concentration Reduces It**

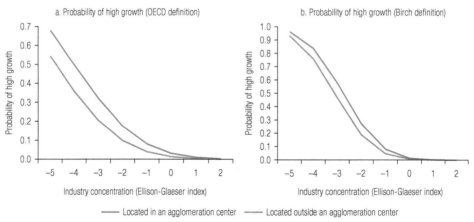

*Source:* Grover Goswami 2018.

*Note:* The figure shows the probability of experiencing a high-growth event in an agglomeration center and at different values of industry concentration (measured by the Ellison-Glaeser index and its interaction with the agglomeration center dummy variable). Agglomeration centers are Ethiopia's top five cities: Addis Ababa, Hawassa, Bahir Dar, Dire Dawa, and Mekelle. Estimates control for three-year lagged values of firm total factor productivity (estimated using the Levinsohn and Petrin 2003 approach), size, age, interaction of age and size, average wage, ownership, foreign direct investment and export status, as well as location, industry, and time effects. Following Shiferaw (2016), estimates also control for bank ties using a dummy variable for whether the plant has bank loans listed as one of the sources of working capital. Robust standard errors are clustered at the plant level. All variables other than the agglomeration dummy and industry concentration are held at their means. Estimates are performed with a pooled static probit model, and robust standard errors are clustered at the plant level. Height of vertical lines corresponds to the 95 percent confidence interval. Data cover the period from 1996 to 2009. OECD = Organisation for Economic Co-operation and Development.

Public policy can counteract these pressures and enhance the growth benefits of agglomeration and spatial connectivity. For example, the relative prevalence of HGFs in Addis Ababa increased substantially following Ethiopia's 2003–04 export promotion reforms, which were targeted at high-value agricultural exports (for example, horticulture products and meat) and labor-intensive manufacturing products (for example, clothing, textile, leather, and leather products). Figure 3.11 shows that the effect of being located in Addis Ababa (conditional on a wide range of firm characteristics) changed from statistically insignificant in the prereform period to positive and statistically significant in the postreform period, suggesting that policy reforms may have influenced the growth probabilities of plants located in the capital city.[24]

Just as spatial clustering benefits firms through connectivity and knowledge spillovers, companies operating within a network of related firms can leverage their in-network relationships to achieve higher growth. A unique data set from Thailand allows for formal testing of this hypothesis. The legal mandate that Thai households have unique surnames enables one to trace all registered firms to their ownership network or business group. In particular, the data allow for tracing two main types of networks: horizontal, which connect firms owned by the same person or entity,

**FIGURE 3.11** **Policy Reforms Strengthened the Links between Agglomeration and High Firm Growth in Ethiopia**

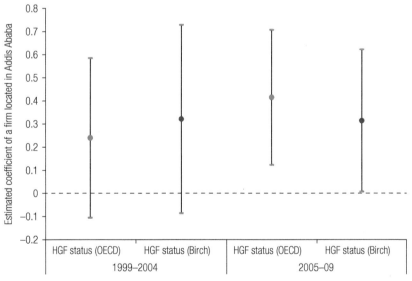

*Source:* Grover Goswami 2018.

*Note:* The figure is a rope-ladder representation of estimated marginal effects and 95 percent confidence bands from a probit regression of employment-based high-growth status on whether a firm is located in Addis Ababa. Additional controls include three-year lagged values of total factor productivity, size, age, interaction of age and size, average wage, ownership, foreign direct investment and export status, along with location, industry, and time effects. Standard errors are clustered at the plant level. HGF = high-growth firm; OECD = Organisation for Economic Co-operation and Development.

## FIGURE 3.12 In-Network Thai Firms Are Larger and More Likely to Experience High Growth

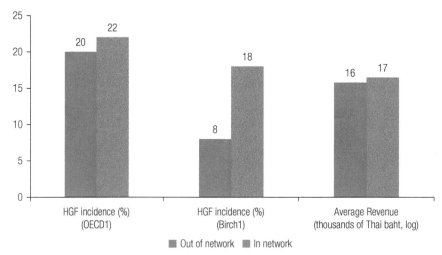

*Source:* Banternghansa and Samphantharak 2018.

*Note:* HGFs are defined using a sales-based metric, and HGF shares are calculated as OECD1 and Birch1 (using all firms in the denominator, see note to Figure 1.1). Only firms above a minimum sales cut-off are included in the estimates, see Section 1.1 for additional details. All differences between in-network and out of network firms are statistically significant. Shares and firm revenue are averages over the 1999-2015 period, revenue is expressed in million Baht.

and vertical, which connect firms that are indirectly owned by the same person or entity through parent or subsidiary companies.[25] The results, shown in figure 3.12, demonstrate that in-network firms are indeed larger than out-of-network firms and are significantly more likely to experience high-growth events.[26] Moreover, firms in larger networks tend to have higher revenue and are more diversified than firms in smaller groups.

Separating the results by type of network reveals that participation in both horizontal and vertical networks significantly increases the probability of high growth. However, within vertical networks, results differ importantly according to the firm's position (figure 3.13). Conditional on participating in a vertical network, firms that have a greater number of connections with other firms—both through receiving connections (in-degree centrality, or the number of firms that have ownership shares in a given firm) and sending connections (out-degree centrality, or the number of firms in which a given firm has an ownership share)—are more likely to experience high growth, although this holds only for the OECD definition and not the Birch definition. By comparison, betweenness—a measure of how many connections pass through a given firm (for example, a central node versus a node on the outskirts of a network)—is significantly associated with a greater likelihood of high growth only for the larger firms captured by the Birch definition. Finally, eigen centrality, which measures the importance of the nodes a firm is connected to by differentiating between

## FIGURE 3.13   Participation in Networks Increases the Likelihood of High Firm Growth in Thailand

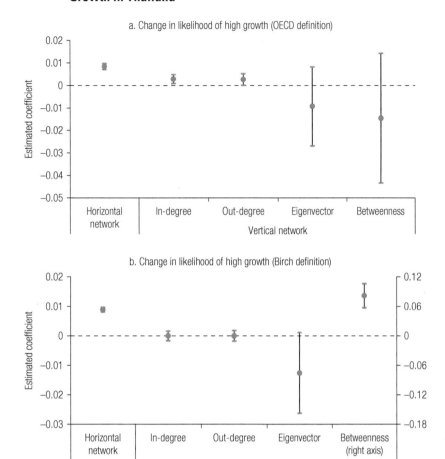

a. Change in likelihood of high growth (OECD definition)

b. Change in likelihood of high growth (Birch definition)

*Source:* Banternghansa and Samphantharak 2018.

*Note:* The figure is a rope-ladder representation of estimated coefficients and 95 percent confidence bands from a regression of high-growth status on network participation variables. The four aspects of participation in vertical networks draw on concepts from network theory: in-degree centrality refers to the number of firms that have ownership shares in a given firm (number of connections a firm receives), out-degree centrality refers to the number of firms in which a given firm has an ownership share (number of connections a firm sends out), betweenness centrality is a measure of how many connections pass through a given firm (for example, a central node versus a node on the outskirts of a network), and eigenvector centrality measures the importance of the nodes a firm is connected to by differentiating between connecting to a lot of nodes versus connecting to fewer but more important or central nodes. Regressions also control for firm revenue, assets, and leverage. OECD = Organisation for Economic Co-operation and Development.

connecting to a lot of nodes versus connecting to fewer but more important or central nodes, has a weakly negative correlation with experiencing a high-growth event. This may mean that some dense ownership networks may lead to "tunneling" of resources out of some firms into others, although the overall impact of being in a vertical network on the probability of high growth—even with the negative "tunneling" penalty—is still significantly positive compared with out-of-network firms.

## Managerial Capabilities and Worker Skills

Managerial capabilities have long been recognized as critical for firm performance.[27] Differences in managerial quality explain as much as one-third of cross-country differences in productivity (Bloom, Sadun, and Van Reenen 2017; Bloom and Van Reenen 2010) whereas other performance measures, such as firm profitability and survival rates, are also positively correlated with good management practices. For example, Bruhn, Karlan, and Schoar (2013) associate adopting modern management practices with more rapid firm growth. One of the more novel findings of Bloom and Van Reenen (2010) is that cross-country variation in management practices is smaller than differences between firms in the same country, suggesting that firm- and sector-specific factors are at least as important as the general business environment in shaping managerial performance.

Several studies have explored the relationship between firm growth and the specific characteristics of firm owners and managers, including education (Nichter and Goldmark 2009; Akcigit, Grigsby, and Nicholas 2017), cognitive test scores (Djankov et al. 2005; McKenzie and Sansone 2017), as well as work experience in the same sector and in a large or foreign firm (Parker 1995). Evidence suggests that high-capability entrepreneurs tend to employ high-quality inputs and use them more effectively to produce high-quality products (Verhoogen 2008; Kugler and Verhoogen 2012; Bastos, Silva, and Verhoogen 2018). And when it comes to the human capital of founding employees, Ouimet and Zarutskie (2014) document that young firms that are able to attract younger, higher ability workers subsequently experience higher growth rates and are more likely to raise venture capital financing (which, according to the results of Hellmann and Puri [2000] could be a proxy for the firm's innovative ability). Box 3.5 provides an example of a Chinese firm that was able to achieve high growth to a large extent due to its investments in human capital.

---

### BOX 3.5

### Firms in Focus: Beijing Genomics Institute, China

Beijing Genomics Institute (BGI) was founded in 1999 as a nonprofit research organization by Wang Jian, Yu Jun, Yang Huanming, and Liu Siqi to participate in the Human Genome Project as China's representative. Since then, the company has grown into a multinational business providing large-scale human, plant, and animal genomics research for the pharmaceutical and clinical markets. Headquartered in Shenzhen, the company defines itself primarily as a company that is "vision driven" (as opposed to revenue or profit driven) and has a number of spin-off for-profit and nonprofit "sub-organizations," including BGI Research, BGI Tech, BGI Diagnosis, BGI Agriculture, and BGI College under BGI Holdings.

*(Box continues on the following page.)*

### Firms in Focus: Beijing Genomics Institute, China *(continued)*

Today, BGI has reported revenues of US$250 million (2016) and employs about 7,000 staff in research and development, manufacturing, and commercial operations in more than 50 countries. The company's path took it through several high-growth episodes. It began with just the four founders, but three years later its employees numbered about 600. The company has further increased its size more than ten-fold since then, including an episode of particularly rapid growth in the late 2000s when firm size grew from about 1,500 to about 4,000 employees in just over two years.

In realizing its growth potential, BGI managed to take full advantage of the extraordinary growth and technology changes in China while capitalizing on the human capital of foreign-educated Chinese researchers who wished to return home. Its founders received graduate scientific training in U.S. and European universities and leveraged their skills to make modest but significant contributions to the Human Genome Project, which, together with subsequent work on programs such as the Rice Genome Project (2002) and sequencing the SARS virus (2003), helped put China on the global map in the genomics scientific community, attracted the attention of the Chinese government, and opened up funding opportunities from the China Development Bank.

Since then, BGI's path continues to be defined by forming research partnerships and attracting top talent. BGI has established partnerships with universities and medical research institutions (including hospitals) in 100 countries to gain access to data (that is, DNA samples) and stress test their sequencing capabilities, while BGI's partners benefit from gaining access to BGI's sequencing capabilities and bioinformatics scale. To maintain its knowledge edge, the company continues to lure Chinese postdoctoral researchers back from the West. It is estimated that BGI has about 2,000 members of staff with PhDs, employed at a fraction of what an equivalent team would cost to assemble in the United States. The company also hires science graduates straight out of university with subsequent in-house training, which has resulted in a drop in the average age of the company's employees to below 30.

*Source:* 10EQS Answers 2017.

Evidence from Ethiopia, Hungary, Mexico, and Brazil confirms a significant positive association between initial average wages and subsequent high growth, although the relationship is not statistically significant in Turkey and Indonesia. To illustrate, panel a of figure 3.14 shows that the probability of experiencing a high-growth event in Ethiopia rises as the firm pays higher initial wages, even after controlling for a wide set of firm characteristics that may also influence firm performance, such as TFP, exports, agglomeration, among others. Panel b shows similar results for Mexico, which are also robust to controlling for a range of fixed effects. Panel b of figure 3.14 also shows that the relationship holds for different types of skills (in this case, measured by the wages of white-collar workers).

**FIGURE 3.14** **Initial Higher Wages among Ethiopian and Mexican Firms Are Correlated with High Growth**

### Ethiopia

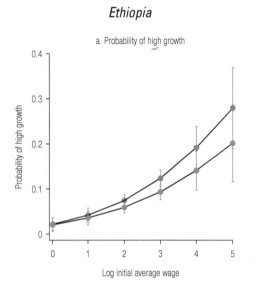

a. Probability of high growth

### Mexico

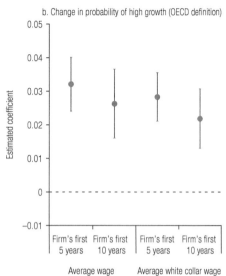

b. Change in probability of high growth (OECD definition)

*Source:* Grover Goswami 2018.

*Note:* The figure shows the probability of experiencing a high-growth event at different values of average initial wages paid by the firm. Estimates control for three-year lagged values of firm total factor productivity (estimated using the Levinsohn and Petrin 2003 approach), size, age, interaction of age and size, average wage, ownership, foreign direct investment and export status, as well as location, industry, and time effects. All variables other than the initial average wage are held at their means. Estimates are performed with a dynamic probit model and robust standard errors are clustered at the plant level. Height of vertical lines corresponds to the 95 percent confidence interval. Data cover the period from 1996 to 2009. OECD = Organisation for Economic Co-operation and Development.

*Source:* Sanchez Bayardo and Iacovone 2018.

*Note:* The figure is a rope-ladder representation of estimated marginal effects and 95 percent confidence bands from a regression of high-growth status (employment-based, OECD) on blue-collar, white-collar, and average wages in a model that includes cohort, industry, and region fixed effects. OECD = Organisation for Economic Co-operation and Development.

For Hungary, figure 3.15 shows that the positive association between average wages and the likelihood of experiencing a high-growth event increases in technology and knowledge intensity for both manufacturing and services sectors. Interestingly, the relationship is statistically significant only after 2003, which may be related to Hungary's accession to the European Union.

In Brazil, a matched employer-employee data set allows for tracking of both firms and workers over a 20-year period, identifying previous employment and earnings trajectories of the workers and managers of future HGFs in a census of manufacturing and service firms. The results show that wages of a firm's founding employees are positively and significantly associated with the likelihood of subsequent high growth, even after controlling for human capital attributes, such as education and previous work experience (figure 3.16). This means that future HGFs are not only able to attract

## FIGURE 3.15 The Relationship between HGF Status and Higher Wages Is Stronger for Hungary's High-Tech Sectors

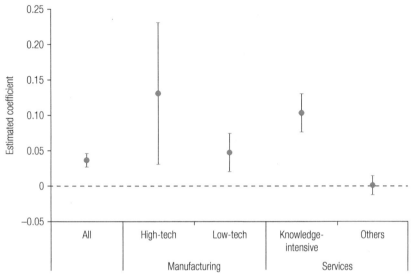

Source: Muraközy, de Nicola, and Tan 2018.

Note: The figure is a rope-ladder representation of estimated marginal effects and 95 percent confidence bands from a regression of average wages on high-growth status (employment-based, OECD) beginning from year *t*. All regressions include firm size, industry, and year fixed effects. The regressions are estimated by ordinary least squares, and standard errors are clustered at the firm level. OECD = Organisation for Economic Co-operation and Development.

## FIGURE 3.16 Employees and Managers of HGFs in Brazil Have Greater Human Capital Endowments

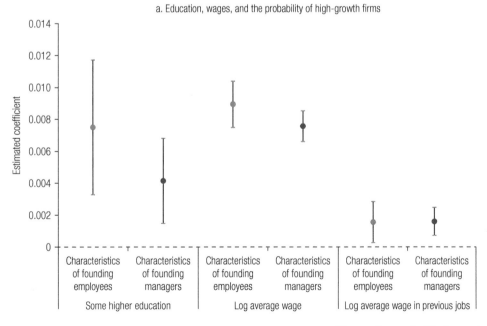

a. Education, wages, and the probability of high-growth firms

(Figure continues on the following page.)

*(Figure continues on the following page.)*

FIGURE 3.16 **Employees and Managers of HGFs in Brazil Have Greater Human Capital Endowments** *(continued)*

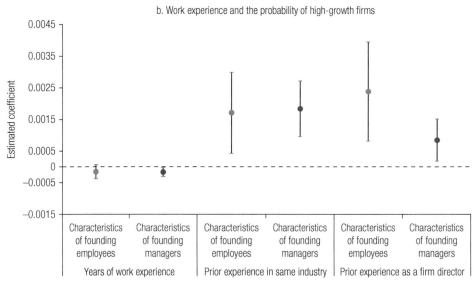

b. Work experience and the probability of high-growth firms

*Source:* Bastos and Silva 2018.

*Note:* The figure is a rope-ladder representation of estimated marginal effects and 95 percent confidence bands from two separate regressions of subsequent high-growth status of firms born in 2000–01 on the characteristics of founding employees and founding managers (measured in the firm's birth year). High-growth firms (HGFs) are defined as those that survived until 2014 and whose employment grew at an annual average rate of 25 percent or more between the year of birth and 2014. Regressions are estimated by ordinary least squares, and standard errors are clustered at the firm level.

workers with better observable qualifications, such as higher levels of education (9.4 years versus 8.3 years) and more valuable experience (for example, from the formal sector, director position, foreign firms), but the wage premium that they offer goes beyond what would be expected given these characteristics, perhaps reflecting a stronger set of less observable employee characteristics.[28] The differences in wages vis-à-vis other firms are particularly stark during the early years of a firm's high-growth experience—for example, in the year of birth, future HGFs pay a nearly a 60 percent wage premium to their workers—but these differences diminish over time as less productive firms (of the same cohort) exit the market (figure 3.17).

Turning to managerial skills, figure 3.16 shows that the human capital of firm managers is similarly associated with a greater likelihood of experiencing a high-growth event (see box 3.6 for details on how firm leaders are identified in the data). Specifically, firms led by individuals with previous experience in the formal sector and in larger firms, with higher education levels, previous management experience, and higher wages in the previous job are more likely to experience a high-growth episode in the subsequent 13-year period; for example, the proportion of leaders with some higher education is 18.2 percent among future HGFs and 7.7 percent in other firms.

**FIGURE 3.17   Future HGFs in Brazil Pay Substantially Higher Wages from the Moment of Birth**

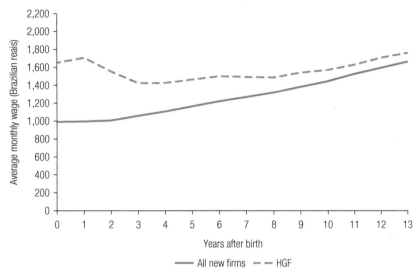

*Source:* Bastos and Silva 2018.

*Notes:* The figure plots the average monthly wage (in Brazilian reais) for the 2000–01 cohort of firms, starting with their birth year. HGF = high-growth firm.

**BOX 3.6**

### Identifying Firm Leaders

To identify the initial leaders of firms from the 2000–01 cohort in Brazil, this book uses information on the wages and type of employment and occupation of each worker. In line with Cardoso and Winter-Ebmer (2010), the following variables are used to identify the firm's leader in the initial years the firm is observed in the data:

1. Owner: Nonsalaried directors for whom the firm pays the FGTS (Fundo de Garantia do Tempo e Serviço) are classified as owners of the firm. The variable type of employment in the Relação Annual de Informações Sociais (RAIS) data set makes it possible to identify the firm leader on the basis of this criterion.
2. Director: Salaried workers whose occupational category refers to any position of director in the firm (occupation categories are coded at the 5-digit level in the 1994 version of the Brazilian Classification of Occupation and at the 6-digit level in the 2002 version).
3. Manager: Salaried workers whose occupational category refers to any position of manager (*gerente*) within the firm.
4. Highest wage in the firm: The top wage earner in the firm.

Using information on these variables, the first step was to verify whether for a given firm any owner was identified in the RAIS data set. If so, the owner was classified as the leader of the firm. If not, information on directors was used. If these were not listed, information on managers was used. For firms whose leadership could not be identified using any of these criteria, the top wage earner in the firm was used. If two or more individuals meet these criteria similarly, all of them were classified as leaders.

*Source:* Bastos and Silva 2018.

## Global Linkages

Relative to their local counterparts, firms with international exposure—measured through exports or foreign ownership—tend to be larger, more productive, and better managed; pay higher wages; and have higher rates of technology adoption (Haddad and Harrison 1993; Girma, Greenaway, and Wakelin 2001; Conyon and Wright 2002; Lipsey and Sjöholm 2004; Bloom and Van Reenen 2010). This is partly due to self-selection, given that better-performing firms are more likely to choose to become exporters or seek out foreign partnerships (for example, Melitz 2003; Greenaway and Kneller 2007). However, international exposure can also affect firm performance more directly: for example, firms that participate in global value chains benefit via the transfer of technological, managerial, and foreign market-related knowledge through capital investment as well as hiring of foreign managers (Tan, Winkler, and Yde-Jensen 2018). Local firms can also imitate foreign technologies or managerial practices either through observation or by hiring workers trained by the foreign company (see, for example, Kokko, Zejan, and Tansini [2001] for Uruguay and Aitken, Hanson, and Harrison [1997] for Mexico). Competition from more productive exporters and multinationals may also induce some firms to become more efficient while others may exit the market altogether (see, for example, Keller and Yeaple [2009] for the United States, Dries and Swinnen [2004] for Poland, and Haskel, Pereira, and Slaughter [2007] for the United Kingdom).[29]

Although most firm-level analyses have focused on the association between international exposure and increases in productivity, some studies have also found a significant, positive relationship between foreign linkages and firm growth (Robson and Bennett 2000; Beck, Demirgüç-Kunt, and Maksimovic 2005). Using the World Bank Enterprise Survey data for 121 developing countries, Reyes (2018) shows that HGFs that are able to internalize FDI spillovers also significantly increase their output. Specifically, a 10 percent increase in the share of local inputs sourced by multinationals or the share of foreign output in the sector is associated with, respectively, a 6 percent and 1.2 percent increase in the output of HGFs. Boxes 3.7 and 3.8 provide examples of Indian and Kenyan firms that were able to achieve high growth to a large extent through stronger foreign investment and export linkages.

---

### BOX 3.7

### Firms in Focus: AAA Growers, Kenya

AAA Growers was born out of a small trial project of growing tomatoes, set up as a microfinance oriented project in collaboration with the International Finance Corporation (IFC). Today, AAA Growers is one of the leading producers of premium and prepared vegetables from Kenya, exporting 95–99 percent of its production (more than 4,000 metric tons of fresh produce annually) to leading retailers in Europe and South Africa. AAA Growers started with 50 employees in 2000 and

*(Box continues on the following page.)*

### Firms in Focus: AAA Growers, Kenya *(continued)*

has now grown to employ more than 3,500 workers spread across four geographical locations in Kenya. Approximately 70 percent of the workers are women.

In addition to the high quality of its product, which is valued in international markets, the success of AAA Growers can also be attributed to product diversification. Although the vegetable segment is the core part of the firm's business, the company entered into the floriculture market in 2010 and since 2013 it has also been venturing into the fruits segment. The company expanded from exporting food to horticulture products by forming AAA Roses (a company registered under the name of Forest Gate (EPZ) Ltd.) in 2011. AAA Roses began exporting roses mainly to Europe (Germany, the Netherlands, and the United Kingdom) and the Middle East. In a relatively short time, AAA Roses has built a strong brand image in the Kenyan flower industry because of the high quality of its product and its modern facilities as well as after-sale services. Product innovation and international exposure is clearly an attribute of this high growth business.

The firm faced several challenges during its inception phase, ranging from land registration to the complicated procedures for obtaining business permits. While seeking to enter international markets, the firm invested in adopting product regulations needed for various markets in Europe. Over the years, the firm has not just learned how to deal with these challenges but rather has mastered them by building and institutionalizing an agile and capable management structure.

*Source:* Reyes 2018.

### Firms in Focus: Hi-Tech Gears, India

The Hi-Tech Gears Ltd. (THG), headquartered in Gurugram, India, employs more than 2,100 workers. The company is a Tier 1 automotive supplier of high precision transmission, engine, and driveline components and subsystems to global original equipment manufacturers (OEMs) and top suppliers.

THG began operations in 1986 producing two-wheeler transmission components in northern India. At the time, India's domestic market was just opening up to overseas competitors, and foreign manufacturers were setting up joint ventures with local manufacturers. One of these was Hero Honda (now Hero MotoCorp), an OEM joint venture between Indian Hero and Japanese Honda. THG landed an order with Hero Honda to supply transmission components. Over the next few years, the company enhanced its management techniques and production capabilities through backward integration by entering a technical collaboration agreement with Kyushu Musashi of Japan for precision near-net forging. The company's 1990 revenues of 27 million Indian rupees had more than quadrupled by 1995.

In the next five years, THG entered into a technical partnership with GETRAG, the world's largest supplier of transmissions for passenger and commercial vehicles, and became a manufacturer of precision gears for Cummins Engines worldwide. Its revenue grew nearly seven-fold during this period. Subsequently, THG diversified into other automotive components (for example, passenger car transmission parts, Power-Transfer Units) and entered new markets.

Today, THG manufactures high precision powertrain components and subsystems for Daimler, Fiat Chrysler, Ford, General Motor, Honda, Hero MotoCorp, New Holland, JCB, Caterpillar, Cummins, and

*(Box continues on the following page.)*

In the case of Hungary, international exposure—as measured by a firm's exporting status—is strongly and positively correlated with a firm's likelihood of experiencing a high-growth event. Panel a of figure 3.18 shows that exporters are some 1–3 percentage points more likely to experience a high-growth event than nonexporters (in 2003, for example, this translates into a 50 percent increase in the probability of experiencing high growth). The relationship between the likelihood of high growth and foreign share in the firm's industry is less conclusive (figure 3.18, panel b); although it remains statistically insignificant (at the 95 percent level) throughout the recent period, the sign changes from negative in periods prior to Hungary's accession to the European Union in 2004 to positive in the post-accession period.

Similar results hold in Mexico, where firms that have a higher share of exports in sales or imports in total inputs (or both), as well as more access to FDI, are more likely to experience a high-growth event in their first 5–10 years (figure 3.19, panel a).

**FIGURE 3.18**  **Hungarian Firms with Links to Global Markets Are More Likely to Experience High-Growth Events**

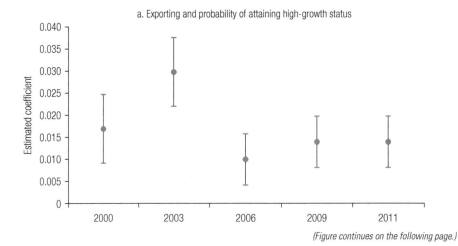

a. Exporting and probability of attaining high-growth status

*(Figure continues on the following page.)*

## FIGURE 3.18 Hungarian Firms with Links to Global Markets Are More Likely to Experience High-Growth Events *(continued)*

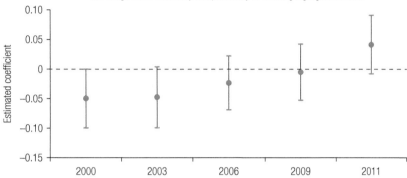

b. Foreign share in industry and probability of attaining high-growth status

*Source:* Muraközy, de Nicola, and Tan 2018.

*Note:* The figure is a rope-ladder representation of estimated coefficients and 95 percent confidence bands from a linear probability regression of high-growth status (employment-based, OECD) on the firm's exporting status (panel a) and foreign share in the firm's industry (panel b). Additional control variables include firm size, age, return on assets, average wages, productivity, and sectoral concentration. OECD = Organisation for Economic Co-operation and Development.

## FIGURE 3.19 International Exposure Is Positively Associated with High Growth in Mexico and Tunisia

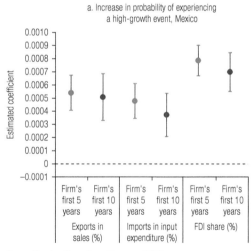

a. Increase in probability of experiencing a high-growth event, Mexico

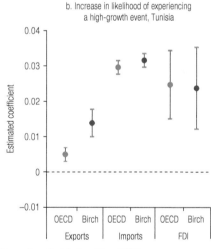

b. Increase in likelihood of experiencing a high-growth event, Tunisia

*Source:* Sanchez Bayardo and Iacovone 2018.

*Note:* The figure is a rope-ladder representation of estimated marginal effects and 95 percent confidence bands from separate probit regressions of high-growth firm status (employment-based, OECD) on the explanatory variables on the X-axis. Estimates control for cohort, industry, and regional effects. OECD = Organisation for Economic Co-operation and Development; FDI = foreign direct investment.

*Source:* Cruz, Baghdadi, and Arouri 2018.

*Note:* The figure is a rope-ladder representation of estimated coefficients and 95 percent confidence bands from a linear probability regression of employment-based high-growth status on the firm's three-year exporting or importing status (in which the maximum value is 3 if the firm has exported or imported for three consecutive years, and analogously, the minimum is 0 if the firm has not exported; the average of the sum of three-year exporting status is 0.21, and the average of the sum of three-year importing status is 0.4). Foreign direct investment (FDI) is a dummy variable that takes the value 1 if the firm is foreign owned and 0 otherwise. Additional controls include firm size, age, region, time, and sector fixed effects. OECD = Organisation for Economic Co-operation and Development.

In terms of magnitude, the FDI channel appears to be more important than exporting: whereas a 1 percent increase in exports as a share of total sales raises the probability of a firm becoming an HGF in the next 5–10 years by 0.05 percentage point, a 1 percent increase in FDI share raises the odds by 0.07 percentage point. Additional unreported estimates suggest that the presence of FDI (measured as a categorical variable) raises the likelihood of experiencing high growth by 3.6–11.6 percentage points in the firm's first five years, with the results robust to controlling for additional firm characteristics such as value added per worker, capital per worker, average wages, and share of imports in input expenditure. Likewise, in Tunisia, exports, imports, and foreign ownership are significantly associated with greater likelihood of experiencing a high-growth event, with the relationship being robust to controlling for various firm characteristics and alternative definitions of high growth (figure 3.19, panel b).

Results from India suggest that the relationship between exporting and the likelihood of experiencing high growth may vary by sector. Controlling for a range of firm characteristics, exporters in both manufacturing and services sectors have a greater likelihood of experiencing a sales-based high-growth event (figure 3.20), although the relationship for manufacturing is statistically significant only at the 10 percent level. Similarly, use of foreign technology (measured through imports of foreign capital goods) is also positively and significantly associated with

**FIGURE 3.20    Foreign Exposure in India Increases the Likelihood of High Growth…
More So in Services**

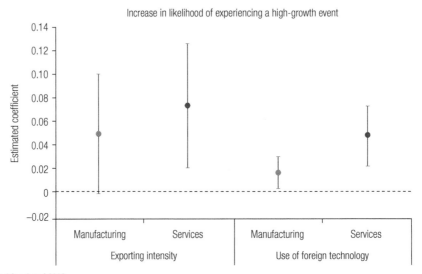

Source: Manghnani 2018.

Note: The figure is a rope-ladder representation of estimated coefficients and 95 percent confidence bands from a linear probability regression of high-growth status (sales-based, OECD) on three-year lagged values of a firm's exporting intensity, measured as the share of sales exported, and a dummy variable for the use of foreign technology. Additional controls include size, age, research and development, product scope, firm and year fixed effects, and industry-year interactions. Robust standard errors are clustered at the firm level. OECD = Organisation for Economic Co-operation and Development.

a greater likelihood of high growth, with the effect stronger in services compared with manufacturing.

Beyond foreign participation affecting firm performance directly, estimates from Mexico also show that firms operating in states and industries with greater presence of FDI are significantly more likely to experience a high-growth event in the first 5–10 years of their life cycle (figure 3.21, horizontal spillovers). Likewise, co-locating with upstream or downstream FDI-intensive firms or exporters in the same state is similarly associated with a higher likelihood of achieving high growth (figure 3.21, vertical spillovers). The results are particularly strong for upstream FDI spillovers, which hold even after controlling for a range of firm-specific observable and unobservable characteristics.

**FIGURE 3.21** **FDI Linkages Increase the Likelihood of High Growth in Mexico**

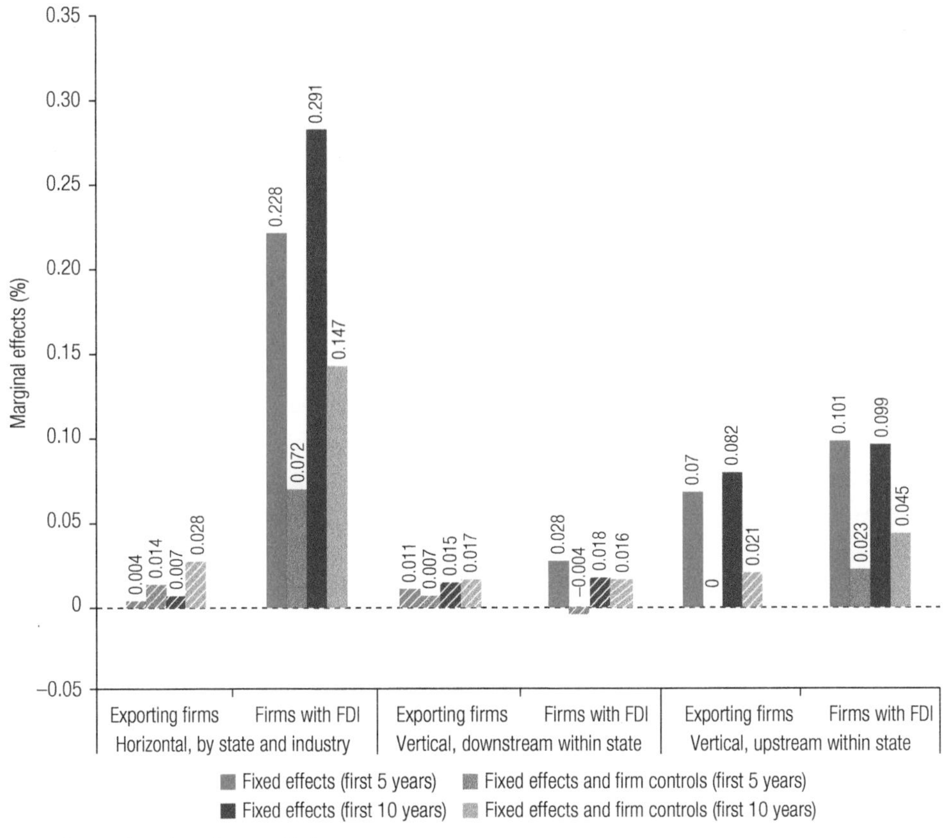

Source: Sanchez Bayardo and Iacovone 2018.

Note: The figure shows the marginal effects of initial value of exporting or foreign direct investment (FDI) spillovers (at the level of state, industry both) on the probability of attaining high-growth status (employment-based, OECD definition), in percentage points. Estimates are obtained from a probit regression that includes cohort, industry, and region fixed effects in the "Fixed effects" model; the "Fixed effects and firm controls" model adds firm characteristics such as value added per worker, average wages, average blue-collar wages, capital per worker, FDI dummy, and share of exports in sales. Solid bars indicate statistical significance at 10 percent level or higher; shaded bars are not statistically significant. OECD = Organisation for Economic Co-operation and Development.

What Makes for High Growth?

## Financial Development

A growing body of empirical evidence confirms the importance of financial development for firm growth. For example, Evans and Jovanovic (1989) show that entrepreneurial choices and firm growth can be affected by differences in access to finance. Cross-country evidence suggests that greater financial development is associated with higher growth in sectors that are more financially dependent (Rajan and Zingales 1998) and in sectors that have a higher share of small firms (Beck et al. 2008). Using a data set of nearly 70,000 firms from 107 counties, Aterido, Hallward-Driemeier, and Pages (2007) show that better access to finance has a significant, positive impact on employment growth for all firms, but smaller firms benefit the most. Similarly, Aghion, Fally, and Scarpetta (2007) show that the impact of financial development on growth of new entrants is much stronger than the impact on incumbents,[30] whereas Bottazzi, Secchi, and Tamagni (2014) find that financing constraints among Italian manufacturing firms prevent potentially fast-growing firms, particularly young ones, from taking advantage of growth opportunities. Duranton et al. (2015a) find that potentially productive firms in Indian manufacturing are unable to obtain financing because of misallocation in land markets, which is the principal form of collateral in business loans.

To what extent might the level of financial development affect the likelihood of high-growth episodes? Because HGFs tend to be disproportionately young, banks may be reluctant to lend to these companies based on their perceived riskiness and lack of collateral. Thus, firms in countries with more developed financial markets may exhibit a higher likelihood of experiencing high-growth events, particularly in sectors that are more dependent on external finance. Using sectoral data aggregated from firm-level surveys for 11 high-income economies, Bravo-Biosca, Criscuolo, and Menon (2016) show that this channel—along with higher banking competition and better contract enforcement—is associated with a more dynamic growth distribution, with a lower share of stable firms and higher shares of growing (but also shrinking) firms.[31]

For a sample of 71,000 firms in 122 developing economies using the World Bank Enterprise Survey data, figure 3.22 shows that—controlling for a range of country, industry, and firm characteristics—firms in sectors that are more dependent on external finance do not generally perform better in countries with more developed financial sectors.[32] The effect of the interaction between the country's degree of financial development and the sector's dependence on external finance is somewhat stronger for the sample of HGFs in these countries but still not statistically significant.[33] However, when the model is estimated separately for low-, lower-middle-, and upper-middle-income countries, the relationship between financial development and the performance of HGFs in upper-middle-income countries is

FIGURE 3.22 **Financial Development Improves Firm Performance in Upper-Middle-Income Countries**

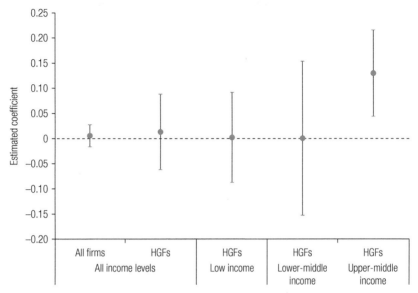

*Source:* Reyes, Grover Goswami, and Abuhashem 2018.

*Note:* The figure is a rope-ladder representation of estimated coefficients and 95 percent confidence bands from a regression of firm growth on an interaction between the country's degree of financial development and the sector's dependence on external finance (following Rajan and Zingales 1998). Regressions also control for firm age, labor productivity, and exporting status and include sector and country fixed effects. Standard errors are clustered at the sector level. The model includes 122 countries and 54 sectors at the 2-digit level (ISIC revision 4). HGF = high-growth firm.

positive and statistically significant. A potential explanation for this result is that firms in low- and lower-middle-income countries tend to face a broader range of performance bottlenecks—such as deficiencies in the basic set of institutional and regulatory factors and poor availability of complementary inputs—and therefore financial development can be more readily identified as a binding constraint for HGFs only at higher levels of development.

**TABLE 3A.1   Background Paper Definitions and Key Correlates of HGFs**

| Country | Period | HGF definition | HGF metrics | Time window to define HGFs | Key correlates of HGF | Measurement of correlates |
|---|---|---|---|---|---|---|
| Brazil | 1994–2014 | Firms born in 2000–01 that had at least 25 percent compound annual growth in employment for the next 13 years, firms born in 2000–01 that were in the 95th percentile of the Birch over the next 13 years for robustness checks[a] | Employment | 13 years | Managerial capabilities and worker skills | Current and prior wages, and previous employment experience |
| Côte d'Ivoire | 2003–2012 | OECD, minimum five employees | Employment | 3 years | Productivity | Revenue- and quantity-based TFP (estimated following Hsieh and Klenow [2009]) |
| Ethiopia | 1996–2009 | OECD without the 10-employee threshold (although, with few exceptions, that is inherently built into the CSA data), Birch for robustness checks | Employment | 3 years | Productivity<br><br>Agglomeration | Revenue-based TFP<br><br>Plant location in an agglomeration center as well as a measure of spatial concentration (the Ellison-Glaeser index) |
| Hungary | 2000–2015 | OECD, minimum five employees at the beginning of the period[b] | Employment and sales | 3, 5, and 10 years | Worker skills<br>Productivity<br><br>International exposure | Average wages<br>TFP, return on assets, wages (a proxy for marginal product of labor), and output per worker<br>Exporting status |
| India | 2004–05 and 2011–12 | Annual rate of revenue growth of 25 log points or higher (approximately a 25 percent rate of growth) between 2004–05 and 2011–12 | Sales | 6 years | Infrastructure | Proximity to the highway system (GQ and NS-EW highways) |
| | 1990–2013 | OECD, sales-based | Sales | 3 years | Innovation<br><br>International exposure | R&D, introduction of a new product or service<br><br>Exporting status |
| Indonesia | 1990–2014 | OECD (data are limited to firms with 20 or more employees), OECD with additional requirement of 15 percent minimum growth per annum, Birch index larger than 50 | Employment | 3 years | Firm size and age | Employment count and firm age |

*(Table continues on the following page.)*

**TABLE 3A.1  Background Paper Definitions and Key Correlates of HGFs** (*continued*)

| Country | Period | HGF definition | HGF metrics | Time window to define HGFs | Key correlates of HGF | Measurement of correlates |
|---|---|---|---|---|---|---|
| Mexico | 1993, 1998, 2003, 2008, 2013 | Firms that grow at an annual average rate of 12 percent per year for five years (equivalent to OECD 20 percent per year for three years), top 5 percent of the distribution of the Birch index | Employment | 5 or 10 years | Worker skills<br>Innovation<br><br>FDI<br>International exposure | Average wages<br>R&D personnel dummy or R&D activities dummy<br>FDI, dummy<br>Exporting status |
| Thailand | 2004–2015 | OECD, Birch | Sales | 3 years | Networks | Horizontal and vertical networks |
| Tunisia | 1996–2015 | OECD, Birch | Employment | 3 years | International exposure | Foreign exposure (exports, imports, and FDI) |
| Turkey (using TurkStat data) | 2005–2014 | OECD, Birch | Employment and sales (OECD) and employment (Birch) | 3 years | Productivity | Revenue-based TFP (using ordinary least squares and Levinsohn and Petrin [2003] methodology) |

*Note:* CSA = Central Statistical Agency; FDI = foreign direct investment; GQ = Golden Quadrilateral; HGF = high-growth firm; NS-EW = North-South-East-West; OECD = Organisation for Economic Co-operation and Development; R&D = research and development; TFP = total factor productivity.

a. HGF definitions follow Haltiwanger et al. (2017). The 2000–01 cohort is chosen to track prior employment and wage history of founding HGF employees and managers.

b. For robustness, two additional variables: (1) firms that grow by at least 20 percent in each year of the three- or five-year period; (2) the top 5 percent of firms with respect to their three- or five-year growth rate.

## Notes

1. See, for example, Foster, Haltiwanger, and Syverson (2008) and Katayama, Lu, and Tybout (2009), who argue that firm selection and success are based on profitability, whereas technical efficiency is just one of several factors determining profits. Melitz (2000), De Loecker (2005), Gorodnichenko (2005), and Katayama, Lu, and Tybout (2003) offer some alternative empirical methods to back out the technical efficiency term when micro-data on prices are not available.

2. Productivity growth can be decomposed into two broad components: changes within surviving firms and changes between firms, with the latter further separated into the effects coming from entry, exit, and changes in market shares across firms. Disney, Haskel, and Heden (2003) decompose productivity growth for the United Kingdom over the period 1980–92 using three alternative techniques: Baily, Hulten, and Campbell (1992); Foster et al. (1998); and Griliches and Regev (1995). The within effect measures the increase in productivity of surviving firms, whereas the between-survivors effect is the change in market share of the survivor weighted by productivity (depending on the technique, this could be final period or base period). A positive term on the latter implies that the market share of the more productive firms increased over the measured period. Foster et al. (1998) additionally include a cross term that measures the covariance between market share and productivity, with a positive term reflecting that firms with growing productivity are able to increase their market shares. Disney, Haskel, and Heden (2003) find a negative cross term for the United Kingdom using the Foster et al. (1998) decomposition and a negative between-survivor term using the Griliches and Regev (1995) method. When comparing the decomposition with the United States for the period 1982–87, their decomposition yields a negative between-survivor effect.

3. Foster, Haltiwanger, and Syverson (2008) show that TFPR is positively correlated with TFPQ but confounds the "true" measure with idiosyncratic demand and factor prices effects. For a set of 11 highly homogeneous manufactured products in the United States (for example, ready-mixed concrete, raw cane sugar, boxes, and the like), the authors report a correlation of 0.75 between the two measures.

4. Productivity losses resulting from resource misallocation—distortions preventing the movement of resources from less to more efficient firms—have been documented extensively in several developing countries; see, for example, Hseih and Klenow 2009; Duranton et al. 2015b; Chuah, Loayza, and Nguye 2018.

5. SBA Office of Advocacy (2008) adopts a more restrictive definition of HGFs, focusing specifically on "high-impact firms": firms whose sales have at least doubled over a four-year period and that have an employment growth quantifier (the product of the absolute and percentage change in employment) of two or more over this period.

6. The estimated marginal effect of TFP on the probability of experiencing a high-growth episode is 0.17–0.20 in specifications using the OECD definition of high growth versus 0.21–0.27 in specifications using the Birch definition.

7. For most quantiles of TFP growth, plant age has a positive coefficient but is not significant. Lagged size of the firm shows a positive association with TFP growth, implying that larger firms consistently show higher TFP growth, with the effect rapidly rising along the TFP distribution. These patterns hold for the two alternative definitions of HGFs.

8. Domestic and foreign demand shocks are captured following the approach of Coulibaly, Sapriza, and Zlate (2013), who use domestic and foreign GDP growth weighted by export shares.

9. Quantity-based TFP (TFPQ) is calculated following Hsieh and Klenow (2009).

10. Proxies for firms' ability to reorganize and restructure that have been used in the literature include managers' self-assessment on the organizational flexibility of the firm and measures of managerial and workforce skills that are complementary to restructuring (Caroli and Van Reenen 2001; Bresnahan, Brynjolfsson, and Hitt 2002; Bloom, Sadun, and Van Reenen 2012).

11. That human capital is crucial to productivity is observed in many studies (for example, Abowd et al. 2005; Ilmakunnas, Maliranta, and Vainiomäki 2004; Fox and Smeets 2011). In addition, innovation differences also explain the gap between the European and U.S. productivity experiences over the past few decades (van Ark, O'Mahoney, and Timmer 2008).

12. Theoretical models include, for example, Nelson and Winter (1982); whereas recent empirical studies are found in Coad and Rao (2008, 2010), Hölzl (2009), and Bos and Stam (2014).

13. Although employment-based HGFs are characterized by organizational innovation and incremental product innovation (Janczak et al. 2006), some studies find a negative association between employment growth in the context of process innovation. See, for example, Coad (2007, 2009), Harrison et al. (2014), Coad and Rao (2011), Hall, Lotti, and Mairesse (2008), and Hall, Jaffe, and Trajtenberg (2005).

14. For example, the negative link between product innovation and firm growth may emerge because HGFs may avoid new product development to channel resources into penetrating existing markets (for example, Parker Storey, and van Witteloostuijn 2010).

15. The period of study affects the direction of the result because it is inherently time consuming for innovative ventures to transform into successful growth opportunities, if at all (Niefert 2005; Stam and Wennberg 2009). Identification of the impact is challenging because innovative activity (for example, R&D investments) usually takes time to translate into growth, making it difficult for an econometrician to detect a statistically significant impact.

16. Literature suggests that new products could create new markets, such as the frozen potato industry, the personal computer, or the software industry (Rigby, Burton, and Young 2006). Evidence supports the view that innovating firms are not only more productive (for example, Wieser 2001) but also grow faster than noninnovators.

17. For example, Jorgenson, Ho, and Stiroh (2008) document the growth in output (and productivity) in the United States during the period 1959–2006 and find that the average annual growth rate in output increased from 3.1 percent during 1973–95 to 4.8 percent during 1995–2000. This resurgence in growth is attributed largely to innovations in information technology.

18. The data for this study is sourced from Centre for Monitoring Indian Economy Prowess, in which employment figures are not available for many firms. Growth is calculated as the log difference in firm sales of goods or services between two consecutive years. The dummy variable for product innovation can also be interpreted as a measure of product diversification. For instance, the higher extent of innovation among gazelles is rooted in product diversification (Hölzl and Friesenbichler 2007). Some studies not specifically focused on HGFs find a positive correlation between product diversification and employment growth in the pre-diversification period but a negative one after diversification (Coad and Guenther 2013).

19. These models contend that access to larger markets through exports allows firms to invest in innovative activities and improve productivity (see Bustos 2011; Lileeva and Trefler 2010; Melitz and Costantini 2007).

20. Kilinç (2018) estimates a difference in difference model controlling for firm heterogeneity using the propensity score matching method for each 2-digit industry. Within manufacturing sectors, the effects are most pronounced in transport equipment, leather, and computer and electronics, whereas among services it is construction, architectural, and engineering services that benefit the most from innovation.

21. Clustering matters because firms located in cities may benefit from thicker markets for capital, labor, and material inputs (Fujita, Krugman, and Venables 1999); and knowledge spillovers and reduced transaction costs (Audretsch and Feldman 1996; Jaffe, Trajtenberg, and Henderson 1993; Anna Lee Saxenien 1990). Clustering of economic activity can also yield dynamic benefits, such as increased innovation (Matsuyama 1991), and may reduce the scope for opportunistic behavior (Collier and Venables 2008; Audretsch and Dohse 2004). On specific work pertaining to geography and HGFs, Anyadike-Danes, Bonner, and Hart (2013) focus on the

type of location but not specifically on clustering. Likewise, Bogas and Barbosa's (2015) finding of a positive correlation of HGF status with human capital, industrial specialization, and services agglomeration speaks to locational traits rather than the importance of firm clustering.

22. Manufacturing in Ethiopia is concentrated in five main towns, with Addis Ababa hosting more than 61 percent of plants in 1996, while the other four towns add another 10 percent to total plant count. The importance of the capital city declined to less than 40 percent in 2009, while the share of the top five locations dropped to 51 percent during the same period.

23. Plants located in towns that are within 50 kilometers of the nearest agglomeration center also have a higher chance of experiencing a high-growth episode relative to those located farther away, although these results are not always significant for the HGFs defined using the Birch index.

24. There is an ongoing debate about the influence of local geography on economic activity and economic development. Local geography, often referred to as first nature characteristic or locational fundamental, represents a time-invariant, location-specific characteristic. These results suggest that although the geographical characteristic, as such, does not change over time, its values can. Industrial policy reforms appear to have enhanced the values of locational fundamentals important for high growth.

25. See Banternghansa (2017) for a more detailed description of Thai horizontal networks and Samphantharak (2006) on vertical networks.

26. The differences in size are driven primarily by firms in vertical networks, given that the size distribution of firms in horizontal networks is not very different from out-of-network firms.

27. This literature dates back at least to Walker (1887). Managerial capabilities are central to the Lucas (1978) model of firm size and have been given new prominence by the work of Bloom and Van Reenen (2007) and studies that have followed their approach.

28. Another possible reason why future HGFs pay higher wages over and above the premium expected considering education and experience, is that their growth puts them under time pressure, whereby they need to find a match more promptly and cannot afford to wait in the labor market to find a better deal.

29. A recent study shows that the mere prospect of foreign firms entering the local market induces local firms to be more productive in various countries (Bao and Chen 2018).

30. Their work draws on firm-level data from 16 countries: Argentina, Chile, Colombia, Denmark, Finland, France, Germany, Hungary, Italy, Mexico, the Netherlands, Portugal, Romania, Slovenia, the United Kingdom, and the United States.

31. These 11 countries include Canada, New Zealand, the United States and eight European countries: Austria, Denmark, Finland, Italy, the Netherlands, Norway, Spain, and the United Kingdom. Results regarding the share of HGFs are more ambiguous, varying with the indicator used. The share of HGFs is lower with higher financial development relative to GDP; however, the HGF contribution to job creation rises with stock market capitalization and falls with private bond market development. Banking competition is associated with a higher share of job creation by HGFs but also with a lower share of growing firms.

32. The degree to which firms are dependent on external finance at the sectoral level, following the approach first proposed by Rajan and Zingales (1998), is taken from Bravo-Biosca, Criscuolo, and Menon (2016). The authors capture the different needs for financial intermediation at the sectoral level with Leontief's coefficients on the input from the finance and insurance sector from input-output tables across 10 OECD countries. The level of financial development is captured by the share of domestic credit to the private sector (financial resources provided to the private sector by financial corporations, such as loans, purchases of nonequity securities, and trade credits and other accounts receivable, that establish a claim for repayment) in GDP. For some countries these claims include credit to public enterprises. Financial corporations include monetary authorities and deposit money banks, as well as other financial corporations for which data are available (including corporations that do not accept transferable deposits but

do incur such liabilities as time and savings deposits). Examples of other financial corporations are finance and leasing companies, money lenders, insurance corporations, pension funds, and foreign exchange companies.

33. For the purposes of these regressions, firm growth $g_{t,t-2}^{ijc}$ is calculated as the midpoint employment growth rate following Davis, Haltiwanger, and Schuh (1996). HGFs are defined as enterprises in the top decile of the distribution of firm growth $(g_{t,t-2}^{ijc})$ across all countries.

## References

Abowd, J. M., J. Haltiwanger, R. Jarmin, J. Lane, P. Lengermann, K. McCue, and K. Sandusky. 2005. "The Telation among Human Capital, Productivity, and Market Value: Building Up from Micro Evidence." In *Measuring Capital in the New Economy*, edited by Carol Corrado, John Haltiwanger, and Daniel Sichel, 153–204. Chicago: University of Chicago Press.

Ackerberg, D. A., K. Caves, and G. Frazer. 2015. "Identification Properties of Recent Production Function Estimators." *Econometrica* 83 (6): 2411–51.

Aghion, P., T. Fally, and S. Scarpetta. 2007. "Credit Constraints as a Barrier to the Entry and Post-Entry Growth of Firms." *Economic Policy* 22 (52): 731–79.

Aitken, B., G. H. Hanson, and A. E. Harrison. 1997. "Spillovers, Foreign Investment, and Export Behavior." *Journal of International Economics* 43 (1–2): 103–32.

Akcigit, U., J. Grigsby, and T. Nicholas. 2017. "The Rise of American Ingenuity: Innovation and Inventors of the Golden Age." Working Paper 23047, National Bureau of Economic Research, Cambridge, MA.

Alchian, A. A. 1950. "Uncertainty, Evolution, and Economic Theory." *Journal of Political Economy* 58: 211–22.

Anyadike-Danes, M., K. Bonner, and M. Hart. 2013. "Exploring the Incidence and Spatial Distribution of High Growth Firms in the UK and Their Contribution to Job Creation." Working Paper 13/05, National Endowment for Science, Technology and the Arts, London.

Arkolakis, C. 2015. "A Unified Theory of Firm Selection and Growth." *The Quarterly Journal of Economics* 131 (1): 89–155.

Asplund, M., and V. Nocke. 2006. "Firm Turnover in Imperfectly Competitive Markets." *Review of Economic Studies* 73 (2): 295–327.

Aterido, R., M. Hallward-Driemeier, and C. Pages. 2007. "Investment Climate and Employment Growth: The Impact of Access to Finance, Corruption, and Regulations across Firms." IZA Discussion Paper 3138, Institute for the Study of Labor, Bonn.

Audretsch, D. B., and D. Dohse. 2004. "The Impact of Location on Firm Growth." Discussion Paper 4332, Centre for Economic Policy Research, London.

Audretsch, D. B., and M. P. Feldman. 1996. "Innovative Clusters and the Industry Life Cycle." *Review of Industrial Organization* 11 (2): 253–73.

Baily, M. N., and D. Farrell. 2006. "Breaking Down Barriers to Growth." *Finance and Development* 43 (1): 23.

Baily, Martin, Charles Hulten, and David Campbell. 1992. "Productivity Dynamics in Manufacturing Plants." *Brookings Papers on Economic Activity: Microeconomics* 1992: 187–249.

Banternghansa, C. 2017. "Multi-Firm Entrepreneurship and Financial Frictions." PIER Discussion Paper 56, Puey Ungphakorn Institute for Economic Research, Bangkok, Thailand.

———, and K. Samphantharak. 2018. "How Does Ownership Network Affect High-Growth Firms in Thailand." Background paper for *High-Growth Firms*, World Bank, Washington, DC.

Bao, C. G., and M. X. Chen. 2018. "Foreign Rivals Are Coming to Town: Responding to the Threat of Foreign Multinational Entry." *American Economic Journal: Applied Economics* 10 (4): 120–57.

Bastos, P., and J. Silva. 2018. "The Origins of High-Growth Firms: Evidence from Brazil." *Background paper for High-Growth Firms*, World Bank, Washington, DC.

Bastos, P., J. Silva, and E. A. Verhoogen. 2018. "Export Destinations and Input Prices." *American Economic Review* 108 (2): 353–92.

Beck, T., A. Demirgüç-Kunt, L. Laeven, and R. Levine. 2008 "Finance, Firm Size, and Growth." *Journal of Money, Credit and Banking* 40 (7): 1379–405.

Beck, T., A. Demirgüç-Kunt, and V. Maksimovic. 2005. "Financial and Legal Constraints to Growth: Does Firm Size Matter?" *Journal of Finance* 60 (1): 137–77.

Bento, P., and D. Restuccia. 2017. "Misallocation, Establishment Size, and Productivity." *American Economic Journal: Macroeconomics* 9 (3): 267–303.

Bloom, N., R. Sadun, and J. Van Reenen. 2012. "Americans Do IT Better: US Multinationals and the Productivity Miracle." *American Economic Review* 102 (1): 167–201.

———. 2017. "Management as Technology?" Working Paper 22327, National Bureau of Economic Research, Cambridge, MA.

Bloom, N., and J. Van Reenen. 2007. "Measuring and Explaining Management Practices across Firms and Countries." *Quarterly Journal of Economics* 122 (4): 1341–408.

———. 2010. "Why Do Management Practices Differ across Firms and Countries?" *Journal of Economic Perspectives* 24 (1): 203–24.

Bogas, P., and N. Barbosa. 2015. "High-Growth Firms: What Is the Impact of Region-Specific Characteristics?" In *Entrepreneurship, Human Capital, and Regional Development,* edited by Rui Baptista and João Leitão, 295–308. Cham, Switzerland: Springer.

Bos, J., and E. Stam. 2014. "Gazelles and Industry Growth: A Study of Young High-Growth Firms in the Netherlands." *Industrial and Corporate Change* 23 (1): 145–69.

Bottazzi, G., E. Cefis, and G. Dosi. 2002. "Corporate Growth and Industrial Structures: Some Evidence from the Italian Manufacturing Industry." *Industrial and Corporate Change* 11 (4): 705–23.

Bottazzi, G., A. Secchi, and F. Tamagni. 2006. "Financial Fragility and Growth Dynamics of Italian Business Firms." Working Paper 2006/07, LEM-Scuola Superiore Sant'Anna, Pisa, Italy.

———. 2014. "Financial Constraints and Firm Dynamics." *Small Business Economics* 42 (1): 99–116.

Bravo-Biosca, A., C. Criscuolo, and C. Menon. 2016. "What Drives the Dynamics of Business Growth?" *Economic Policy* 31 (88): 703–42.

Bresnahan, T. F., E. Brynjolfsson, and L. M. Hitt. 2002. "Information Technology, Workplace Organization, and the Demand for Skilled Labor: Firm-Level Evidence." *Quarterly Journal of Economics* 117 (1): 339–76.

Bruhn, M., D. Karlan, and A. Schoar. 2013. "The Impact of Consulting Services on Small and Medium Enterprises: Evidence from a Randomized Trial in Mexico." Policy Research Working Paper 6508, World Bank, Washington, DC.

Bustos, P. 2011. "Trade Liberalization, Exports, and Technology Upgrading: Evidence on the Impact of MERCOSUR on Argentinian Firms." *American Economic Review* 101 (1): 304–40.

Cabral, L. 2007. "Small Firms in Portugal: A Selective Survey of Stylized Facts, Economic Analysis, and Policy Implications." *Portuguese Economic Journal* 6 (1): 65–88.

Cardoso, Ana Rute, and Rudolf Winter-Ebmer. 2010. "Mentoring and Segregation: Female-Led Firms and Gender Wage Policies." *Industrial and Labor Relations Review* 64 (1): 143–63.

Caroli, E., and J. Van Reenen. 2001. "Skill-Biased Organizational Change? Evidence from a Panel of British and French Establishments." *Quarterly Journal of Economics* 116 (4): 1449–92.

Chuah, L. L., N. V. Loayza, and H. Nguye. 2018. "Resource Misallocation and Productivity Gaps in Malaysia." Policy Research Working Paper 8368, World Bank, Washington, DC.

Cirera, X., R. Fattal Jaef, and N. Gonne. 2018. "High-Growth Firms and Misallocation in Low-Income Countries: Evidence from Côte d'Ivoire." Background paper for *High-Growth Firms*, World Bank, Washington, DC.

Coad, A. 2007. "Testing the Principle of 'Growth of the Fitter': The Relationship between Profits and Firm Growth." *Structural Change and Economic Dynamics* 18 (3): 370–86.

———. 2009. *The Growth of Firms: A Survey of Theories and Empirical Evidence.* Cheltenham, UK: Edward Elgar.

———, and C. Guenther. 2013. "Diversification Patterns and Survival as Firms Mature." *Small Business Economics* 41 (3): 633–49.

Coad, A., and R. Rao. 2008. "Innovation and Firm Growth in High-Tech Sectors: A Quantile Regression Approach." *Research Policy* 37 (4): 633–48.

———. 2010. "Firm Growth and R&D Expenditure." *Economics of Innovation and New Technology* 19 (2): 127–45.

———. 2011. "The Firm-Level Employment Effects of Innovations in High-Tech US Manufacturing Industries." *Journal of Evolutionary Economics* 21 (2): 255–83.

Coase, R. 1937. "The Nature of the Firm." *Economica* 4 (16): 386–405.

Collier, P., and A. J. Venables. 2008. "Managing the Exploitation of Natural Assets: Lessons for Low Income Countries." Paper prepared for the African Research Consortium annual conference, Nairobi, Kenya.

Conyon, M., and P. Wright. 2002. "The Productivity and Wage Effects of Foreign Acquisition in the United Kingdom." *Journal of Industrial Economics* 50 (1): 85–102.

Coşar, A. K., N. Guner, and J. Tybout. 2010. "Firm Dynamics, Job Turnover, and Wage Distributions in an Open Economy." Working Paper 16326, National Bureau of Economic Research, Cambridge, MA.

Coulibaly, B., H. Sapriza, and A. Zlate. 2013. "Financial Frictions, Trade Credit, and the 2008–09 Global Financial Crisis." *International Review of Economics and Finance* 26 (1): 25–38.

Cruz, M., L. Baghdadi, and H. Arouri. 2018. "The Dynamics of High-Growth Firms: Evidence from Tunisia." Background paper for *High-Growth Firms*, World Bank, Washington, DC.

Czarnitzki, D., and J. Delanote. 2013. "Young Innovative Companies: The New High-Growth Firms?" *Industrial and Corporate Change* 22 (2): 1315–40.

Daunfeldt, S.-O., N. Elert, and D. Johansson. 2010. "The Economic Contribution of High-Growth Firms: Do Definitions Matter?" Working Paper 151, Ratio Institute, Stockholm.

Davis, Steven J., John Haltiwanger, Ronald S. Jarmin, C. J. Krizan, Javier Miranda, Alfred Nucci, and Kristin Sandusky. 2009. "Measuring the Dynamics of Young and Small Businesses: Integrating the Employer and Nonemployer Universes." In *Producer Dynamics: New Evidence from Micro Data*, edited by Timothy Dunne, Bradford J. Jensen, and Mark J. Roberts, 329–68. Chicago: University of Chicago Press for NBER.

Davis, S., J. Haltiwanger, and S. Schuh. 1996. *Job Creation and Destruction.* Cambridge, MA: MIT Press.

Decker, R. A., J. Haltiwanger, R. S. Jarmin, and J. Miranda. 2016. "Where Has All the Skewness Gone? The Decline in High-Growth (Young) Firms in the U.S." *European Economic Review* 86 (July): 4–23.

De Loecker, J. 2005. "Product Differentiation, Multi-Product Firms and Structural Estimation of Productivity." Unpublished manuscript, KU Leuven, Leuven, Belgium.

de Wit, G. 2005. "Firm Size Distributions: An Overview of Steady-State Distributions Resulting from Firm Dynamics Models." *International Journal of Industrial Organization* 23 (5–6): 423–50.

Disney, R., J. Haskel, and Y. Heden. 2003. "Restructuring and Productivity Growth in UK Manufacturing." *Economic Journal* 113 (489): 666–94.

Djankov, S., E. Miguel, Y. Qian, G. Roland, and E. Zhuravskaya. 2005. "Who Are Russia's Entrepreneurs?" *Journal of the European Economic Association* 3 (2–3): 587–97.

Dranove, D., C. Forman, A. Goldfarb, and S. Greenstein. 2014. "The Trillion Dollar Conundrum: Complementarities and Health Information Technology." *American Economic Journal: Economic Policy* 6 (4): 239–70.

Dries, L., and J. F. Swinnen. 2004. "Foreign Direct Investment, Vertical Integration, and Local Suppliers: Evidence from the Polish Dairy Sector." *World Development* 32 (9): 1525–44.

Du, J., Y. Gong, and Y. Temouri. 2013. "High Growth Firms and Productivity—Evidence from the United Kingdom." Working Paper 13/04, National Endowment for Science, Technology and the Arts, London.

Du, J., and Y. Temouri. 2015. "High-Growth Firms and Productivity: Evidence from the United Kingdom." *Small Business Economics* 44 (1): 123–43.

Duranton, G., E. Ghani, A. Grover Goswami, and W. Kerr. 2015a. "Effects of Land Misallocation on Capital Allocations in India." Policy Research Working Paper 7451, World Bank, Washington, DC.

———. 2015b. "The Misallocation of Land and Other Factors of Production in India." Policy Research Working Paper 7221, World Bank, Washington, DC.

Eaton, J., S. S. Kortum, and S. Sotelo. 2012. "International Trade: Linking Micro and Macro." Working Paper 17864, National Bureau of Economic Research, Cambridge, MA.

Eslava, M., and J. Haltiwanger. 2017. "The Life-Cycle of Plants in Colombia: Fundamentals vs Distortions." Research Department Working Paper 1105, CAF, Development Bank of Latin America.

Evans, D. S., and B. Jovanovic. 1989. "An Estimated Model of Entrepreneurial Choice under Liquidity Constraints." *Journal of Political Economy* 97 (4): 808–27.

Falk, M. 2012. "Quantile Estimates of the Impact of R&D Intensity on Firm Performance." *Small Business Economics* 39 (1): 19–37.

Foster, L., J. Haltiwanger, C. J. Krizan, and A. P. Growth. 1998. "Lessons from Microeconomic Evidence." Working Paper 6803, National Bureau of Economic Research, Cambridge, MA.

Foster, L., J. Haltiwanger, and C. Syverson. 2008. "Reallocation, Firm Turnover, and Efficiency: Selection on Productivity or Profitability?" *American Economic Review* 98 (1): 394–425.

———. 2016. "The Slow Growth of New Plants: Learning about Demand?" *Economica* 83 (329): 91–129.

Fox, J. T., and V. Smeets. 2011. "Does Input Quality Drive Measured Differences in Firm Productivity?" *International Economic Review* 52 (4): 96–89.

Friedman, M. 1953. "The Methodology of Positive Economics." In *Essays In Positive Economics.* Chicago: University of Chicago Press.

Fujita, M., P. Krugman, and A. J. Venables. 1999. *The Spatial Economy: Cities, Regions, and International Trade.* Cambridge, MA: MIT Press.

Gandhi, A., S. Navarro, and D. Rivers. 2016. "On the Identification of Production Functions: How Heterogeneous Is Productivity?" Working Paper 2017–27, Centre for Human Capital and Productivity, University of Western Ontario, London, ON.

Ghani, E., W. Kerr, and S. O'Connell. 2011. "Who Creates Jobs?: New Evidence from India." CEPR Policy Portal. http://www.voxeu.org/article/who-creates-jobs-new-evidence-india.

Gilbert, B. A., P. P. McDougall, and D. B. Audretsch. 2006. "New Venture Growth: A Review and Extension." *Journal of Management* 32 (6): 926–50.

Gibrat, R. 1931. *Les Inégalités Économiques.* Paris: Recueil Sirey.

Girma, S., D. Greenaway, and K. Wakelin. 2001. "Who Benefits from Foreign Direct Investment in the UK?" *Scottish Journal of Political Economy* 48 (2): 119–33.

Glaeser, E. L., and W. R. Kerr. 2009. "Local Industrial Conditions and Entrepreneurship: How Much of the Spatial Distribution Can We Explain?" *Journal of Economics and Management Strategy* 18 (3): 623–63.

Goedhuys, M., and L. Sleuwaegen. 2010. "High-Growth Entrepreneurial Firms in Africa: A Quantile Regression Approach." *Small Business Economics* 34 (1): 31–51.

Gorodnichenko, Y. 2005. "Reduced-Rank Identification of Structural Shocks in VARs." Working Paper, Department of Economics, University of Michigan, Ann Arbor.

Greenaway, D., and R. Kneller. 2007. "Firm Heterogeneity, Exporting and Foreign Direct Investment." *Economic Journal* 117 (517): F134–61.

Griliches, Z., and H. Regev. 1995. "Firm Productivity in Israeli Industry 1979–1988." *Journal of Econometrics* 65 (1): 175–203.

Grover Goswami, A. 2018. "Firms Far Up! Productivity, Agglomeration, and Growth Entrepreneurship in Ethiopia." Background paper for *High-Growth Firms*, World Bank, Washington, DC.

Haddad, M., and A. Harrison. 1993. "Are There Positive Spillovers from Direct Foreign Investment? Evidence from Panel Data for Morocco." *Journal of Development Economics* 42 (1): 51–74.

Hall, B. H., A. Jaffe, and M. Trajtenberg. 2005. "Market Value and Patent Citations." *RAND Journal of Economics* 36 (1): 16–38.

Hall, B. H., F. Lotti, and J. Mairesse. 2008. "Employment, Innovation, and Productivity: Evidence from Italian Microdata." *Industrial and Corporate Change* 17 (4): 813–39.

Haltiwanger, J. 1997. "Measuring and Analyzing Aggregate Fluctuations: The Importance of Building from Microeconomic Evidence." Federal Reserve Bank of St. Louis Economic *Review* 79 (3): 55–78.

———, R. S. Jarmin, R. Kulick, and J. Miranda. 2017. "High-Growth Firms: Contribution to Job, Output and Productivity Growth." In *Measuring Entrepreneurial Businesses: Current Knowledge and Challenges,* edited by John Haltiwanger, Erik Hurst, Javier Miranda, and Antoinette Schoar, 11–62. Chicago: University of Chicago Press.

Hannan, M. T. 2005. "Ecologies of Organizations: Diversity and Identity." *Journal of Economic Perspectives* 19 (1): 51–70.

———, and J. Freeman. 1977. "The Population Ecology of Organizations." *American Journal of Sociology* 82 (5): 929–64.

Harrison, R., J. Jaumandreu, J. Mairesse, and B. Peters. 2014. "Does Innovation Stimulate Employment? A Firm-Level Analysis Using Comparable Micro-Data from Four European Countries." *International Journal of Industrial Organization* 35 (July): 29–43.

Haskel, J. E., S. C. Pereira, and M. J. Slaughter. 2007. "Does Inward Foreign Direct Investment Boost the Productivity of Domestic Firms?" *Review of Economics and Statistics* 89 (3): 482–96.

Hellmann, T., and M. Puri. 2000. "The Interaction between Product Market and Financing Strategy: The Role of Venture Capital." *Review of Financial Studies* 13 (4): 959–84.

Hölzl, W. 2007. "Intellectual Property Rights, Innovation and European IPR Policy." *Austrian Economic Quarterly* 12 (1): 71–82.

———. 2009. "Is the R&D Behaviour of Fast-Growing SMEs Different? Evidence from CIS III Data for 16 Countries." *Small Business Economics* 33 (1): 59–75.

———, and K. Friesenbichler. 2007. "Are Gazelles More Innovative than Other Firms?" Unpublished manuscript, WIFO Austrian Institute of Economic Research, Vienna.

Hopenhayn, H. A. 1992. "Entry, Exit, and Firm Dynamics in Long Run Equilibrium." *Econometrica* 60 (5): 1127–50.

Hsieh, C.-T., and P. J. Klenow. 2009. "Misallocation and Manufacturing TFP in China and India." *Quarterly Journal of Economics* 124 (4): 1403–48.

———. 2014 "The Life Cycle of Plants in India and Mexico." *Quarterly Journal of Economics* 129 (3): 1035–83.

Ilmakunnas, P., M. Maliranta, and J. Vainiomäki. 2004. "The Roles of Employer and Employee Characteristics for Plant Productivity." *Journal of Productivity Analysis* 21 (3): 249–76.

Itskhoki, O., and E. Helpman. 2014. "Firms, Trade and Labor Market Dynamics." Working Paper, Princeton University, Princeton, NJ.

Jaffe, A. B., M. Trajtenberg, and R. Henderson. 1993. "Geographic Localization of Knowledge Spillovers as Evidenced by Patent Citations." *Quarterly Journal of Economics* 108 (3): 577–98.

Janczak, S., F. Barès, S. Boiteux, and M.-F. Clerc-Girard. 2006. "Entrepreneurship and the High Growth Companies: The Evolution of the Gazelles and Their Ties to the Territory." Working Paper 2006–02, ICN Business School, Nancy, France.

Jorgenson, D. W., M.S. Ho, and K. J. Stiroh. 2005. *Information Technology and the American Growth Resurgence*, vol. 3. Cambridge, MA: MIT Press.

———. 2008. "A Retrospective Look at the US Productivity Growth Resurgence." *Journal of Economic Perspectives* 22 (1): 3–24.

Jovanovic, B. 1982. "Selection and the Evolution of Industry." *Econometrica* 50 (3): 649–70.

Katayama, H., S. Lu, and J. Tybout. 2003. "Why Plant-Level Productivity Studies Are Often Misleading, and an Alternative Approach to Interference." Working Paper 9617, National Bureau of Economic Research, Cambridge, MA.

———. 2009. "Firm-Level Productivity Studies: Illusions and a Solution." *International Journal of Industrial Organization* 27 (3): 403–13.

Keller, W., and S. R. Yeaple. 2009. "Multinational Enterprises, International Trade, and Productivity Growth: Firm-Level Evidence from the United States." *Review of Economics and Statistics* 91 (4): 821–31.

Kılınç, U. 2018. "Assessing Productivity Gains from International Trade in a Small Open Economy." *Open Economies Review* 29 (5): 953–80.

Kokko, A., M. Zejan, and R. Tansini. 2001. "Trade Regimes and Spillover Effects of FDI: Evidence from Uruguay." *Review of World Economics* 137 (1): 124–49.

Kugler, Maurice, and Eric Verhoogen. 2012. "Prices, Plant Size, and Product Quality." *Review of Economic Studies* 79 (1): 307–39.

Lall, S. V., J. V. Henderson, and A. J. Venables. 2017. *Africa's Cities: Opening Doors to the World.* Washington, DC: World Bank.

Lechner, C., and M. Dowling. 2003. "Firm Networks: External Relationships as Sources for the Growth and Competitiveness of Entrepreneurial Firms." *Entrepreneurship and Regional Development* 15 (1): 1–26.

Levinsohn, J., and A. Petrin. 2003. "Estimating Production Functions Using Inputs to Control for Unobservables." *Review of Economic Studies* 70 (2): 317–41.

Lileeva, A., and D. Trefle. 2010. "Improved Access to Foreign Markets Raises Plant-Level Productivity for Some Plants." *Quarterly Journal of Economics* 125 (3): 1051–99.

Lipsey, R., and F. Sjoholm. 2004. "Foreign Direct Investment, Education and Wages in Indonesian Manufacturing." *Journal of Development Economics* 73 (1): 415–22.

Liu, J., M. Tsou, and J. Hammit. 1999. "Do Small Plants Grow Faster? Evidence from the Taiwan Electronics Industry." *Economics Letters* 65 (1): 121–29.

Lopez-Acevedo, G., D. Medvedev, and V. Palmade, eds. *South Asia's Turn: Policies to Boost Competitiveness and Create the Next Export Powerhouse.* Washington, DC: World Bank.

Lööf, H., M. Andersson, B. Johansson, and C. Karlsson. 2012. "R&D Strategy and Firm Performance: What Is the Long-Run Impact of Persistent R&D." In *Innovation and Growth: From R&D*

*Strategies of Innovating Firms to Economy-Wide Technological Change*, edited by Martin Andersson, Borje Johansson, Charlie Karlsson, and Hans Lööf, 182–207. Oxford: Oxford University Press.

Lucas, R. 1978. "On the Size Distribution of Business Firms." *Bell Journal of Economics* 9 (2): 508–23.

Luttmer, E. G. 2007. "Selection, Growth, and the Size Distribution of Firms." *Quarterly Journal of Economics* 122 (3): 1103–44.

———. 2011. "On the Mechanics of Firm Growth." *Review of Economic Studies* 78 (3): 1042–68.

Manghnani, R. 2018. "High-Growth Firms and Innovation: Evidence from India." Background paper for *High-Growth Firms*, World Bank, Washington, DC.

Marris, R. 1963. "A Model of the Managerial Enterprise." *Quarterly Journal of Economics* 77 (2): 185–209.

———. 1964. *The Economic Theory of Managerial Capitalism*. London: Macmillan.

Mason, C., and R. Brown. 2010. "High Growth Firms in Scotland." Scottish Enterprise, Glasgow.

Mason, G., K. Bishop, and C. Robinson. 2009. "Business Growth and Innovation: The Wider Impact of Rapidly-Growing Firms in UK City-Regions." NESTA Research Report, National Endowment for Science, Technology and the Arts, London.

Mason, G., C. Robinson, and C. Rosazza-Bondibene. 2012. "Sources of Labour Productivity Growth: Sectoral Decompositions for Britain, 1998–2007." NESTA Research Report, National Endowment for Science, Technology and the Arts, London.

Matsuyama, K. 1991. "Increasing Returns, Industrialization, and Indeterminacy of Equilibrium." *Quarterly Journal of Economics* 106 (2): 617–50.

Mazzucato, M., and S. Parris. 2015. "High-Growth Firms in Changing Competitive Environments: The US Pharmaceutical Industry (1963 to 2002)." *Small Business Economics* 44 (1): 145–70.

McKenzie, D., and D. Sansone. 2017. "Man vs. Machine in Predicting Successful Entrepreneurs: Evidence from a Business Plan Competition in Nigeria." Policy Research Working Paper 8271, World Bank, Washington, DC.

Melitz, M. J. 2000. "Estimating Firm-Level Productivity in Differentiated Product Industries." Unpublished manuscript, Harvard University, Cambridge, MA.

———. 2003. "The Impact of Trade on Intra-Industry Reallocations and Aggregate Industry Productivity." *Econometrica* 71 (6): 1695–725.

———, and J. Constantini. 2008. "The Dynamics of Firm-Level Adjustment to Trade Liberalization." In *The Organization of Firms in a Global Economy*, edited by Elhanan Helpman, Dalia Marin, and Thierry Verdier, 107–41. Cambridge, MA: Harvard University Press.

Mueller, D. C. 1969. "A Theory of Conglomerate Mergers." *Quarterly Journal of Economics* 83 (4): 642–659.

Mukim, M. 2011. "Does Exporting Increase Productivity? Evidence from India." Working Paper, London School of Economics, London.

Muraközy, B., F. de Nicola, and S. W. Tan. 2018. "High-Growth Firms in Hungary." Background paper for *High-Growth Firms*, World Bank, Washington, DC.

Nelson, R. R. 1981. "Research on Productivity Growth and Productivity Differences: Dead Ends and New Departures." *Journal of Economic Literature* 19 (3): 1029–64.

———, and S. G. Winter. 1982. "The Schumpeterian Tradeoff Revisited." *American Economic Review* 72 (1): 114–32.

NESTA (The National Endowment for Science, Technology and the Arts). 2009. "The Vital 6 Percent: How High-Growth Innovative Businesses Generate Prosperity and Jobs." London.

Nichter, S., and L. Goldmark. 2009. "Small Firm Growth in Developing Countries." *World Development* 37 (9): 1453–64.

Niefert, M. 2005. "Patenting Behaviour and Employment Growth in German Start-Up Firms: A Panel Data Analysis." Discussion Paper 05-03, Centre for European Economic Research, Mannheim, Germany.

Oliner, S. D., D. E. Sichel, and K. J. Stiroh. 2008. "Explaining a Productive Decade." *Journal of Policy Modeling* 30 (4): 633–73.

Ouimet, P., and R. Zarutskie. 2014. "Who Works for Startups? The Relation between Firm Age, Employee Age, and Growth." *Journal of Financial Economics* 112 (3): 386–407.

Pakes, A., and R. Ericson. 1998. "Empirical Implications of Alternative Models of Firm Dynamics." *Journal of Economic Theory* 79 (1): 1–45.

Parker, J. "Patterns of Business Growth: Micro and Small Enterprises in Kenya." PhD diss., Michigan State University, 1995.

Parker, S. C., D. J. Storey, and A. van Witteloostuijn. 2010. "What Happens to Gazelles? The Importance of Dynamic Management Strategy." *Small Business Economics* 35 (2): 203–26.

Pavcnik, N. 2002. "Trade Liberalization, Exit, and Productivity Improvements: Evidence from Chilean Plants." *Review of Economic Studies* 69 (1): 245–76.

Penrose, E. T. 1959. *The Theory of the Growth of the Firm*. Oxford: Basil Blackwell.

Pozzi, A., and F. Schivardi. 2016. "Demand or Productivity: What Determines Firm Growth?" *RAND Journal of Economics* 47 (3): 608–30.

Rajan, R. G., and L. Zingales. 1998. "Financial Dependence and Growth." *American Economic Review* 88 (3): 559–86.

Reyes, J.-D. 2018. "Effects of FDI on High-Growth Firms in Developing Countries." In *Global Investment Competitiveness Report 2017/2018: Foreign Investor Perspectives and Policy Implications*. Washington, DC: World Bank.

————, A. Grover Goswami, and Y. Abuhashem. 2018. "Financial Sector Development and High-Growth Firms." Background paper for *High-Growth Firms*, World Bank, Washington, DC.

Rigby, D., M. Burton, and T. Young. 2006. "Precaution and Protectionism: 'Likeness' and GM Food at the WTO." Paper prepared for the 2006 Annual Meeting of the International Association of Agricultural Economists, Queensland, Australia, August 12–18.

Robson, P. J., and R. J. Bennett. 2000. "SME Growth: The Relationship with Business Advice and External Collaboration." *Small Business Economics* 15 (3): 193–208.

Rosenthal, S. S., and W. C. Strange. 2004. "Evidence on the Nature and Sources of Agglomeration Economies." In *Handbook of Regional and Urban Economics*, vol. 4, 2119–71. Amsterdam: Elsevier.

Samphantharak, K. 2006. "Internal Capital Markets in Business Groups." Unpublished manuscript, University of California, San Diego.

Sanchez Bayardo, L. F., and L. Iacovone. 2018. "High-Growth Firms and Spillovers in Mexico." Background paper for *High-Growth Firms*, World Bank, Washington, DC.

Saxenian, A. 1990. "Regional Networks and the Resurgence of Silicon Valley." *California Management Review* 33 (1): 89–112.

SBA Office of Advocacy. 2008. "High-Impact Firms: Gazelles Revisited," by Z. J. Acs, W. Parsons, and S. Tracy. Small Business Research Summary 328, Washington, DC.

Shiferaw, A. 2016. "Constraints to Private Investment in a High-Growth Environment: Firm-Level Evidence from Ethiopia." Working Paper 168, Department of Economics, College of William and Mary, Williamsburg, VA.

Siba, E., M. Söderbom, A. Bigsten, and M. Gebreeyesus. 2012. "Enterprise Agglomeration, Output Prices, and Physical Productivity: Firm-Level Evidence from Ethiopia." WIDER Working Paper 2012/85, World Institute for Development Economic Research, Helsinki.

Sleuwaegen, L., and M. Goedhuys. 2002. "Growth of Firms in Developing Countries: Evidence from Côte d'Ivoire." *Journal of Development Economics* 68 (1): 117–35.

Stam, E., and K. Wennberg. 2009. "The Roles of R&D in New Firm Growth." *Small Business Economics* 33 (1): 77–89.

Syverson, C. 2004. "Market Structure and Productivity: A Concrete Example." *Journal of Political Economy* 112 (6): 1181–222.

———. 2011. "What Determines Productivity?" *Journal of Economic Literature* 49 (2): 326–65.

Tan, S. W., H. Winkler, and T. Yde-Jensen. 2018. "Connectivity and Firms." In *Critical Connections: Why Europe and Central Asia's Connections Matter for Growth and Stability*. Washington, DC: World Bank.

van Ark, B., M. O'Mahoney, and M. P. Timmer. 2008. "The Productivity Gap between Europe and the United States: Trends and Causes." *Journal of Economic Perspectives* 22 (1): 25–44.

Verhoogen, Eric. 2008. "Trade, Quality Upgrading and Wage Inequality in the Mexican Manufacturing Sector." *Quarterly Journal of Economics* 123 (2): 489–530.

Viner, J. 1932. "Cost Curves and Supply Curves." *Zeitschrift für Nationalökonomie* 3 (1): 23–46.

Walker, F. 1887. "The Source of Business Profits." *Quarterly Journal of Economics* 1 (3): 265–288.

Wieser, R. 2001. "R&D and Productivity: Evidence for European and US Firms in the 1990s." Working Paper 159, WIFO Austrian Institute of Economic Research, Vienna.

# 4. Searching for Winners

Based on the evidence of the disproportionate contribution of high-growth firms (HGFs) to job creation such as that presented in this book, policy makers in developed and developing countries alike continue to seek to identify and support high-potential firms. However, as the analysis in this book shows, the benefits from HGFs are real but also transient because few firms are able to sustain rapid growth beyond several years, and many exit the market altogether soon after the high-growth episode. In order to link these findings to policy makers' priorities, this chapter identifies shortcomings in the current approaches to supporting HGFs and proposes a reorientation of policy priorities going forward. It begins with discussing the programs and instruments used to support firm growth in developing countries. The chapter continues with a review of evidence on the effectiveness of different approaches to targeting and develops an alternative framework to supporting high firm growth, grounded in the empirical results of the earlier chapters.

The evidence on the benefits of HGFs has often been used selectively by policy makers to justify ad hoc actions and interventions, instead of building a comprehensive, evidence-based foundation on which to develop appropriate policies (Nightingale and Coad 2014). A review of policy initiatives targeting HGFs in 14 low- and middle- income economies, including most of the countries analyzed earlier in the book, reveals that these policies generally lack the features of good policy design, such as a results framework, clear objectives, well-defined eligibility and selection criteria, and robust monitoring and evaluation (M&E) systems (many programs in high-income countries suffer from similar problems). Such design and implementation gaps do not bode well for the success and scalability of public efforts to support HGFs. The lack of strong M&E systems (including program impact evaluations) also means that it is unclear whether these programs generate benefits equal to their costs; the risk is that the poor record of active labor market policies, which McKenzie (2017a) argues rarely yield individual or social benefits that exceed the cost of training, may also apply in this context.

The policy agenda to support high firm growth has so far failed to reflect its elusive nature. To be successful, a policy maker must not only identify the "right" firm but also the precise moment in its life cycle when it is about to embark on a high-growth episode—a very tall order. Moreover, high firm growth can be driven by strong fundamentals or fortuitous demand conditions, and the detailed firm-level data needed to differentiate between the two are often not available at all and in the best case come with a lag of a year or more. Finally, although some countries have successfully experimented with tiered approaches to firm support based on meeting certain performance milestones, these have programs usually been implemented on a small scale in strong institutional settings—raising questions about broad replicability in countries with weaker implementation capacity.

The arguments in favor of targeting firms usually rest on some combination of two assertions: that selectivity is required since complex and expensive support cannot be provided to all firms that may express interest, and that policy can be more effective if it targets firms with the greatest potential. This chapter highlights two sets of fundamental challenges to implementing this vision. First, a growing number of studies that apply rigorous evaluation methods find that the ability to predict high growth on the basis of any set of measurable firm or entrepreneur characteristics—for example, business plans, demographics, intelligence, socio-emotional skills—remains very low. Second, many of the available criteria, for example, targeting based on previous success in business, may not be appropriate filters for public policy because they would direct public funds to those who are already better off, potentially perpetuating rather than addressing existing inequities.

With these concerns in mind, this book argues for a reorientation of public policy away from actively searching for high-potential firms toward the ABCs of growth entrepreneurship: improving Allocative efficiency, encouraging Business-to-business spillovers, and strengthening firm Capabilities. A large body of literature—some of it reviewed earlier in this book—shows that interventions aimed at supporting these ABCs are positively correlated with furthering desirable outcomes such as firm productivity. The evidence presented in this book shows that they are also associated with greater likelihood of a high-growth episode. Policy makers wishing to reap the benefits of high firm growth should therefore pursue policies that support and encourage good practices, such as healthy firm entry, exit, and reallocation; improved access to finance and flexible labor markets; better flows of knowledge across firms through tighter linkages to external markets, denser networks, and agglomeration; and stronger firm capabilities, including innovation, managerial, and entrepreneurship skills. The chapter also draws policy makers' attention to three critical crosscutting themes: improving the quality of firm-level data, strengthening the rigor in policy evaluation, and building institutional capabilities to implement policies.

## Programs and Instruments to Support Firm Growth

Governments across the world have adopted a wide range of policies to support the emergence and expansion of HGFs. Many such efforts go beyond the traditional boundaries of an enterprise, recognizing that growth entrepreneurs thrive in environments where multiple factors work together to form a dynamic entrepreneurship ecosystem (Zacharakis et al. 2003; Napier and Hansen 2011; Malecki 2011; Kantis and Federico 2012; Feld 2012; Isenberg 2010). The Babson framework—focusing on conducive policy, efficient markets, human capital, finance, culture, and supporting services (for example, legal, accounting, technical expertise)—is one example of a comprehensive approach to defining the necessary components of an entrepreneurship ecosystem (Isenberg 2011; see box 4.1 for a discussion of the origins and the evolution of the ecosystem approach).

## BOX 4.1

### Communities, Networks, and Ecosystems

Following Granovetter's (1976, 1985) work on embeddedness, a substantial literature has developed around the concept of entrepreneurs as economic actors in their environments (Aldrich and Zimmer 1986; Ruef 2010; Garud and Karnøe 2003). There are three terms relevant to this environmental perspective—*networks, communities, and ecosystems*—although there is considerable overlap across them.

*Networks* consist of actors that are connected directly or indirectly and that interact through those connections (Brass 1992, cited in Hoang and Antoncic 2003). These actors can be similar to or different from each other, and network members may cooperate, compete, or engage in both competition and cooperation. They may do so formally (according to explicit rules) or informally (Malerba 2007). Despite the wealth of studies examining the potential impact of network structure on firm and entrepreneurial outcomes, there is no general agreement among researchers on what constitutes an entrepreneurship network, nor on how a firm is included in or excluded from a network (this applies more broadly to other networks; see Lynn, Reddy, and Aram [1996]).

*Communities* have been studied in the context of entrepreneurial regions and social groupings, with geography and social networks as the two primary conceptualizations of community (Thornton and Flynn 2006, cited in Jennings et al. 2013). Indeed, much of the literature has explicitly made references to networks in the effort to define community. Most recently, Thornton, Ocasio, and Lounsbury (2012) have suggested that community should be understood as a set of logics and orders that influence entrepreneurial activity.

The term "business *ecosystem*" was introduced by Moore in 1993, drawing an analogy to the concept used in natural sciences. The most recent entrepreneurship-related discussion, summarized by Autio et al. (2015), consider ecosystems as policy tools, clusters, and geographic systems, among other notions. The authors identify two major streams of ecosystems research: one on innovation ecosystems and the other on regional ecosystems, both occurring in the context of networks of "co-specialized organizations that play complementary roles to advance value co-creation" (Finland, Ministry of Trade and Industry 2105, 1).

Notwithstanding the overlaps and lack of precision, one way of ordering the three concepts is the following ranking in order of scope:

- An entrepreneurship network is the broadest of the three terms and includes any set of connections between actors involved in entrepreneurial activity, whether directly or indirectly.
- A community refers to a shared sense of belonging, which gives entrepreneurs the confidence to pursue their goals.
- An ecosystem is the most narrowly defined of the three terms requiring participation by organizations (and, optionally, individuals) that are united in their pursuit of value creation through entrepreneurship.

*Source:* Andjelkovic 2018.

Policies to encourage HGFs form a subset of a broader set of initiatives to facilitate growth entrepreneurship and healthy ecosystems. Motivated in part by studies that advocate targeting firms with high growth potential (for example, Storey 1994; SBA Office of Advocacy 2008; Shane 2009; Lerner 2010; Mason and Brown 2013), policy makers in both developed and developing countries are increasingly attempting to identify and support these firms (see also Bos and Stam 2014; Lee 2014; Autio and Rannikko 2016). Such initiatives also draw on conclusions from studies such as Bravo-Biosca, Criscuolo, and Menon (2016), who find that more stringent employment protection legislation and weaker financial systems have a negative effect on the growth of top performers, and Haltiwanger, Jarmin, and Miranda (2013, 30), who make the case for prioritizing the resolution of bottlenecks that are particularly binding for HGFs: "[t]o the extent that market failures are found to underlie these frictions, there might be a role for well-designed corrective policies that help entrepreneurs start and grow dynamic young firms that boost overall net job creation."

Despite the many calls for such interventions, studies and policy documents give little guidance on the type of support that should be provided, how to identify prospective HGFs, or the timing of assistance (Anyadike-Danes et al. 2009; Mason, Bishop, and Robinson 2009; Lerner 2010). Most of the instruments used in the early 2000s, when policy initiatives for encouraging HGFs had just begun to take shape, were hard to distinguish from more general initiatives for promoting entrepreneurship. Although many proposals to support HGFs remain fairly broad and mostly similar to standard policies targeting small and medium enterprises (SMEs), some more focused initiatives catering to HGFs have been developed in the past decade or so. Examples include public and private initiatives in the Netherlands (such as Masterclasses, Angel Program, Port4Growth), the United Kingdom (such as High-Growth Start-Up), and Finland (such as Growth Firm Service; Finland, Ministry of Trade and Industry 2007). Other programs target outcomes that have often been associated with high firm growth: for example, iNNpulsa in Colombia and the GVFL state-backed venture fund in India target firm-level innovation through the provision of grants and equity investments. Others, such as a set of programs in the Philippines providing support to firms from start-up to expansion of exports, draw on evidence that links export orientation to firm performance (see Du, Gong, and Temouri 2013; Bernard and Jensen 1999; Girma, Greenaway, and Kneller 2004; Harris and Li 2007).

To better understand the range and design of support programs in low- and middle-income economies, we considered HGF policy interventions in 14 countries: Angola, Brazil, Colombia, Côte d'Ivoire, Ghana, India, Jamaica, Jordan, Malaysia, Mexico, the Philippines, Senegal, South Africa, and Turkey. These countries were selected based on the existence, diversity, and scope of HGF-related interventions, public access to information about these interventions, as well as alignment with the firm-level analysis used earlier in the book.[1] The review identified 54 public interventions with components to support HGFs, captured via an extensive literature survey, Internet searches, and review of public agency websites and media content.

Among the 14 countries and 54 public interventions, programs in Mexico and South Africa are the most ambitious in the use of national-level interventions that specifically target HGFs (box 4.2). Several countries—Brazil, Colombia, India, Jamaica, and Malaysia—have at least four programs to support HGFs, some of which are large-scale. The interventions themselves may be classified into five areas of focus according to the market failure they seek to address (following Audretsch, Grilo, and Thurik 2007): strengthen firm *capabilities*, improve access to *finance*, help firms reach new *markets*, resolve *regulatory* obstacles, and provide critical *infrastructure*. There does not appear to be any pattern between the choice of interventions across countries and GDP per capita, population size, or the entrepreneurial ecosystem ranking of the country (using the Global Entrepreneurship and Development Index), although, within this sample, lower-income countries in Africa are somewhat more likely than others to use infrastructure provision as an explicit lever to

---

### BOX 4.2

**National Programs to Support High Firm Growth in Mexico and South Africa**

*Mexico's High Impact Entrepreneurship Program (HIEP)*, launched in 2013, supports innovative small and medium enterprises (SMEs) through a matching grants scheme. HIEP funds both start-ups and scale-ups and provides matching grants up to 70–80 percent of the costs for a firm to invest in information technology and software, certifications, consulting and professional services, and machinery and equipment. Grant amounts for scale-ups can reach 5 million pesos (about US$280,000). The program uses strict eligibility criteria to target firms with either high growth potential or high social and environmental impact, and firms are required to have an innovation component in their business model. In 2016, the program screened a pool of approximately 1,000 applicants through expert panels and reduced the pool by about half. Additional screening then identified close to 200 firms that ultimately received the matching grant. A randomized controlled trial evaluation, supported by the World Bank, to identify program impacts on firm outcomes is ongoing.

*South Africa's National Gazelles program* is a new business growth acceleration program that identifies SMEs with growth potential and provides them with financial and nonfinancial support. Member gazelles are selected competitively through a two-stage process and gain access to personalized support services, networking, marketing, and business analysis. Businesses from all over South Africa that meet certain age and turnover conditions are eligible to apply to the program, with a focus on black-owned businesses aligned with the country's national transformation agenda. The selection process is a combination of an application and interview with business experts (the regional distribution is also taken into account when approving firms). The core "high care" program accepts 40 new members every year from a short list of 200 applicants; the remaining 160 become part of a group that receives assistance to enter into the core program in the future.

support firm growth. Two additional trends include a preference for (1) innovation or firms in "innovative sectors" and (2) technology and high-tech sectors (although, as was shown earlier, rapid firm growth is not necessarily linked to high-tech sectors; see also Henrekson and Johansson [2010]; Anyadike-Danes et al. [2009]).

A majority of countries use interventions to build firm *capabilities*. The more commonly offered programs are business support and business development services, mentoring and networking, and access to technology. Incubators and accelerators, which combine the provision of physical space with business support services, mentoring, and so on, are also a popular instrument.

Programs to support access to *finance* include loans at concessional or market terms, grants, venture capital, and nonfinancial support (for example, networking with funders). Most countries that provide public venture capital funds also have private venture capital and private angel investors; the coexistence of public and private venture capital firms is also a feature of some high-income economies. Governments also boost access to finance indirectly through the establishment of dedicated alternate financing exchanges for SMEs (these often run parallel to the main stock exchange) and vehicles such as funds of funds, or facilitate equity finance through associations or accreditation (box 4.3).

Efforts aimed at improving access to *markets* are used somewhat less frequently, although this is partly an artifact of excluding export and trade promotion interventions from this category for the purpose of the analysis. Identified interventions focus primarily on support for partnership opportunities and networks to widen market access. For example, Brazil's Tech Sampa and the Philippine's Shared Services Facilities provide information services to support access to markets.

The broad set of regulations affecting HGFs encompasses labor, tax, property rights, standards, trade, foreign direct investment (FDI), contracts, spatial, industrial, and competition policies (see also the discussion later in this chapter in the section titled, "Toward an Evidence-Based Approach to Supporting High Firm Growth"). Within the set of identified programs in the 14 countries, targeted *regulatory* interventions involve the creation of new regulatory structures or incentives for equity financing, collaboration, and new platforms for trade and finance. Examples include tax incentives—such as exemptions, reductions, or credits—that lower the risk for angel investors (as in Malaysia).

Finally, some targeted interventions focus on improving *infrastructure*, for example, through technology parks or free or special economic zones. The services involved may range from basic infrastructure (energy, water, roads, access to ports, and so on) to high-grade manufacturing technology, educational installations, or access to labs (for example, Côte d'Ivoire's ZBTIC biotechnology and information and communication technology free zone).

## Public Facilitation of Equity Finance

Public facilitation of equity finance, either through venture capital, angel investing, or the fund-of-funds approach, seeks to develop the private equity industry. For example, Turkey's angel network accreditation program carried out through the Treasury provides tax incentives to angel investors. In Latin America, Brazil's INOVAR program supports venture capital and angel associations, whereas the industry association ColCapital in Colombia offers its members, who are fund managers, services that include advocacy and regulatory reform, shared spaces for events, generation of content and information about the private equity environment, information dissemination, and training and education on industry best practices and international standards.

Similarly, fund-of-funds instruments are more than just investment vehicles. They serve the larger purpose of developing (and in some cases, starting) the venture capital industry in the country or region. By providing technical support, fund manager assistance, training, and partnerships, as well as co-investment, funds of funds are a unique way to leverage public resources to build sustainable and competitive venture capital markets. In the process, they can reach more firms than if the government had invested directly in the firms. Examples of such programs include the following:

*Istanbul Venture Capital Initiative (iVCi)*. iVCi was Turkey's first dedicated fund of funds and co-investment program, comprising a number of development-oriented investors, such as the Small and Medium Enterprise Development Organization of Turkey, the Technology Development Foundation of Turkey, the Development Bank of Turkey, and the European Investment Fund. In addition to making profitable investments, the fund aimed to be a crossroads location and industry leader for the venture capital (VC) industry in southeastern Europe and Central Asia, serving as a catalyst for the development of the VC industry, providing advice and insights to its investee funds. The structure allowed an international adviser to be intimately involved with the local funds and promoted networking within the Turkish VC and industrialist environment.

*SME Fund of the Sovereign Fund for Strategic Investments (FONSIS)*. FONSIS is an innovative instrument in Senegal where the state serves as a sovereign investor and majority shareholder of the fund. The fund has US$1 billion in state-owned assets, with 20 percent earmarked for SMEs. In some cases, FONSIS also directly invests in SMEs or other projects. Its investment strategy with regard to sectors is guided by the priorities identified in the National Development Plan, such as agriculture, fishing, infrastructure, logistics, energy, social housing, mining, and information technology services.

*Small Industries Development Bank of India (SIDBI) Venture Fund*. SIDBI Venture Fund is a fund of funds channeling finance to venture funds that ultimately reach micro, small, and medium enterprises (MSMEs). SIDBI has invested in 88 different VC funds in India, which have catalyzed an average investment of more than US$860 million to over 472 MSMEs. SIDBI has created a panel of experts in various fields who are available to advise on investment decisions and form part of the Venture Capital Investment Committee.

*Jamaica Venture Capital Programme (JVCP)*. JVCP was coestablished by the Development Bank of Jamaica, a public sector financial institution, and the Inter-American Development Bank. JVCP has supported the VC sector in Jamaica through the establishment of a fund of funds,

*(Box continues on the following page.)*

programs that foster partnerships between the public and private sectors, and efforts to lobby for appropriate legal and regulatory frameworks for private equity and venture capital. JVCP also supports training and capacity building of SMEs and entrepreneurs to improve their investment readiness and efforts to build the expertise of local fund managers and investors. JVCP also partners with eligible fund managers in the development of local venture funds.

*Source:* Desai, Olafsen, and Cook 2018.

Several countries have interventions that offer multiple types of support, such as ZBTIC in Côte d'Ivoire, Accelerate with JEDCO in Jordan, and iNNpulsa in Colombia.[2] A mix of support for firm capabilities, such as combining business support services with networking or access to networks, is often packaged in incubators or accelerators. Interestingly, although the ZBTIC free zone appears to be the only targeted intervention in Côte d'Ivoire, it is set up to deliver multiple types of support for firm capabilities. Other types of instruments, such as dedicated SME exchanges, are not normally packaged with direct support in the other areas of intervention.

Two common weaknesses across the reviewed initiatives are a lack of a clearly defined results framework and inadequate M&E processes. A well-defined results framework is a necessary condition for good program design, implementation, and scalability. Figure 4.1 shows an indicative results framework of a science, technology, and innovation (STI) intervention, which establishes a clear results chain from program inputs to measurable outputs, outcomes, and ultimate intended impact. In reality, few programs follow such good practice, even in high-income countries.

The lack of clearly stated objectives and a well-developed theory of change also manifests itself in inconsistent and limited measurement of results, as well as lack of an evaluation of costs and inputs. This makes it difficult to identify strategies and interventions that are successful and hinders transferability of lessons across countries. Some instruments, such as business plan competitions, define outputs in terms of the number of funded firms or ideas or the amount of funding provided, making it more difficult to assess outcomes and impacts in terms of long-term growth.[3] Another challenge is that many public interventions offer several mechanisms for support—for example, a public-private partnership free zone might provide access to infrastructure, communication technologies, support with regulatory and administrative requirements, and even an incubator—so it is difficult to identify the impact of each separately. Table 4.1 provides some examples of results-monitoring frameworks for a select group of interventions in developing countries, highlighting challenges in tracking higher-level outcomes, limited reliance on counterfactual designs, and limited availability of data.

## FIGURE 4.1 Results Framework for a Science, Technology, and Innovation Intervention

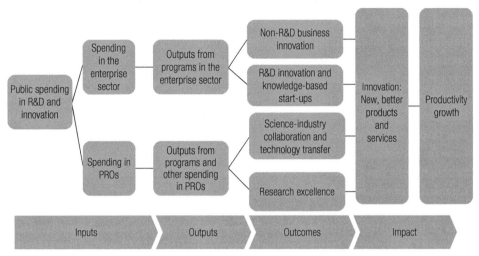

*Source:* Correa 2014.

*Note:* PRO = public research organization; R&D = research and development.

## TABLE 4.1 Results Framework and Measurement for a Sample of Growth-Oriented Interventions

| Program | Stated goal | Measurement framework | Reported results |
|---|---|---|---|
| *Tech Sampa (Brazil)* | Promote innovation and start-ups in the city of São Paulo. | Track usage and uptake of programs, number of event participants, plus qualitative questions about firm performance. | Interviews with start-ups have asked about job creation, investment, earnings, and access to accelerator programs. |
| *Manizales Más (Colombia)* | Develop the entrepreneurship ecosystem in Manizales City. | Track monthly results for participant firms, including sales, number of new employees, what kind of employees, hiring term, investment in new assets, innovation, new markets access, what they have learned from program, and debt acquisitions. | 46 percent growth among 73 high-potential companies in five years. Participating companies registered an average of US$39 million in sales, created 1,392 new jobs, and attracted 1,679 new customers. Eight companies began exporting. |
| *National Gazelles (South Africa)* | Identify and support small and medium enterprises with growth potential; assist members to grow faster and more profitably than they would normally do. | Track firm-level accounting information of participating companies at regular intervals. Participating firms are benchmarked at the start of the program so change can be tracked. | The first class of 40 gazelles was accepted in 2016. Of those, 68% increased business performance by 17%; 45% had 10% more cash flow; 71% increased growth potential by 17%, and 37% de-risked the business. |
| *ColCapital (Colombia)* | Promote the development of the venture capital and private equity industry in Colombia. | Track year-by-year results of the work plan, in addition to tracking results of the venture capital industry itself. Track capital commitments, employment numbers from the funds they work with, number of people that attend events, number of association members by year, and corporate governance of funds. | Difficult to track fund performance because of confidentiality. ColCapital attributes the expansion of the private equity industry to its programs. The annual compound growth in volume of private equity funds since 2005 is 41.2 percent. |

*Source:* Desai, Olafsen, and Cook 2018.

Policy interventions aimed at stimulating HGFs rarely undergo rigorous evaluations even in high-income country settings. One exception is an evaluation of the NIY Program of the Finnish National Technology Agency, Tekes, by Autio and Rannikko (2016). The program provides participant firms with buffering and bridging support, solicits active public-private collaboration, and combines improved access to finance with capacity-boosting initiatives.[4] It also exhibits a high degree of selectiveness by staging support according to milestone achievement to focus on "retaining winners." An evaluation of this program found that participants experienced 120 percent faster sales growth than comparable (propensity score matched) nonparticipant firms, with differences persisting over three years (Autio and Rannikko 2016).[5] Denmark's Growth Houses and the Dutch Growth Accelerator are two other examples of programs with impact evaluations, although none have relied on randomized controlled trials (RCTs), which are usually regarded as the gold standard in evaluation practices. In the context of large-scale initiatives in developing countries, RCTs have been used to evaluate Nigeria's YouWiN! business plan competition (McKenzie 2017b) and Mexico's High Impact Entrepreneurship Program (jointly by the Institute of the Entrepreneur [INADEM] and the World Bank).

## Selection of Beneficiaries

It is almost axiomatic that the success of an intervention depends critically on the selection of beneficiaries. Once a set of market failures justifying an intervention has been identified, a policy maker must decide who is going to form the target population and how members of this population are going to be selected. Although much of the literature on beneficiary selection focuses on the "how," the "who" is equally important, both to program design and to measurement of results.

Consider figure 4.2, which illustrates a hypothetical difference between two firms, A and B, with and without an intervention targeting high firm growth in sales. In this example, high-performing firm A has faster sales growth compared with firm B with or

**FIGURE 4.2    High Performance versus High Program Impact**

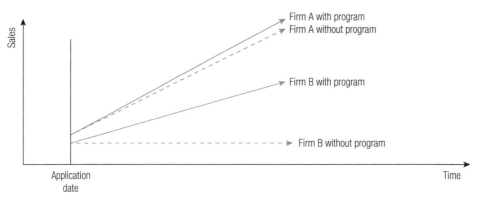

*Source:* Buba, Gonzalez, and Kokas 2018.

without the program, but the gains from the program are much larger for firm B than for A. Programs that seek only to maximize sales growth should target the best performer A, even though the firm was already doing well without the program and the gains from the program are minimal. On the other hand, a program could choose to target those who would benefit the most from an intervention—for example, population groups that may have a more difficult time starting and sustaining businesses, while acknowledging that even with the program, beneficiaries may not reach high-growth status. For the purposes of this book, the key difference to consider is whether the role of the government in supporting HGFs is that of a venture capitalist (maximizing profit, output, or employment) or a social planner with a wider set of objectives (that also include equity considerations). A related distinction is whether the success of a program in this example should be measured by rates of overall sales growth among beneficiaries (leading to targeting firm A) or the marginal improvement in sales growth from the intervention (leading to targeting firm B).

McKenzie (2017b) provides an empirical illustration of such trade-offs with results from a YouWin! business plan competition in Nigeria (figure 4.3). In the control group of semifinalists who did not receive a grant, male applicants were more likely to start a new business than female applicants three years following the competition. However, among those who received a grant, female entrepreneurs benefited much more than males, although not enough to fully close the initial gender gap.[6] Therefore, targeting solely based on the likelihood of starting a business would suggest focusing on male participants, whereas targeting to maximize the benefits from the program would suggest focusing on female beneficiaries.

**FIGURE 4.3  Grants to Start New Businesses in Nigeria Benefited Women More than Men**

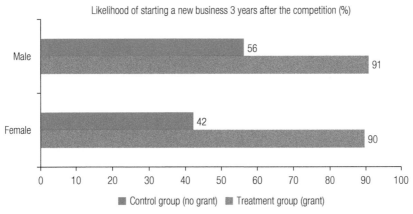

*Source:* McKenzie 2017b.

*Note:* The figure shows the mean likelihood, estimated from a linear regression, of starting a new business after the YouWin! business plan competition in Nigeria. The figure presents results from the third round of follow-up survey data collection, which took place between September 2014 and February 2015. This corresponds to 3 years after application and between 12 and 18 months after firms had received their last tranche payment from the program. Data on enterprise ownership are available for 88.5 percent of the experimental winners and 82.5 percent of the experimental control group.

Moving on to the "how," the rigor of the selection process varies substantially across programs. A review of 24 acceleration programs in Sub-Saharan Africa found that fewer than half used a rigorous selection process (Buschmann et al. 2017). On the other hand, the National Gazelles program in South Africa uses external auditors to assess firms and manage the selection process and uses another external firm to independently verify the selection process. The Finland NIY program relies on inputs from an external expert panel of new venture experts and VCs who interview each applicant. Endeavor, a private non-profit that runs high-impact entrepreneurship programs in countries, including Brazil, Chile, Colombia, the Arab Republic of Egypt, Jordan, Malaysia, and Turkey, uses a multi-stage selection process with participation from local and international experts (box 4.4). A review of RCTs of the impact of business and personal initiative training, consulting services, technical assistance, and grant programs shows that screening intensity is positively associated with the likelihood of significant program impact, although nearly all studies were conducted with micro and small firms (table 4A.2).

Selection of participants is often the result of a two-part process. First, entrepreneurs or firms must meet certain *eligibility* criteria, which are the basic minimum requirements to apply for the intervention. Second, eligible participants go through a *filtering* process to determine who meets the standards and expectations to participate in the program. In many programs targeting HGFs or entrepreneurs, the eligibility stage already excludes likely low performers from the set of applicants. For instance, although programs are usually marketed to the whole population of firms through radio, television spots, flyers, road shows, and the like, firms that have better access to information or that are located in cities are more likely to be aware of an intervention and hence more likely to register. Furthermore, most programs—in particular in countries where the number of potential participants is high—are Internet-based and require that the firms register online, therefore excluding those without access and at

---

**BOX 4.4**

**Endeavor's Selection Process**

Endeavor is a private nongovernmental organization that runs high-impact entrepreneurship programs in many countries, including Brazil, Chile, Colombia, the Arab Republic of Egypt, Jordan, Malaysia, and Turkey. The selection process begins with research within the Endeavor network, resulting in several recommendations. An Endeavor team screens the recommended high-impact potential entrepreneurs to determine preliminary suitability for the program. This step is followed by a first opinion review (staff interview entrepreneurs) and then a second opinion review (senior mentors conduct interviews with candidates on business strategy, innovation, growth potential, challenges, opportunities, and personal characteristics). After the completed reviews, the entrepreneur meets with a local selection panel of 10–15 mentors and local board members. Finally, an international selection panel meets to finalize the new class of entrepreneurs. Each of these steps conforms to specific internal assessment criteria.

least rudimentary information technology skills. Thus, the pool of applicants is often not representative of the population of firms.

For example, in the YouWin! business plan competition in Nigeria, the program limited the access to grants to "young" entrepreneurs who were asked to fill out a concept note in Excel and register online. Consequently, applicants were older and more educated than an average person in the target range. The Ghana Alternative Market program, which is an alternative exchange specifically for SMEs, requires firms to have a minimum stated capital and a minimum of 20 shareholders, as well as publicly float a minimum 25 percent of issued shares—all of which make the participant firms substantially different from an average SME in the country.

The most common eligibility criteria across instruments appear to be based on the sector of the firm, with either a strong preference or requirement for technology and innovation (for example, biotech, health, agribusiness, energy, media, and information and communication technology). This emphasis is common in developing and developed countries alike, although this book and other related literature finds that HGFs do not tend to be particularly concentrated in high-tech sectors. For example, several programs in the Netherlands seek to stimulate the growth of new firms in biotech (Biopartner Program) (The Hague, Ministry of Economic Affairs of the Netherlands 2005) and information and communication technology (Twinning Program) (Hulsink and Elfring 2000), whereas the NIY program in Finland mostly attracts firms in the knowledge-intensive services sector (Autio and Rannikko 2016). Other interventions complement priority sectors in the broader national agenda; for example, South Africa's National Gazelles program prioritizes 10 key sectors identified in the national economic strategy.

When it comes to the *filtering* stage, programs often rely on the company's pitch, delivered via a business plan or an interview with a selection panel of experts. Other potential characteristics for selecting participants include the entrepreneur's demographics, background, prior experience, personality traits, and cognitive abilities. The following discussion briefly reviews the evidence on the effectiveness of each of these approaches in selecting high performers.

*Business plan competitions* have become a popular method for selecting program participants, although with mixed results. On the one hand, Fafchamps and Woodruff (2017) find that a panel of judges' evaluation of a written business plan and oral presentation had a significant and positive association with subsequent firm performance for small firms in Ghana. However, the scores explained only a third of the variance in outcomes, and evaluations of a thorough baseline survey on each entrepreneur (in terms of a measure of ability, two measures of attitudes, management practices, and access to credit) were more effective in predicting firm growth and much less costly.[7] On the other hand, McKenzie (2017b) finds that evaluations of the business plans were not good predictors of the success of new or existing businesses among semifinalists of Nigeria's YouWiN! program, with the exception of job creation.

Entrepreneur *demographic characteristics* such as age tend to be a mixed predictor of success. Some studies have found that young entrepreneurs perform better because they changed and grabbed opportunities faster (for example, Amran [2011] for Malaysia and Sinha [1996] for India). On the other hand, Kristiansen, Furuholt, and Wahid (2003) find that Internet café entrepreneurs in Indonesia who were older than 25 were significantly more successful than younger ones. Akcigit, Grigsby, and Nicholas (2017), using a rich data set of inventors in the United States, show that innovators were most productive between the ages of 36 and 55. Family background can also play a substantial role in influencing the intention of a person to start a business and the potential for success (Duchesneau and Gartner 1990; Mungai and Velamuri 2010). For example, Djankov et al. (2005) and Djankov et al. (2006a, 2006b) find evidence that entrepreneurs in Russia, China, and Brazil have more relatives and friends who are themselves entrepreneurs than do wage workers, whereas Shittu and Dosunmu (2014) obtain similar results for new business graduates in Nigeria.

The evidence on the importance of *prior work experience* is more positive. Although Mazzarol et al. (1999) find that respondents with previous government employment experience were less likely to be successful founders of small businesses, Maxwell and Westerfield (2002) show that entrepreneurs' managerial experience has a positive impact on firm performance—similar to the results presented in the section in chapter 3 of this book titled, "Managerial Capabilities and Worker Skills." Wadhwa et al. (2009) conclude that more successful entrepreneurs (in a group of 540 firm founders) came with wide sectoral experience.

The literature on the importance of *educational background* of the entrepreneur for firm performance is divided. In a review of 42 studies, van der Sluis, van Praag, and Vijverberg (2008) document a positive and significant effect of formal education on firm performance, as measured by business survival, firm growth, and firm returns on investment. Harada (2004) finds a strong relationship between the entrepreneur's education and total factor productivity for firms in Japan. In a meta-analysis of 70 studies, covering a range of developing and developed countries and industries, Unger et al. (2011) find a positive and significant, albeit small, association between education and entrepreneurial success.[8] On the other hand, Jalbert, Jalbert, and Furumo (2011), focusing on a large sample of U.S. firms during 1997–2006, conclude that the effect of educational background of the CEO on firm performance is insignificant or weak. Isaga (2015) finds similar results in Tanzania for the relationship between firm performance (measured by employment, sales, and asset growth) and education.

Although the literature has long argued for the importance of entrepreneur *personality traits* (for example, Robinson, Shaver, and Wrightsman 1991; McCline, Bhat, and Baj 2000), most of the empirical evidence focuses on the intention to become entrepreneurs rather than subsequent performance.[9] One exception is Campos et al. (2017), who show that a psychology-based personal initiative training program in Togo (which teaches a proactive mindset and focuses on entrepreneurial behaviors) increased firm profits by 30 percent in two years versus a statistically insignificant effect of a business training program—and paid for itself within one year. Similar results are emerging from a large ongoing impact evaluation to teach hard versus soft business skills to high school students in Uganda.

Several studies have found that entrepreneurs' *cognitive abilities*, as measured by psychometric tests (see box 4.5), can be useful in predicting the success of businesses. For example, McKenzie and Sansone (2017), using data from Nigeria's YouWin! competition, show that an IQ test (Raven's score) alone can predict business success nearly as well as business plan scores from a panel of judges or any combination of predictive variables. Related evidence, such as Arráiz, Bruhn, and Stucchi (2015), shows that psychometric tests can lower the risk of the loan portfolio when used as a secondary screening mechanism for entrepreneurs with a credit history in Peru and can enable increased loans to entrepreneurs with no credit history without increasing portfolio risk. Klinger, Khwaja, and LaMonte (2013) find that such tests were useful in predicting

---

**BOX 4.5**

### Measuring Cognitive Abilities

In the entrepreneurship literature, cognitive abilities are usually measured using the digit span recall, the Raven progressive nonverbal reasoning test, and a localized version of Frederick's three question cognitive reflection test (Frederick 2005).

A *digit span test* is used to measure the ability of an individual's working memory to recall numbers. Participants hear or see a sequence of numerical digits and are asked to recall the sequence correctly (forward or backward), with increasingly longer sequences being tested in each trial. The participant's span is the longest number of sequential digits that can accurately be remembered. Digit span tasks are the most commonly used test for memory span (that is, a common measure of short-term memory), partly because performance on a digit span task cannot be affected by factors such as semantics, frequency of appearance in daily life, complexity, and so on (Jones and Macken 2015).

*Raven's Progressive Matrices* is a nonverbal group test typically used in educational settings. It is a 60-item test used in measuring abstract reasoning and regarded as a nonverbal estimate of fluid intelligence (that is, the capacity to reason and solve novel problems, independent of any knowledge from the past). It is the most common and popular test administered to groups ranging from 5-year-olds to seniors.

Frederick's *Cognitive Reflection Test* is a three-question task designed to measure a person's tendency to override an initial automatic or "gut" response that is incorrect and to engage in further reflection to find a correct answer. The test has been found to correlate with many measures of economic thinking, such as numeracy (Szaszi et al. 2017), temporal discounting, risk preference, and gambling preference (Frederick 2005). It has also been found to correlate with measures of mental heuristics, such as the gambler's fallacy, understanding of regression to the mean, the sunk cost fallacy, and others (Toplak, West, and Stanovich 2011).

risk in a sample of preapproved applicants in Peru, and Klinger et al. (2013) obtain similar results for SME loan clients of Banco Ciudad de Buenos Aires, one of the top three public banks of Argentina.

Overall, the predictive power of any of the existing approaches to assessing the likelihood of good firm performance—even the more successful ones such as cognitive abilities—is low. In a review of business plan scores, economic models based on firm and entrepreneur characteristics, and machine learning approaches, McKenzie and Sansone (2017) show that even the best techniques can identify only one-fifth of the top performers (see also Fafchamps 2010; McKenzie 2015). Similarly, studies show that less than 10 percent of the differences in growth among firms can be explained by factors that can be observed (Coad 2009; Hölzl 2009, 2014; Storey 1994). These results echo the findings of Kerr, Nanda, and Rhodes-Kropf (2014) regarding the challenges of professional investors in identifying high-potential businesses. Most firms selected by VCs eventually fail, and VCs make money only because a few of those that succeed earn very high returns: about 60 percent of investments are terminated at a loss, whereas 10 percent generate a return equivalent to five times the capital invested. Likewise, Nanda, Samila, and Sorenson (2018) argue that consistent VC success is not a function of the managers' inherent ability to identify good performers but is instead explained by better access to deal flow after an initial profitable investment (that is, "doubling down" on the initial success by investing in later rounds and larger syndicates).[10] Thus, current approaches to selecting firms or entrepreneurs appear to be more effective at screening out likely poor performers than identifying high-potential beneficiaries.

## Toward an Evidence-Based Approach to Supporting High Firm Growth

The evidence in this book presents policy makers with a dilemma. On the one hand, the appeal of supporting HGFs based on their direct contributions to job and output creation as well as the additional spillover benefits documented in chapter 1 is strong. On the other hand, evidence in chapter 2, as well as the earlier discussion on targeting in this chapter, points to a lack of reliable predictors of high growth and the episodic nature of high-growth episodes. Even experienced venture capital investors struggle to distinguish successful start-ups from the ones that will fail (Nanda 2016). Thus, the likely outcomes of an approach that channels significant public resources into targeted policies in search of high growth can range from investing in known good performers (potentially crowding out private resources), to losing a large share of the investments, to creating a culture of rent-seeking and politically connected firms. One may always believe that he or she can do better than average or that the unique circumstances of a particular country, region, or sector may warrant public intervention. But, much like the venture capital industry, such a belief is likely to represent a "triumph of hope over experience" (Mulcahy, Weeks, and Bradley 2012).

The comparison with the venture capital industry is apt for several reasons. First, a wide distribution of returns with a high share of failures may be acceptable to a private investor but may not represent a prudent approach to managing public funds on a large scale. Second, as shown in chapter 3, the observed high growth among firms may be only weakly correlated with desirable fundamentals such as productivity—the distinction is likely moot for a private investor whose primary (or only) metric is profitability but is critical for a policy maker whose objective set is wider and whose time horizon is longer (that is, investing in profitable but unproductive companies is likely to reduce income growth and erode profitability over the long run). Third, the few characteristics that have some explanatory power in predicting high growth—for example, age, gender, IQ scores—can lead to investment strategies that select the already better-off beneficiaries. Recent evidence from Mexico shows that even the take-up of interventions is higher among better-off entrepreneurs (that is, those with initially higher profits and sales and better management; see Iacovone, Calderon, and MacGregor [2018]). Although this may serve as perfectly reasonable guidance for a private investor, a policy maker is often guided by considerations of equity and addressing deeply rooted institutional and cultural barriers that may give rise to observed performance differences (for example, those between male and female entrepreneurs).

This book proposes that a solution to this dilemma lies in a reorientation of public policy away from searching for high-potential firms toward the ABCs of growth entrepreneurship: improving Allocative efficiency, encouraging Business-to-business spillovers, and strengthening firm Capabilities (illustrated in the top portion of figure 4.4).

**FIGURE 4.4    The "ABC" Framework to Support Firm Dynamism and Growth**

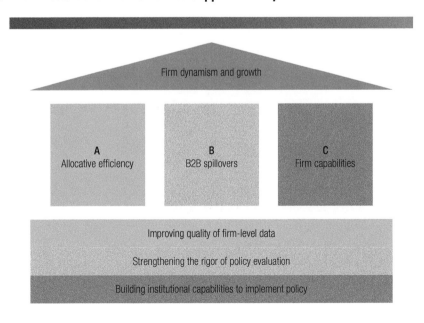

A large body of literature—some of it reviewed in earlier parts of this book—shows that interventions aimed at supporting these ABCs are positively correlated with furthering desirable outcomes such as firm productivity, and the evidence presented in this book shows that they are also associated with greater likelihood of a high-growth episode without the costs and perils of active firm targeting. Therefore, rather than targeting "growth for growth's sake" (Lee, Sissons, and Jones 2016), which may lead policy makers to aim for some "target" share of HGFs without recognizing that the incidence of HGFs can be driven by economic dynamism or distortions, policies following the ABC framework aim to strengthen the fundamentals that are likely to lead to high, sustainable firm growth. Policy actions and instruments under each component of the ABCs—some supported explicitly by the empirical findings of this book and others identified based on existing literature and more general insights—are detailed in the discussion below and color-coded in figure 4.5. The presentation of specific instruments draws heavily on Cirera, Frias, and Hill (forthcoming), who provide a detailed discussion of each instrument, including design and implementation modalities as well as the evidence on their likely impact.

In addition to the ABCs of policy interventions, three crosscutting themes form a necessary foundation for successful policies to support high firm growth (see the bottom portion of figure 4.4). One is the critical importance of improving the quality of firm-level data. Unlike household surveys, which have become nearly ubiquitous across the developing world in the past three decades because of growing demand for measuring poverty and increasing capacities of statistical agencies, high-quality

**FIGURE 4.5  Policy Instruments to Support Firm Growth**

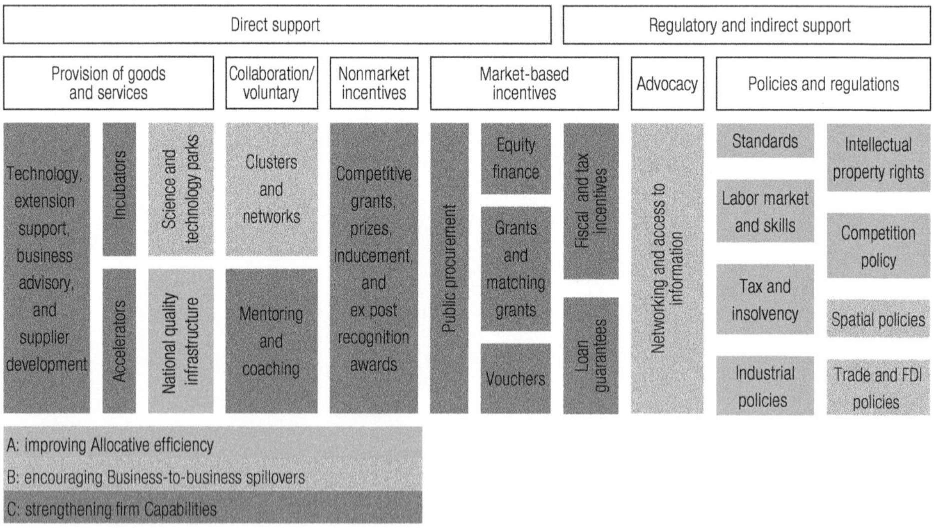

*Source:* Adaptation of figure 7.1 (The Innovation Policy Space) in Cirera and Maloney (2017).

national firm-level data (particularly of the panel variety) remain rare. And, unlike efforts to construct moving snapshots of the global distribution of income (Milanovic 2002; Bussolo, De Hoyos, and Medvedev 2010; Lakner and Milanovic 2016), few similar efforts exist when it comes to the distribution of firms.[11] While this book—together with Cusolito and Maloney (2018)—represents one of the first steps in this direction, it is also a call for action to national statistical agencies, donors, and international organizations to make high-quality firm data a priority. If we agree that productivity is all that matters in the long run, we should be serious about measuring it.

The second theme is strengthening the rigor in policy evaluation. As discussed earlier, few business support or development programs, even in high-income countries, rely on robust logical frameworks and theory of change or use counterfactual evaluation designs to measure effectiveness, which is why most of the evidence on beneficiary selection in the annex to this chapter comes from academic literature setting up RCTs with micro-entrepreneurs rather than evaluations of larger-scale firm-support programs. Similarly, as the following discussion will reveal, evidence on the impact of most policy instruments is scarce and largely limited to high-income countries. Given these limitations on what does and does not work to support firm growth, embedding rigorous impact evaluations as part of program design and implementation can help ensure that public resources achieve the desired outcomes efficiently and effectively and allow policy makers to correct and adapt program implementation along the way. The World Bank's Competitiveness Policy Evaluation Lab is one example of an international initiative to integrate impact evaluations into the design and implementation of competitiveness and business support programs (box 4.6).

The third crosscutting theme is institutional capabilities to implement policies. Cirera and Maloney (2017) propose an "escalator" approach to gradually build the institutional capabilities of developing countries to match the ambition of policy instruments in support of the science, technology, and innovation agenda (often taken from high-income countries). Similar concerns apply to policies in support of high firm growth. A study of policy initiatives for encouraging HGFs in nine, primarily high-income countries by the Finland, Ministry of Trade and Industry (2007) finds that these initiatives tend to be characterized by siloed approaches and poor coordination across departments and ministries.[12] Ensuring that the relevant institutions have the necessary human and financial resources and the right mandate and they communicate effectively in implementing the ABCs of growth entrepreneurship will be critical to success. It will also require that policy initiatives from other countries are adapted to local contexts and the capabilities of firms and implementing agencies rather than copied and pasted into a new environment. Relatedly, policies also must take into account the quality of governance and guard against the risk that targeted interventions could be channeled on the basis of political connections (for example, Rijkers, Freund, and Nucifora 2017; Akcigit, Grigsby, and Nicholas 2017).

## Competitiveness Policy Evaluation Lab (ComPEL)

The Competitiveness Policy Evaluation Lab (ComPEL) is an umbrella program at the World Bank to support and coordinate impact evaluation efforts in the areas of competitiveness and private sector development. Its main objective is to generate high-quality evidence to inform policy making on firm productivity, job creation, and investment to continuously and systematically improve the impact of projects. This is achieved by using impact evaluations and inferential research strategically to identify the features or mechanisms that maximize impact of existing programs and to develop and pilot new policy solutions in developing countries.

ComPEL follows a cluster approach to impact evaluation, with clusters identified through an extensive consultation process among government stakeholders, economists from academia, donor partners, and World Bank staff. The clusters currently under implementation include (1) connecting businesses to markets, (2) improving regulatory efficiency for firms, and (3) targeting firms with high-growth potential.

The ongoing evaluations in the high-growth potential cluster include different approaches to screening mechanisms as well as bundling different types of support to treatment recipients.

| Country | Targeting mechanism | Firm support | Sample size (firms) |
|---------|---------------------|--------------|---------------------|
| Balkans | Experts' assessment of business pitch | Basic online training and intense support (including individualized mentoring, master classes, and pitch support) | 346 |
| Georgia | Competition that allocates more resources to high achievers | Based on training results, provide incentive to get broadband and mentoring to establish online retail | 1,012 |
| Kenya | Screening of business plans | Training and grants to prepare plans and invest in inputs | 9,000 |
| Mexico | Expert's assessment of application and screening of application by government officials | Large grants for innovations | 339 |
| Nigeria | Screening of application, workshop participation, and score on business practices | Training, consulting, insourcing, and outsourcing to improve skills, practices, and access to credit | 2,000 |

More information available at http://www.worldbank.org/en/programs/competitiveness-policy-impact-evaluation-lab /brief/targeting-and-promoting-businesses-with-high-growth-potential.

## Allocative Efficiency

To grow, firms need to be able to access resources, such as labor, capital, land, intermediate inputs, and so on. The literature on firm growth has long emphasized the role of competition in forcing inefficient firms to exit and transfer their resources to the more efficient ones, thus boosting economywide productivity.[13] In particular, economies that have been generally recognized as more productive and dynamic, such as the

United States, are characterized by high rates of industry turnover: "a hallmark of the U.S. economy has been a high pace of job and worker reallocation with a high pace of business entry and exit ... this dynamism and flexibility of the U.S. labor market has been important for productivity growth, earnings growth and job creation" (Haltiwanger 2015; see also Haltiwanger 2011). On the other hand, developing-country economies are often characterized by muted firm dynamics that keep resources locked in unproductive firms that neither exit nor grow (Tybout 1996; Li and Rama 2015; Akcigit, Alp, and Peters 2016). This gives rise to the now well-known problem of resource misallocation, whereby distortions to allocative efficiency not only lower economywide productivity but also reduce the likelihood of high-growth episodes (chapter 3).

Hsieh and Klenow (2014) quantify the economic impact of misallocation by showing that firms in India and Mexico grow almost four times slower than firms in the United States—and that these differences are responsible for as much as 25 percent of the gaps in aggregate productivity between these countries and the United States. Hsieh and Klenow (2009) show that if distortions in China and India were lowered to levels observed in the United States, productivity could rise by 40–60 percent in India and 30–50 percent in China.[14] The challenge in translating these findings into policy recommendations is that these and other studies do not precisely identify the nature of distortions, and an exhaustive list is likely to be difficult to compile and will vary substantially by country and sector circumstances. One way to conceptually separate the issue into policy-actionable areas is to follow the standard productivity decomposition approaches to consider the three margins of entry, exit, and reallocation (figure 4.6).

**FIGURE 4.6  Decomposition of Productivity Growth**

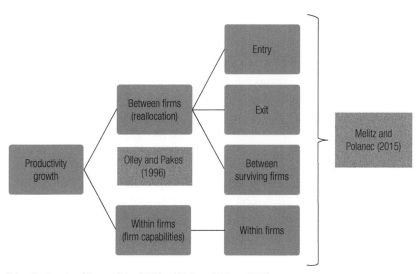

*Source:* Elaboration based on Olley and Pakes (1996) and Melitz and Polanec (2015).

Policies along the *entry* margin seek to improve allocative efficiency by making it easier for new, potentially more productive firms, to enter the market. Much of the policy attention in the growth entrepreneurship space has already been dedicated to this margin through initiatives aimed at facilitating start-ups through easier registration and licensing procedures, access to various forms of seed capital, mentorship, and other means of facilitating start-up ecosystems. Many interventions along this margin, such as steps to ease new business registration—often supported by the World Bank Group through its Doing Business advisory services—have a rather long track record and allow for peer-to-peer learning and international benchmarking. Others, such as initiatives to support ecosystems, are in relatively early stages with limited evidence on effectiveness. However, in most instances policies that reduce the regulatory burden on new firms and allow entrepreneurs to focus on bringing their ideas to market and building a customer base rather than complying with arduous rules and regulations are likely to increase the likelihood that more productive firms are able to enter and stay in the market.

Conversely, policies along the *exit* margin seek to ensure that less productive firms release their resources for more efficient use. Indeed, Akcigit, Alp, and Peters (2016) argue that new firms in India have difficulty growing precisely because inefficient incumbents are not pushed out of the market, starving new firms of the necessary resources to grow. Adalet McGowan, Andrews, and Millot (2017) refer to a specific subset of these inefficient incumbents as "zombie" firms—firms 10 years old or older that cannot cover their interest payments with profits for three consecutive years— and argue that they contribute substantially to capital misallocation. Their results for a sample of OECD countries show that reforms to insolvency regimes—that is, steps to reduce barriers to corporate restructuring and the personal cost associated with entrepreneurial failure—reduce the share of capital sunk in "zombie" firms and spur the reallocation of capital to more productive firms. Combined with other evidence on the benefits to reforming insolvency regimes— for example, that lower costs to close a business are associated with more innovation and experimentation with risky technologies (Andrews, Criscuolo, and Menon 2014), more rapid spillover of new innovations from the frontier (Saia, Andrews, and Albrizio 2015), and greater adoption of existing technologies (Westmore 2013)—these results suggest that pursuing more flexible bankruptcy regulations, for example, by reducing the legal burden and social stigma associated with business failures, can be an effective means of improving allocative efficiency, boosting productivity, and increasing the likelihood of high firm growth.

Policies along the *reallocation* margin seek to improve the ability of existing firms to access resources through more flexible labor and financial market policies. The findings in chapter 3 emphasize the role that the accumulation of human capital by workers and managers (through previous labor market experience) plays in increasing the likelihood of high-growth episodes. Therefore, flexible labor market policies that facilitate the ability of employees to bring their experience from one firm to the next, rather than restricting mobility, are likely to support high firm growth. Similarly, chapter 3 also shows that the level of financial development, as measured by the share of domestic credit to the private sector in GDP, is positively correlated with high firm growth in the sample of upper-middle-income countries, suggesting that further steps along the financial reform agenda can have important benefits to firm growth. Focusing on complementary institutions (for example, securities laws, investor protection) and strengthening banking competition could therefore improve the allocation of resources by making it easier for innovative and productive firms to access financing (Nanda 2016).[15] Last but not least, policies such as standards, national quality infrastructure, and intellectual property rights can further strengthen the reallocation margin by lowering the risk of investing in new technology and ensuring that firms are able to reap the benefits of their investment in research and product development.

### B2B Spillovers

The evidence presented in chapter 3 of this book shows that connections between firms—through spatial clusters, value chains, or ownership networks, including FDI—matter for the probability of experiencing high growth. For example, spatial clustering of firms may generate positive externalities through localization economies (for example, firms in the same industry locating close together to pool inputs such as specialized labor sourcing) or urbanization economies (for example, firms from different industries locating close together to benefit from a diverse supplier network, common infrastructure, increased scale of markets, and so on).[16] The spillover benefits from FDI are well documented in the literature and include transfer of technology and managerial knowledge, either directly through supplier networks or indirectly through demonstration effects (Djankov and Hoekman 2000; Görg, Strobl, and Walsh 2007; Javorcik 2004; Arnold and Javorcik 2009). Participation in global markets through exporting, particularly as part of global value chains, offers similar benefits as well as diversification of the customer base and quality upgrading through learning-by-doing (Atkin, Khandelwal, and Osman 2017); product shedding, which forces firms to focus on their core competency (Bernard, Jensen, and Schott 2006); and enhanced access to higher-quality intermediate inputs (Goldberg et al. 2010).

Good *spatial policies* can support high firm growth by maximizing the benefits of agglomeration while minimizing congestion externalities and resolving coordination failures (Duranton, Gobillon, and Overman 2011). However, the literature cautions that "the mere existence of agglomeration externalities does not indicate which places should be subsidized" (Glaeser and Gottlieb 2008, 2). Instead, when it comes to urban agglomerations, studies suggest establishing functional land markets, improving land use, providing urban transport and other basic public services, and fostering housing finance markets. These are the key components of policies for addressing the urban order in cities (Bird et al. 2018; Brueckner and Lall 2015; Duranton and Venables 2018; Ellis and Roberts 2015; Lall, Henderson, and Venables 2017).

One specific set of reforms in this area is improving the efficiency of land use.[17] Zoning laws, for instance, can aid in mitigating the distortive effects of externalities generated by the proximity of "incompatible" industries or firms and also help contain urban sprawl via green belts or assist in curbing congestion.[18] Similarly, an urban growth boundary can be assigned with the objective of controlling sprawl and directing land use to certain activities, whereas density regulations, such as lot size zoning,[19] floor area ratio,[20] or building height regulation, can work to control sprawl and density.

Complementary transport policies to reach spatially optimal outcomes represent another set of reforms to improve spatial connectivity and facilitate agglomeration economies, particularly in light of growing evidence that cities that exhibit more urban sprawl may experience faster growth and more job creation. It is well documented that physical infrastructure and transportation play a critical role in explaining changes in economic activity and firm productivity.[21] Theory suggests that a decline in transport costs tends to untangle the location of firms and households and can lead to a more efficient organization of economic activity (Fujita and Ogawa 1982; Lucas and Rossi-Hansberg 2002; Glaeser and Kohlhase 2004) directly through a reduction in the cost of workers' commute and indirectly through the concentration of business areas.

Evidence from developed and developing countries alike indicates that better connectivity and reductions in transport costs—for example, through the implementation of transport corridors and corridor policies—can support firm growth.[22] However, outcomes tend to vary by sector and location: studies have shown that the Chinese national highway system brought large gains to major metropolitan areas while adversely affecting peripheral counties (Faber 2014; Roberts et al. 2012), whereas U.S. cities with more highways tend to specialize in the production of heavier goods (Duranton, Morrow, and Turner 2014). Therefore, when considering spatial policies, policy makers must be mindful that agglomeration gains in some locations may come at the expense of displacement in others. For example, studies show that some of the agglomeration gains to firm growth come from firms and factors of production moving from one location to another (Chandra and Thompson 2000; Duranton, Morrow, and Turner 2014; Redding and Turner 2015).

The first best set of *policies to attract quality FDI* include reforms to strengthen the regulatory climate, ensure a stable macro and political environment, and facilitate access to resources, including infrastructure and workers with the right skills (OECD 2003). These issues are difficult to resolve at large scale, which is why many countries resort to the use of regulatory exemptions and fiscal and financial incentives to offset broader deficiencies in the investment climate in order to attract multinational enterprises. Such incentives take many forms—for example, lower corporate tax rates, tax holidays, preferential tariff regimes, single-window customs clearance, subsidized land and buildings, stepped-up investment in infrastructure, and educational measures—and are often confined to specific economic sectors or geographic zones, but they all share unfortunate features of a poor evidence base on the costs versus benefits as well as a tendency to engender a "race to the bottom" across jurisdictions. OECD (2003, 10–11) cautions that, at most, the use of such incentives may "tip the balance in favour of one location among a group of economies that are perceived to have broadly equivalent enabling environments."

Similar logic applies to *trade and export promotion policies*. Exporters often rely on imported inputs—for example, Bastos, Silva, and Verhoogen (2018) show that Portuguese exporters to richer destinations demand higher-quality inputs whereas Van Assche and Van Biesebroeck (2018) link capital goods imports to faster productivity growth and product upgrading in China—which makes further efforts to reduce tariffs and nontariff measures an important priority. Although the spotlight of trade liberalization efforts often falls on the manufacturing sector, services liberalization is equally important because of the sector's growing prominence as a production input,[23] as well as to take advantage of growing opportunities in services trade (Grover Goswami, Mattoo, and Sáez 2011; Dihel and Grover Goswami 2016) and the possibility of bundling services with goods production.[24] Improving trade logistics and helping potential exporters connect with foreign buyers is also high on this agenda, which also often includes similar types of incentives as mentioned earlier for FDI, and the same caveats apply.

Beyond regulatory measures, several direct support instruments have been used to facilitate B2B spillovers. One example is *science and technology parks*, which are professionally managed physical spaces offering infrastructure and other support services to facilitate intra-industry, research-industry, and government-industry collaboration. The key challenge in implementing science and technology park projects is to avoid turning them into "just" real estate developments by ensuring the parks are located in areas that have skilled workers and well-functioning job markets, provide an attractive residential and living environment, and offer a package of services, such as sources of financing, management and marketing advice, and fostering of collaboration between firms. As with all instruments, clear identification of the target group and the challenges facing this group is required a priori to develop the package of services offered by the park, which should also seek to attract complementary businesses, such as consultancy firms and other technical services providers.

*Clusters*, including industrial parks and economic zones, similarly aim to foster firm collaboration through geographical co-location and removal of institutional and financial constraints that cannot be fully addressed at the national level. Despite their long history, the evidence on the effectiveness of clusters remains limited because of the complexity and variety of the initiatives. The available guidance suggests that clusters tend to have a positive effect on interfirm collaboration, innovation, employment, sales, and exports, but the effects generally take at least several years to manifest, and the absence of a control group makes these conclusions less robust than findings regarding other initiatives that have undergone more rigorous evaluations.

One of the best-known success stories is China's state-level special economic zones. These zones have been associated with significant subsequent GDP growth in their host cities —driven by physical capital accumulation as well as modest growth in TFP and human capital investments—and positive spillovers to neighboring regions or cities (Alder, Shao, and Zilibotti 2016). However, the same study showed that province-level zones, which are characterized by less autonomy and a patchwork of different policies, do not have a significant effect on economic development. Similarly, evidence outside of East Asia is mixed (Farole 2011; Khandelwal and Teachout 2016), and one of the few rigorous evaluations of cluster initiatives, the Local Productive Systems in France, found little evidence of a positive impact on employment growth and productivity (Martin, Mayer, and Mayneris 2011). This suggests that the success of economic zones is very much contextual, and, indeed, examples of successful policies are usually those in which the initiatives targeted an already formed and well-functioning cluster.

Programs to strengthen *networks* are similar to cluster policies but aim more specifically to resolve coordination failures across firms through virtual initiatives by distributing risk, fostering knowledge flows, and enabling participants to tackle challenges that no single firm may be able to address on its own. Relative to research-based networks, the evidence on the effectiveness of business networks is very limited: of the four studies of networks identified in Cirera, Frias, and Hill (forthcoming), only one found a positive impact of participation on the likelihood of innovation, whereas the results of others were mixed.

### Firm Capabilities

Firm capabilities are those elements of the production process that a firm cannot readily buy in the market and must therefore learn (Sutton 2012). Innovation and managerial competencies are the most common examples of firm capabilities. Although the recognition of their importance to firm performance goes back more than a century (for example, Walker 1887), recent advances in the measurement of these practices and their link to improvements in firm productivity have shone a new spotlight on policy interventions that can help firms build these capabilities. In the specific context of HGFs, findings in chapter 3 of this book highlight the importance of innovation and managerial skills to increased likelihood of a high-growth event. Policy instruments to help firms build their capabilities mostly tend to be direct rather than regulatory and include market-based financial incentives, nonmarket incentives, such as inducement mechanisms and awards, and direct provision of goods and services, including technology transfer and business advisory services.

*Financial incentives* to build firm capabilities include direct instruments, such as vouchers, grants and matching grants, equity financing, and public procurement, and indirect interventions, such as fiscal and tax incentives and loan guarantees. These market-based instruments encourage behavior change by nudging firms to undertake activities they would otherwise not do (for example, innovate, upgrade management, or find new markets for products). Vouchers aim to achieve this by stimulating demand; successful programs therefore combine relatively low-value awards with simple application procedures and minimal administration costs. Grants, equity financing, fiscal incentives, and loan guarantees address credit market imperfections and incomplete appropriability of undertaking certain projects and usually follow a competitive process. Most often, the complexity of application procedures and the cost of program administration increases with the size of awards (for example, with tax credits); however, even in the more expensive cases, administrative costs as a share of total project budget (or per unit of resources transferred) tend to be below direct provision of services. Finally, public procurement programs address similar market failures through a "demand pull" mechanism by having the government act as lead buyer.

Evidence reviewed in Cirera, Frias, and Hill (forthcoming) shows that vouchers tend to be effective at stimulating behavior change, but evidence of sustained impact is mixed, suggesting that voucher programs are likely to work best as an initial step toward more complex support programs. Likewise, grants are generally effective in producing intended outcomes (for example, business innovation) and encouraging firms to invest their own resources in the process—and competition-based grants generally outperform entitlement-based grants. However, fewer studies find significant increases in sales, employment, and value added due to grant programs, and outcomes in terms of productivity growth are mixed. Similarly, Cirera, Frias, and Hill (forthcoming) document that fiscal incentives usually have a positive impact on outcomes (for example, higher R&D investment and greater probability of developing new products for R&D tax credits) with effects becoming stronger in the long run, but the evidence is mixed when it comes to productivity. Findings on the relative effectiveness of grants versus tax incentives are mixed, although evidence from developing countries shows that smaller firms may be less likely to participate in tax incentives.

When it comes to loan guarantees, studies show positive but weak effects on outcomes (for example, R&D spending) and similarly weak support for increases in firm sales and productivity. Government-backed early-stage equity investment is a relatively new policy tool. Although it is rapidly gaining acceptance in developing countries (see box 4.3), Cirera, Frias, and Hill (forthcoming) caution that evidence regarding improved access to finance, exit rates or values, and increased sales compared with private funds is mixed, and when the impact is positive, it tends to be linked to private co-participation in the scheme. Finally, evidence shows that public procurement programs help participants generate new intellectual property and contribute to new firm creation, but effects on employment vary and are limited to the short term.

*Inducement instruments* and *recognition awards* are nonmarket incentive mechanisms to encourage additional efforts by participants to address a specific challenge. They share some similarities with financial incentive mechanisms but transfer the risk of failure from the government to participant firms. Although prize competitions may struggle to attract established firms and instead draw unconventional participants, evidence cited in Cirera, Frias, and Hill (forthcoming) suggests that total investment by prize seekers is at least as large as the amount of the prize. Moreover, prizes tend to be successful in developing new technologies and solutions as well as raising public awareness of the issues underpinning the competition, although none of the studies examining their impact are performed in a rigorous counterfactual setting. The cost of award initiatives may be even lower than prizes, and they can be similarly effective in drawing society's attention to specific issues, although the administration and governance of awards requires care to ensure fairness, transparency, and sufficient quality of winning projects. Because prizes and awards cannot offset institutional and capability weaknesses, these instruments are unlikely to work well if businesses are financially or technically constrained from making the needed investments.

*Technology, extension support, and advisory services* programs advise firms on process improvements, workforce training, supply chain development, customer acquisition, exporting, and technology transfer. They are common in a number of high-income countries; some of the better-known examples include the Manufacturing Extension Partnership in the United States, Fraunhofer Institutes and Steinbeis Centers in Germany, Japan's Kohsetsushi Centers and Productivity Centers, and SPRING and A*STAR in Singapore. These initiatives help firms resolve information asymmetries regarding their own capabilities (for example, studies such as Bloom et al. [2013] have shown that firms often do not seek out consulting services because they do not know what they are missing), address shallow markets (for example, the quality of available consulting services may vary, and firms may have difficulty distinguishing between potential suppliers, whereas extension programs often provide some consulting in-house and use their networks of private sector providers for others), and improve access to technology or services that the firms may not be able to purchase on their own (for example, prototyping, 3D printing, and the like). With few exceptions (for example, Bloom et al. [2013, 2018] for India and Bruhn Karlan, and Schoar [2018] for Mexico), the evidence on the effectiveness of these interventions comes from high-income countries. Cirera, Frias, and Hill (forthcoming) show that the impact on sales, employment, and productivity tends to be positive, although constant adaptation and changes in the design of these programs makes attribution difficult. Since a lack of demand for these services is an important bottleneck inhibiting firm growth and productivity, key factors for the success of these interventions include ensuring consistent quality of advice and services provided, strong outreach and engagement with potential clients, and agile application processes.

*Incubators* and *accelerators* are instruments most often associated with HGFs given that their primary purpose is to support the development and scaling of growth-oriented, early-stage businesses by providing access to physical space, advisory services, mentorship, and sometimes access to finance for a predefined period (typically one to five years for incubators and three to six months for accelerators). Their services are offered either stand-alone or embedded in science and technology parks, clusters, and technology transfer intermediaries. As with other instruments, most of the evidence on the effectiveness of these initiatives is from high-income countries. Studies reviewed by Cirera, Frias, and Hill (forthcoming) suggest that incubated firms can be successful in generating additional revenue and employment, although the impact on innovation (for example, patents) is insignificant. Accelerators can be successful in increasing company survival rates, revenue, and (more modestly) employment growth, as well as improving deal flow in the regional ecosystems, although the evidence is even more limited than for incubators. On a cautionary side, although incubation and acceleration programs exist in agribusiness, health care, and other industries, the tech sector by and large remains the primary focus of these programs, placing them at odds with the literature and the findings in this book that HGFs are found in all sectors of the economy. To be successful, these initiatives must also generate a critical mass of clients, which makes them ill-suited to nascent ecosystems (as a potential solution to this issue, box 4.7 discusses regional approaches to incubation and acceleration). On the other hand, the proliferation and limited connections between individual incubator and

---

### BOX 4.7

#### Cross-Border Incubation and Acceleration Initiatives

Regional interventions can facilitate resource pooling and knowledge sharing, particularly in nascent entrepreneurial ecosystems. Regional coverage expands offerings in countries with less developed ecosystems overall, and entrepreneurs can gain access to instruments that do not require the full-time presence of a provider in a market with emerging (but not yet critical mass) high-potential firms. Regional interventions can reduce the costs of accessing foreign markets by connecting entrepreneurs to mentors, markets, and networks in neighboring countries, whose experiences may be similar to that of the participants.

There are several examples of regional interventions to deliver incubation and acceleration services. The education-based incubator MEST in Ghana sources entrepreneurs-in-training from Ghana as well as Kenya, Nigeria, and South Africa. LatAm Startups is a not-for-profit accelerator program for Latin American start-ups seeking to expand in the North American market. Through the LatAm Hub in Toronto, Latin American firms from Argentina, Brazil, Mexico, and Uruguay are offered three-month accelerator residencies in Toronto, with mentorship, connections, and community. The program also offers conferences, speaker events, and information technology platforms designed to connect entrepreneurs, investors, and ecosystem leaders between Canada and Latin America. Flat6Labs is a private accelerator-incubator model with coworking space; it invests in "bright and passionate entrepreneurs with cutting-edge ideas" in several cities in the Middle East, including Cairo, Jeddah, and Abu Dhabi, with plans to expand into Beirut and Tunis. Flat6Labs looks for start-ups across sectors as well as founding teams (up to four members) and targets ideas before the minimum viable product stage.

accelerator programs across locations mean that some firms might go through the programs multiple times, highlighting the importance of effective selection mechanisms, particularly when public funds are involved.

Given the wide range of instruments and varying evidence on effectiveness, how should a policy maker attempt to package the set of measures to support firm growth? Cirera and Maloney (2017) develop a hierarchy of the sophistication of instruments to support the strengthening of firm capabilities along the "capabilities escalator," which matches the complexity of instruments with the needs of firms and their ability to benefit from the instruments as well as the ability of public institutions to deliver these programs. For example, the majority of firms in low- and lower-middle-income countries struggle with the adoption of basic managerial and organizational practices and machinery upgrading and undertake little to no formal R&D. In these instances, the "capabilities escalator" approach suggests a focus on encouraging firms to adopt existing technology and invest in simple organizational changes rather than providing them with incentives to undertake advanced research.

Similarly, the reliance on policies such as matching grants or other financial incentives are based on the (often empirically untested) assumption that the main obstacle to firm upgrading is poor access to capital, whereas firms may also face difficulties in collaborating and accessing new markets and new technology, and other challenges that require a more comprehensive mix of instruments. In this regard, the World Bank Group's Public Expenditure Reviews for Science, Technology, and Innovation offer practical guidance to policy makers on how to improve the alignment of the policy mix with national development objectives and the specific constraints faced by firms, as well as on how to improve the design and implementation of individual policy instruments for enhanced efficiency and effectiveness (box 4.8). The same methodological framework has now been successfully applied to a broader range of business development policies, including support to SMEs.

An agency such as SPRING provides an example of the "capabilities escalator" approach, in which relatively low-cost interventions (for example, online toolkits and consultancy vouchers) are available to a large population of firms, while more sophisticated and costly ones (for example, loans, capability development grants, and productivity and innovation tax credits) are geared toward a smaller number of firms that have "graduated" from previous interventions and are recommended for enhanced levels of support by their SPRING account manager (Cirera and Maloney 2017). At a higher level of sophistication, A*STAR offers even more complex services to support technological upgrading. Similarly, the NIY initiative in Finland relies on a milestone design that sets performance targets for participant firms to remain in the program and move on to the next phase of support.

### Science, Technology, and Innovation Public Expenditure Reviews

Science, Technology, and Innovation Public Expenditure Reviews (STI PERs) can help countries improve the quality of their innovation policy making, improve resource allocation across programs, achieve budget savings, and enhance program impact. STI PERs evaluate four stages of innovation policy interventions:

1. *General evaluation of the quality and coherence of the policy mix* based on the conditions of the country and its innovation system, including the portfolio mapping of STI programs and their assessment based on coherence with existing innovation policy objectives
2. *Evaluation of the quality of design, implementation, and governance (functional analysis)* of existing instruments based on international good practices
3. *Evaluation of the efficiency of existing instruments*, meaning their ability to produce the expected outputs with reasonable levels of resources
4. *Evaluation of the effectiveness of existing instruments and the system* by analyzing their ability to generate the desired impact.

Unlike traditional PERs, STI PERs have the individual innovation policy instrument as the unit of analysis, which allows evaluators to identify what is spent with what objectives, and therefore assess efficiency and effectiveness at a more detailed level. Their main objectives are to do the following:

- Support the process of redesigning and shaping public innovation policies by using data and information on existing instruments
- Improve the ability of governments to coordinate innovation policies by evaluating the design and implementation process and assessing the quality of the monitoring and evaluation system
- Support the adoption of good practices in design, implementation, and coordination of innovation policy instruments by benchmarking instruments across countries (where appropriate)
- Formulate policy recommendations to strengthen the innovation policy mix by eliminating redundancies and leveraging complementarities across the portfolio of instruments.

For example, in Colombia, the World Bank provided a comprehensive evaluation of more than 120 instruments, assessing the effectiveness of the policy mix, the degree of redundancies, and existing gaps in the current policy support. The analysis was used to inform the new innovation policy strategy. Furthermore, the project evaluated the quality of design, implementation, and coordination of existing instruments and worked with the authorities to improve the quality of evaluation and project management practices. In Chile, the World Bank evaluated the quality of the innovation and entrepreneurship policy mix and worked with two government agencies to identify good practices and weaknesses in design and implementation practices. The results of the PER were used to inform the current restructuring of innovation instruments.

**TABLE 4A.1   List of 54 Targeted Interventions in 14 Developing Countries**

| Country | Intervention |
|---|---|
| Angola | 1. Fundo Activo de Capital de Risco Angolano (FACRA) |
| Brazil | 2. Tech Sampa<br>3. Primeira Empresa Inovadora (PRIME)<br>4. INOVAR<br>5. SEED (Startups and Entrepreneurship Ecosystem Development)<br>6. Start-Up Brasil |
| Colombia | 7. FCP Innovación<br>8. Manizales Más:<br>9. Fondo Emprender<br>10. Apps.co<br>11. iNNpulsa<br>12. ColCapital |
| Côte d'Ivoire | 13. ZBTIC free zone and incubator: Biotechnology and Information and Communication Technology Free Zone |
| Ghana | 14. Venture Capital Trust Fund<br>15. Ghana Alternative Market |
| India[a] | 16. BSE-SME; NSE-Emerge<br>17. SIDBI fund of funds (e.g., ASPIRE, Fund of Funds for Start-ups, India Aspiration Fund)<br>18. Venture capital funds: SIDBI Venture Capital; targeted venture capital funds (e.g., IFCI Venture Capital Fund for Scheduled Castes)<br>19. Technology Upgradation and Quality Certification Program<br>20. Nonbanking finance company (e.g. Cheraman)<br>21. Incubator/accelerator (e.g. Ginserv)<br>22. State-based MSME technology facilitation project (e.g., Kolkata) |
| Jamaica | 23. SME Growth Initiative<br>24. Jamaica Stock Exchange – Junior Market<br>25. Champions Assist<br>26. Jamaica Venture Capital Programme<br>27. Start Up Jamaica |
| Jordan | 28. Accelerate with Jordan Enterprise Development Corporation (JEDCO)<br>29. SME Observatory |
| Malaysia | 30. ACE Market<br>31. Groom Big (Product and Services Quality Enhancement Programme)<br>32. Business Acceleration Program<br>33. Bumiputera Enterprise Enhancement Program (BEEP)<br>34. Angel Tax Incentive Office<br>35. Women Entrepreneur Financing Program (WEP-LEAP) |
| Mexico | 36. Negocios Extrabursátiles<br>37. US-Mexico Foundation for Science Business Acceleration Program<br>38. NAFIN Entrepreneurs Fund<br>39. Fondo de Fondos Corporación Mexicana de Inversiones de Capital<br>40. High Impact Entrepreneurship Program (HIEP) |
| Philippines | 41. SME Board (Stock Exchange)<br>42. Shared Service Facilities<br>43. SME Roving Academy<br>44. Mentor ME |

*(Table continues on the following page.)*

**TABLE 4A.1  List of 54 Targeted Interventions in 14 Developing Countries *(continued)***

| Country | Intervention |
|---|---|
| Senegal | 45. SME Fund of the Sovereign Fund for Strategic Investments (FONSIS)<br>46. CTIC Dakar (MLabs) |
| South Africa | 47. National Gazelles (NG)<br>48. AltX<br>49. Seda Technology Programme (STP)<br>50. National Empowerment Fund |
| Turkey | 51. Turkish Growth and Innovation Fund (TGIF); Istanbul Venture Capital Initiative (iVCi; predecessor to TGIF)<br>52. Borsa – Second National Market<br>53. Business angel licensing (tax incentive)<br>54. Angel network accreditation |

*Source:* Desai, Olafsen, and Cook 2018.

*Note:* This table includes interventions that explicitly target firm growth. This is representative and does not include a complete list of all relevant interventions in a given country. This includes only interventions that are partly or wholly funded or implemented by public agencies or that are operated by private entities that co-invest with, originated from, or serve as extensions of public sector agencies (for example, FCP Innovación in Colombia). It does not include export promotion and innovation policy interventions, unless they are explicitly linked to entrepreneur or small and medium enterprise (SME) growth. It does not include private direct targeting interventions, such as private venture capital, and it does not include public indirect targeting interventions, such as general bank reform and infrastructure parks or special development zones, unless there is a specific focus on firm growth or scale (for example, ZBTIC in Côte d'Ivoire). The instruments identified in each intervention reflect their most recognizable activities and may not reflect the entire range of ongoing or changing programmatic activities.

a. Note that for India, because of the decentralized organization of many interventions, those studied are of certain types rather than the complete set of interventions.

**TABLE 4A.2  Intensity of Program Screening and Impacts**

| Study | Country | Intervention | Impact, revenue | Impact, jobs | Screening intensity[a] (0–2) | Business plan (Y/N) | Firm size (workers) | Entre-preneur education[b] |
|---|---|---|---|---|---|---|---|---|
| Anderson, Chandy, and Zia (2016) | South Africa | Training marketing | (+) | (+) | 2 | N | 1.44 | High |
| | | Training finance | (+) | (+) | | | N/A | N/A |
| Berge, Bjorvatn, and Tungodden (2014) | Tanzania | Business training | (+) | | 1 | N | 1.08 | Medium |
| | | Medium-sized grants | (+) | (+) | | | N/A | N/A |
| Blattman et al. (2014) | Uganda | Small-sized grant | (+) | (+) | 2 | Y | New business | Medium |
| Bloom et al. (2013) | India | Consulting | (+) | N/A | 1 | N | 273 | N/A |
| Bruhn and Zia (2018) | Bosnia | Business training – women | (−) | (+) | 1 | N | 2.28 | High |
| | | Business training – men | (−) | (−) | | | N/A | N/A |
| Bruhn, Karlan, and Schoar (2018) | Mexico | Consulting | N/A | (+) | 2 | N | 13.7 | High |

*(Table continues on the following page.)*

**TABLE 4A.2  Intensity of Program Screening and Impacts** *(continued)*

| Study | Country | Intervention | Impact, revenue | Impact, jobs | Screening intensity[a] (0–2) | Business plan (Y/N) | Firm size (workers) | Entre-preneur education[b] |
|---|---|---|---|---|---|---|---|---|
| Calderon, Cunha, and De Giorgi (2013) | Mexico | Short basic business training | (+) | (+) | 0 | N | 1.66 | N/A |
| Campos et al. (2017) | Togo | Business training | (+) | (–) | 2 | N | N/A | N/A |
| | | Personal initiative training | | (+) | 2 | N | | N/A |
| De Mel, McKenzie, and Woodruff (2008) | Sri Lanka | Small-sized grant | | N/A | 0 | N | 1 | Medium |
| De Mel et al. (2014) | Sri Lanka | Business training – new | | N/A | 1 | N | 1 | Medium |
| | | Business training – existing | (–) | N/A | | | | N/A |
| Drexler et al. (2012) | Dominican Republic | Standard finance training | (–) | (+) | 0 | N | 1.8 | Low |
| | | Rule of thumb finance training | | (–) | | | | N/A |
| Fafchamps et al. (2011) | Ghana | Small-sized grant | (+) | N/A | 1 | N | 1 | Medium |
| Giné, Mansuri, and Picón (2011) | Pakistan | Business training | (–) | N/A | 0 | N | N/A | N/A |
| Glaub et al. (2014) | Uganda | Personal initiative training | (+) | (+) | | | 8.09 | N/A |
| Gonzalez-Uribe and Leatherbee (2017) | Chile | Medium/large-sized equity-free cash Space Training | (+) | (+) | 2 | Y | 2.74 | N/A |
| Karlan, Knight, and Udry (2015) | Ghana | Consulting | (–) | (+) | 0 | N | 2.21 | N/A |
| Karlan and Valdivia (2011) | Peru | Business training | (+) | (+) | 0 | N | 1.96 | N/A |
| Klinger and Schundeln (2011) | El Salvador, Guatemala, Nicaragua | Business training | N/A | (+) | 2 | Y | 8.1 | N/A |
| | | Business training and mentoring | N/A | (+) | | | | N/A |
| Macours, Premand, and Vakis (2012) | Nicaragua | Technical assistance and small-sized grants | (+) | N/A | 1 | Y | New business | Low |

*(Table continues on the following page.)*

High-Growth Firms

**TABLE 4A.2  Intensity of Program Screening and Impacts** *(continued)*

| Study | Country | Intervention | Impact, revenue | Impact, jobs | Screening intensity[a] (0–2) | Business plan (Y/N) | Firm size (workers) | Entre-preneur education[b] |
|---|---|---|---|---|---|---|---|---|
| Mano et al. (2012) | Ghana | Business training | (+) | N/A | 0 | N | 4.3 | High |
| McKenzie (2015) | Nigeria | Business training and medium-size grants | (+) | (+) | 2 | Y | 7.7 | High |
| McKenzie et al. (2016) | Republic of Yemen | Matching grant to cover technical assistance | (+) | (−) | 2 | Y | 12.28 | N/A |
| McKenzie and Woodruff (2008) | Mexico | Small-sized grants | (+) | N/A | 1 | N | 1 | Medium |
| Valdivia (2012) | Peru | Business training | (+) | (−) | 1 | N | 2.11 | High |
| | | Business training and consulting | (+) | (−) | | | | N/A |

| Legend: | |
|---|---|
| | Positive and statistically significant coefficients |
| | Not statistically significant coefficients; the sign is indicated in parentheses |
| | Negative and statistically significant coefficients |

*Note:* N/A = not available.

[a] Intensity of screening: 0: no screening; 1: existence of eligibility criteria but loose, short business plan, forms to be filled out, questionnaire to answer as prerequisite; 2: various steps in the selection process, business plan, online application, or numerous eligibility criteria.

[b] Education: Low educational background: below 6 years of schooling; medium: between 6 and 12 years of schooling; high: more than 12 years of schooling.

## Notes

1. The selection also captures countries of different populations—ranging from Jordan with a population of about 9 million to Indonesia with about 258 million—and GDP per capita (in purchasing power parity terms), ranging from about US$2,300 in Senegal to US$25,000 in Malaysia. These countries vary, too, in the policy performance of the overall business climate facing entrepreneurs, as indicated by the Global Entrepreneurship and Development Index score, ranging from Angola, ranked 125th (out of 137), to Turkey, ranked 36th. More than 200 interventions were reviewed, with case research performed on 54 interventions in 14 low- and middle-income countries.

2. The use of multiple instruments in one intervention is common, especially in private incubators, which can offer comprehensive support. The MEST Incubator program in Ghana is a good example. The program accepts applicants from countries across Sub-Saharan Africa. It provides seed financing (about US$50,000–US$ 200,000 for minority equity), access to shared physical infrastructure, dedicated advisers that provide training and mentoring, business development, marketing, sales and distribution, and value-added services (for example, a suite of technology services and programs). Program length is typically 12 to 24 months, with approximately 20 graduated firms in its portfolio history. An online application is followed

by screening and interviews, with program entry on a rolling, year-round basis. The selection process includes evaluation of the entrepreneur's personal attributes and the strength of the idea and the business plan as proxies for high growth potential.

3. For some interventions, it is simply too early to measure the impact effectively. For example, Mexico's recently started High Impact Entrepreneurship Program is in the process of an evaluation in conjunction with the World Bank. There is also the issue of the time horizon of an evaluation; for example, Dejardin and Fritsch (2011) find that the most important growth effects of start-ups tend to occur with a time lag of up to 10 years, but most programs can hardly wait for 10 years to assess results.

4. Buffering policies support new ventures by insulating against negative shocks, whereas bridging policies encourage new types of firms by facilitating access to external resources and enhancing survival and growth. Capacity-boosting policies actively pursue growth by working on the organizational capacity of firms.

5. Notably, the growth among NIY-treated firms was achieved during the financial crisis, when economic activity in the rest of the country was shrinking. The results remain robust to using alternative periods and with different propensity score matching methods, suggesting that the growth-enhancing impact is due to the contribution made by the NIY Program itself, and not because of the selection effect.

6. A related issue is that the choice of the target population may have a bearing on the selection of an appropriate policy instrument. For example, some studies have shown that women tend to achieve lower increases in sales or profits from grant programs than men (Blattman et al. 2014; De Mel, McKenzie, and Woodruff 2008; Fafchamps et al. 2011), whereas training appears to have a larger role in changing the business practices of entrepreneurs with lower financial literacy (Bruhn and Zia 2013) or lower skills (Drexler, Fischer, and Schoar 2014; Karlan and Valdivia 2011).

7. The jury results did add a modest amount of explanatory power to the survey prediction.

8. Based on 70 independent samples (N=24,733), the study finds a significant but small relationship between human capital and success (correlation coefficient equal to 0.098).

9. Kerr, Kerr, and Xu (2017) review the literature on the personality traits of entrepreneurs, indicating a clear gap in understanding of how firm performance connects to entrepreneurial personality.

10. The authors argue that initial VC success is mostly a result of investing in the right place at the right time and does not reflect inherently higher quality of the VC investor. Conditional on the initial positive outcome, VC firms are able to take advantage of their initial success by making subsequent larger and later-stage investments in the same sectors and regions, which tend to be more profitable than smaller, early-stage investments.

11. Two exceptions are the ORBIS database (which collects largely financial records for larger, listed firms) and combining firm-level data across countries from the World Bank Enterprise Surveys.

12. These include Australia; Brazil; Finland; Hong Kong SAR, China; Hungary; Italy; the Netherlands; Spain; and the United Kingdom.

13. For example, Cabral (2007) notes that "one of the most important results from the analysis of time series productivity data is the importance of industry turnover in the process of productivity growth." See also box 3.1 for alternative theories of firm growth.

14. These conclusions are also borne out by a range of other influential studies (for example, see Duranton et al. 2015; Fajnzylber, Maloney, and Montes-Rojas 2006; Fox and Sohnesen 2012; Ghani, Grover Goswami, and Kerr 2015; Grimm, Kruger, and Lay 2011; Kinda and Loening 2008). However, studies have also shown that other factors, such as adjustment costs of capital, coupled with volatility in firms' sales can generate the same type of dispersion on marginal products and revenue total factor productivity (Collard-Wexler and De Loecker 2015) and that differences in approaches to data cleaning across countries can account for much of the variation in measured misallocation (Rotemberg and White 2017).

15. For example, Nanda (2016) argues that the lack of complementary institutions has contributed to the weak presence of biotechnology companies in Germany, where the financial system is more heavily bank-oriented as compared to the market-oriented financial system in the United States.

16. Marshall (1890) argued that the clustering of specialized manufacturing firms increased knowledge sharing through processes such as shared labor markets. Henderson, Kuncoro, and Turner (1995) show that agglomeration effects for mature industries are related to Marshall scale economies, whereas newer industries benefit from diversity akin to Jacobs (1969) economies. Externalities associated with sources such as geographic concentration of human capital, which explains clustering of firms based on labor pooling, is explained in Rauch (1993) and Ciccone and Peri (2006). Duranton and Puga (2004) summarize the gains from agglomeration in terms of sharing, matching, and learning effects. Sharing effects include the gains from a greater variety of inputs and industrial specialization, the common use of local indivisible goods and facilities, and the pooling of risk; matching effects correspond to improvement of either the quality or the quantity of matches between firms and workers; and learning effects involve the generation, diffusion, and accumulation of knowledge. For a more recent survey on the evidence on agglomeration economies, see Combes and Gobillon (2015).

17. Duranton et al. (2015) find that changes in two policies relating to land use (stamp duties and an urban land ceiling act) are associated with better allocation of resources and output. Also see Lall, Henderson, and Venables (2017) for a discussion on how clarifying property rights and strengthening urban planning can help African cities out of the low development trap. They argue that unregulated markets are unlikely to get urban form and density right because the productivity of firms and the job-generating aspects of increased density are positive externalities that can be internalized only when appropriate policies are in place.

18. The problem with the equilibrium with zoning restrictions is that land rents are not continuous at the boundary between business and residential sectors, which motivates some land owners to lobby for changes in zoning restrictions. Zoning has the advantage that it entails relatively low transaction costs and is well-established. But it is inflexible and unresponsive to market signals, and the private gains from rezoning invite rent-seeking behavior and corruption. Alternatives include pricing policies (such as differential property tax rates or impact fees on developers), government creation of previously absent markets (such as that for transferable development rights), or the redefinition of property rights (such as the use of restrictive covenants).

19. Lot size zoning fixes the minimum or the maximum size of the lot in a given part of the city.

20. Floor area ratio refers to the ratio of the total floor area of the building relative to the aggregate size of the plot on which it is built. While lot size zoning can be a first best policy as it directly impacts population density, FAR regulation is a second best policy because it controls only the total floor supply of a building without controlling the per-capita floor space consumption.

21. See Anas, Arnott, and Small (1998) and Glaeser and Kahn (2004) for a review of this literature, and Burchfield et al. (2006) for a recent empirical study of urban sprawl in the United States.

22. See Baum-Snow (2007), Donaldson (2018), Donaldson and Hornbeck (2016), and Duranton and Turner (2011) for the United States; Hsu and Zhang (2014) for Japan; López-García, Montero, and Moral-Benito (2013) for Spain; Banerjee, Duflo, and Qian (2012) and Faber (2014) for China; Ghani, Grover Goswami, and Kerr (2016) for India; and Storeygard (2016) for Sub-Saharan Africa.

23. The impact of services inputs on manufacturing outcomes has been a growing topic in recent research. For example, Hoekman and Shepherd (2017) use cross-country data to assess the impact of services productivity on manufacturing productivity and exports. See also Arnold, Javorcik, and Mattoo (2011) for the Czech Republic, Arnold, et al. (2015) for India, Duggan, Rhardja, and Varela (2013) for Indonesia, Dihel and Goswami (2017) for Kenya, and Fernandes and Paunov (2012) for Chile.

24. There is compelling evidence that goods producers are increasingly offering complex engineered products that "bundle" services (Vandermerwe and Rada 1988; Neely, Benedettini, and Visnjic 2011). Crozet and Milet (2015) show that selling services increases profitability of French firms by 3.7–5.3 percent and is correlated with increased levels of employment. Servicification can also be correlated with better trade performance of firms, as exemplified by Lodefalk (2014) for Swedish manufacturing firms.

## References

Adalet McGowan, M., D. Andrews, and V. Millot. 2017. "Insolvency Regimes, Zombie Firms and Capital Reallocation." Economics Department Working Paper 1399, Oganisation for Economic Co-operation and Development, Paris.

Akcigit, Ufuk, Harun Alp, and Michael Peters. 2016. "Lack of Selection and Limits to Delegation: Firm Dynamics in Developing Countries." Working Paper 21905, National Bureau of Economic Research, Cambridge, MA.

Akcigit, U., J. Grigsby, and T. Nicholas. 2017. "The Rise of American Ingenuity: Innovation and Inventors of the Golden Age." Working Paper 23047, National Bureau of Economic Research, Cambridge, MA.

Alder, S., L. Shao, and F. Zilibotti. 2016. "Economic Reforms and Industrial Policy in a Panel of Chinese Cities." *Journal of Economic Growth* 21 (4): 305–49.

Aldrich, H., and C. Zimmer. 1986. "Entrepreneurship through Social Networks." In *The Art and Science of Entrepreneurship*, edited by D. Sexton and R. Smilor, 3–23. Cambridge, MA: Ballinger.

Amran, N. A. 2011. "Corporate Governance Mechanisms and Company Performance: Evidence from Malaysian Companies." *International Review of Business Research Papers* 7 (6): 101–14.

Anas, A., R. Arnott, and K. A. Small. 1998. "Urban Spatial Structure." *Journal of Economic Literature* 36 (3): 1426–64.

Anderson, S., R. Chandy, and B. Zia. 2016. "Pathways to Profits: Identifying Separate Channels of Firm Growth through Business Training." Policy Research Working Paper 7774, World Bank, Washington, DC.

Andjelkovic, M. 2018. "Communities, Networks, and Ecosystems: Definitional Questions for Entrepreneurship Research." Unpublished manuscript, World Bank, Washington, DC.

Andrews, D., C. Criscuolo, and C. Menon. 2014. "Do Resources Flow to Patenting Firms? Cross-Country Evidence from Firm Level Data." Economics Department Working Paper 1127, Organisation for Economic Co-operation and Development, Paris.

Anyadike-Danes, M., K. Bonner, M. Hart, and C. Mason. 2009. "Measuring Business Growth: High Growth Firms and Their Contribution to Employment in the U.K." Research Report MBG/35, National Endowment for Science, Technology and the Arts, London.

Arnold, J. M., and B. S. Javorcik. 2009. "Gifted Kids or Pushy Parents? Foreign Direct Investment and Plant Productivity in Indonesia." *Journal of International Economics* 79 (1): 42–53.

———, M. Lipscomb, and A. Mattoo. 2015. "Services Reform and Manufacturing Performance: Evidence from India." *Economic Journal* 126 (590): 1–39.

Arnold, J. M., B. S. Javorcik, and A. Mattoo. 2011. "Does Services Liberalization Benefit Manufacturing Firms? Evidence from the Czech Republic." *Journal of International Economics* 85 (1): 136–46.

Arráiz, I., M. Bruhn, and R. Stucchi. 2015. "Psychometrics as a Tool to Improve Screening and Access to Credit." Policy Research Working Paper 7506, World Bank, Washington, DC.

Atkin, D., A. Khandelwal, and A. Osman. 2017. "Exporting and Firm Performance: Evidence from a Randomized Experiment." *Quarterly Journal of Economics* 132 (2): 551–615.

Audretsch, D., I. Grilo, and R. Thurik. 2007. *Handbook of Research on Entrepreneurship Policy.* Northampton, MA: Edward Elgar.

Autio, E., S. Nambisan, M. Wright, and L. Thomas. 2015. Call for Papers for a Special Issue: Entrepreneurial Ecosystems. *Strategic Entrepreneurship Journal.* sej.strategicmanagement.net /conf-dl/sej-entrepreneurial-ecosystems.pdf.

Autio, E., and H. Rannikko. 2016. "Retaining Winners: Can Policy Boost High-Growth Entrepreneurship?" *Research Policy* 45 (1): 42–55.

Banerjee, A., E. Duflo, and N. Qian. 2012. "On the Road: Access to Transportation Infrastructure and Economic Growth in China." Working Paper 17897, National Bureau of Economic Research, Cambridge, MA.

Bastos, Paulo, Joana Silva, and Eric Verhoogen. 2018. "Export Destinations and Input Prices." *American Economic Review* 108 (2): 353–92.

Baum-Snow, N. 2007. "Suburbanization and Transportation in the Monocentric Model." *Journal of Urban Economics* 62 (3): 405–23.

Berge, L. I. O., K. Bjorvatn, and B. Tungodden. 2014. "Human and Financial Capital for Microenterprise Development: Evidence from a Field and Lab Experiment." *Management Science* 61 (4): 707–22.

Bernard, A. B., and J. B. Jensen. 1999. "Exceptional Exporter Performance: Cause, Effect, or Both?" *Journal of International Economics* 47 (1): 1–25.

———, and P. K. Schott. 2006. "Trade Costs, Firms and Productivity." *Journal of Monetary Economics* 53 (5): 917–37.

Bird, Julia Helen, Yue Li, Hossain Zillur Rahman, Martin G. Rama, and Anthony J. Venables. 2018. *Toward Great Dhaka: A New Urban Development Paradigm Eastward.* Directions in Development Series. Washington, DC: World Bank.

Blattman, C., E. Green, J. Annan, and J. Jamison. 2014. "The Returns to Cash and Microenterprise Support among the Ultra-Poor: A Field Experiment." Working Paper, Columbia University, New York.

Bloom, N., B. Eifert, A. Mahajan, D. McKenzie, and J. Roberts. 2013. "Does Management Matter? Evidence from India. "*Quarterly Journal of Economics* 128 (1): 1–51.

Bloom, N., A. Mahajan, D. McKenzie, and J. Roberts. 2018. "Do Management Interventions Last? Evidence from India." Working Paper 24249, National Bureau of Economic Research, Cambridge, MA.

Bos, J., and E. Stam. 2014. "Gazelles and Industry Growth: A Study of Young High-Growth Firms in the Netherlands." *Industrial and Corporate Change* 23 (1): 145–69.

Bravo-Biosca, A., C. Criscuolo, and C. Menon. 2016. "What Drives the Dynamics of Business Growth?" *Economic Policy* 31 (88): 703–42.

Brueckner, J. K., and S. V. Lall. 2015. "Cities in Developing Countries: Fueled by Rural-Urban Migration, Lacking in Tenure Security, and Short of Affordable Housing." In *Handbook of Regional and Urban Economics*, vol. 5, 1399–455. Amsterdam: Elsevier.

Bruhn, M., D. Karlan, and A. Schoar. 2018. "The Impact of Consulting Services on Small and Medium Enterprises: Evidence from a Randomized Trial in Mexico." *Journal of Political Economy* 126 (2): 635–87.

Bruhn, M., and B. Zia. 2013. "Stimulating Managerial Capital in Emerging Markets: The Impact of Business Training for Young Entrepreneurs." *Journal of Development Effectiveness* 5 (2): 232–66.

Buba, J., J. Gonzalez, and D. Kokas. 2018. "Entrepreneurship Programs—Screening for Beneficiaries." Background paper for *High-Growth Firms*, World Bank, Washington, DC.

Burchfield, M., H. G. Overman, D. Puga, and M. A. Turner. 2006. "Causes of Sprawl: A Portrait from Space." *Quarterly Journal of Economics* 121 (2): 587–633.

Buschmann, S., L. Heemskerk, K. Racz, and B. V. Enclude. 2017. "Lessons from Business Acceleration Programs in Sub-Saharan Africa: Program-Level Review of 24 Accelerator Programs." infoDev report, World Bank, Washington, DC.

Bussolo, M., R. De Hoyos, and D. Medvedev. 2010. "Global Poverty and Distributional Impacts: The GIDD Model." In *Agricultural Price Distortions, Inequality, and Poverty*, edited by Kym Anderson, John Cockburn, and Will Martin, 87–119. Washington, DC: World Bank.

Cabral, L. 2007. "Small Firms in Portugal: A Selective Survey of Stylized Facts, Economic Analysis, and Policy Implications." *Portuguese Economic Journal* 6 (1): 65–88.

Calderon, G., J. M. Cunha, and G. De Giorgi. 2013. "Business Literacy and Development: Evidence from a Randomized Controlled Trial in Rural Mexico." Working Paper 19740, National Bureau of Economic Research, Cambridge, MA.

Campos, F., M. Frese, M. Goldstein, L. Iacovone, H. C. Johnson, D. McKenzie, and M. Mensmann. 2017. "Teaching Personal Initiative Beats Traditional Training in Boosting Small Business in West Africa." *Science* 357 (6357): 1287–90.

Chandra, A., and E. Thompson. 2000. "Does Public Infrastructure Affect Economic Activity? Evidence from the Rural Interstate Highway System." *Regional Science and Urban Economics* 30 (4): 457–90.

Ciccone, A., and G. Peri. 2006. "Identifying Human-Capital Externalities: Theory with Applications." *Review of Economic Studies* 73 (2): 381–412.

Cirera, X., J. Frias, and J. Hill. Forthcoming. *Instruments to Support Business Innovation: A Guide for Policy Makers and Practitioners.* Washington, DC: World Bank.

Cirera, X., and W. F. Maloney. 2017. *The Innovation Paradox: Developing Country Capabilities and the Unrealized Promise of Technological Catch-Up.* Washington, DC: World Bank.

Coad, A. 2009. *The Growth of Firms: A Survey of Theories and Empirical Evidence.* Cheltenham, UK: Edward Elgar.

Collard-Wexler, Allan, and Jan De Loecker. 2015. "Reallocation and Technology: Evidence from the US Steel Industry." *American Economic Review* 105 (1): 131–71.

Combes, P. P., and L. Gobillon. 2015. "The Empirics of Agglomeration Economies." In *Handbook of Regional and Urban Economics*, vol. 5, 247–348. Amsterdam: Elsevier.

Correa, P. 2014. "Public Expenditure Reviews in Science, Technology, and Innovation: A Guidance Note." World Bank, Washington, DC.

Cusolito, A. P., and W. F. Maloney. 2018. *Productivity Revisited: Shifting Paradigms in Analysis and Policy.* Washington, DC: World Bank.

Dejardin, M., and M. Fritsch. 2011. "Entrepreneurial Dynamics and Regional Growth." *Small Business Economics* 36 (4): 377–82.

De Mel, S., David McKenzie, and Christopher Woodruff. 2008. "Who Are the Microenterprise Owners? Evidence from Sri Lanka on Tokman v. de Soto." In *International Differences in Entrepreneurship*, edited by Josh Lerner and Antoinette Schoar, 63–87. Chicago: University of Chicago Press.

———. 2014. "Business Training and Female Enterprise Start-up, Growth, and Dynamics: Experimental Evidence from Sri Lanka." *Journal of Development Economics* 106 (January): 199–210.

Desai, S., E. Olafsen, and P. A. Cook. 2018. "A Scan of Growth Entrepreneurship Policy in Developing Countries." Background paper for *High-Growth Firms*, World Bank, Washington, DC.

Dihel, N., and A. Grover Goswami. 2016. *The Unexplored Potential of Trade in Services in Africa.* Washington, DC: World Bank.

Dihel, N., and A. Grover Goswami. 2017. "Services in Kenya's Manufacturing: Friend or Foe?" Unpublished manuscript, World Bank, Washington DC.

Djankov, S., and B. Hoekman. 2000. "Foreign Investment and Productivity Growth in Czech Enterprises." *World Bank Economic Review* 14 (1): 49–64.

Djankov, S., E. Miguel, Y. Qian, G. Roland, and E. Zhuravskaya. 2005. "Who Are Russia's Entrepreneurs?" *Journal of the European Economic Association* 3 (2–3): 587–97.

Djankov, S., Y. Qian, G. Roland, and E. Zhuravskaya. 2006a. "Entrepreneurship in China and Russia Compared." *Journal of the European Economic Association* 4 (2–3): 352–65.

———. 2006b. "Who Are China's Entrepreneurs?" *American Economic Review* 96 (2): 348–52.

Donaldson, D. 2018. "Railroads of the Raj: Estimating the Impact of Transportation Infrastructure." *American Economic Review* 108 (4–5): 899–934.

Donaldson, D., and R. Hornbeck. 2016. "Railroads and American Economic Growth: A 'Market Access' Approach." *Quarterly Journal of Economics* 131 (2): 799–858.

Drexler, Alejandro, Greg Fischer, and Antoinette Schoar. 2014. "Keeping It Simple: Financial Literacy and Rules of Thumb."*American Economic Journal: Applied Economics* 6 (2): 1–31.

Du, J., Y. Gong, and Y. Temouri. 2013. "High Growth Firms and Productivity—Evidence from the United Kingdom." Working Paper 13/04, National Endowment for Science, Technology and the Arts, London.

Duchesneau, D. A., and W. B. Gartner. 1990. "A Profile of New Venture Success and Failure in an Emerging Industry." *Journal of Business Venturing* 5 (5): 297–312.

Duggan, V., S. Rahardja, and G. Varela. 2013. "Service Sector Reform and Manufacturing Productivity: Evidence from Indonesia." Policy Research Working Paper 6349, World Bank, Washington, DC.

Duranton, G., E. Ghani, A. Grover Goswami, and W. Kerr. 2015. "The Misallocation of Land and Other Factors of Production in India." Policy Research Working Paper 7221, World Bank, Washington, DC.

Duranton, Gilles, Laurent Gobillon, and Henry G. Overman. 2011. "Assessing the Effects of Local Taxation Using Microgeographic Data." *Economic Journal - Royal Economic Society* 121 (555): 1017–46.

Duranton, G., P. M. Morrow, and M. A. Turner. 2014. "Roads and Trade: Evidence from the US." *Review of Economic Studies* 81 (2): 681–724.

Duranton, G., and D. Puga. 2004. "Micro-Foundations of Urban Agglomeration Economies." In *Handbook of Regional and Urban Economics*, vol. 4, 2063–117. Amsterdam: Elsevier.

Duranton, G., and M. A. Turner. 2011. "The Fundamental Law of Road Congestion: Evidence from US Cities." *American Economic Review* 101 (6): 2616–52.

Duranton, G., and A. J. Venables. 2018. "Place-based Policies for Development." Policy Research Working Paper WPS 8410, World Bank, Washington DC.

Ellis, P., and M. Roberts. 2015. *Leveraging Urbanization in South Asia: Managing Spatial Transformation for Prosperity and Livability*. Washington, DC: World Bank.

Faber, B. 2014. "Trade Integration, Market Size, and Industrialization: Evidence from China's National Trunk Highway System." *Review of Economic Studies* 81 (3): 1046–70.

Fafchamps, M. 2010. "Vulnerability, Risk Management, and Agricultural Development." *African Journal of Agricultural Economics* 5 (1): 243–60.

———, D. McKenzie, S. R. Quinn, and C. Woodruff. 2011. "When Is Capital Enough to Get Female Microenterprises Growing? Evidence from a Randomized Experiment in Ghana." Working Paper 17207, National Bureau of Economic Research, Cambridge, MA.

Fafchamps, M., and C. Woodruff. 2017. "Identifying Gazelles: Expert Panels Versus Surveys as a Means to Identify Firms with Rapid Growth Potential." *World Bank Economic Review* 31 (3): 670–86.

Fajnzylber, P., W. F. Maloney, and G. V. Montes-Rojas. 2006. "Releasing Constraints to Growth or Pushing on a String? The Impact of Credit, Training, Business Associations, and Taxes on the Performance of Mexican Micro-Firms." Policy Research Working Paper 3807, World Bank, Washington, DC.

Farole, T. 2011. *Special Economic Zones in Africa: Comparing Performance and Learning from Global Experiences*. Washington, DC: World Bank.

Feld, B. 2012. *Startup Communities: Building an Entrepreneurial Ecosystem in Your City*. Chichester, UK: John Wiley & Sons.

Fernandes, A. M., and C. Paunov. 2012. "The Risks of Innovation: Are Innovating Firms Less Likely to Die?" *Review of Economics and Statistics* 97 (3): 638–53.

Finland, Ministry of Trade and Industry. 2007. "High-Growth SME Support Initiatives in Nine Countries: Analysis, Categorization, and Recommendations," by E. Autio, M. Kronlund, and A. Kovalainen. Consultant report, Helsinki.

Fox, L., and T. P. Sohnesen. 2012. "Household Enterprises in Sub-Saharan Africa: Why They Matter for Growth, Jobs, and Livelihoods." Policy Research Working Paper 6184, World Bank, Washington, DC.

Frederick, S. 2005. "Cognitive Reflection and Decision Making." *Journal of Economic Perspectives* 19 (4): 25–42.

Fujita, M., and H. Ogawa. 1982. "Multiple Equilibria and Structural Transition of Non-Monocentric Urban Configurations." *Regional Science and Urban Economics* 12 (2): 161–96.

Garud, R., and P. Karnøe. 2003. "Bricolage versus Breakthrough: Distributed and Embedded Agency in Technology Entrepreneurship." *Research Policy* 32 (2): 277–300.

Ghani, E., A. Grover Goswami, and W. R. Kerr. 2015. "Highway to Success: The Impact of the Golden Quadrilateral Project for the Location and Performance of Indian Manufacturing." *Economic Journal* 126 (591): 317–57.

———. 2016. "Highways and Spatial Location within Cities: Evidence from India." *World Bank Economic Review* 30 (Supplement 1): S97–S108.

Giné, X., G. Mansuri, and M. Picón. 2011. "Does a Picture Paint a Thousand Words? Evidence from a Microcredit Marketing Experiment." *World Bank Economic Review* 25 (3): 508–42.

Girma, S., D. Greenaway, and R. Kneller. 2004. "Does Exporting Increase Productivity? A Microeconometric Analysis of Matched Firms." *Review of International Economics* 12 (5): 855–66.

Glaeser, E. L., and J. D. Gottlieb. 2008. "The Economics of Place-Making Policies." Working Paper 14373, National Bureau of Economic Research, Cambridge, MA.

Glaeser, E. L., and M. E. Kahn. 2004. "Sprawl and Urban Growth." In *Handbook of Regional and Urban Economics*, vol. 4, 2481–527. Amsterdam: Elsevier.

Glaeser, E. L., and J. E. Kohlhase. 2004. "Cities, Regions and the Decline of Transport Costs." In *Fifty Years of Regional Science*, edited by Raymond Florax and David Plane, 197–228. Berlin: Springer-Verlag.

Glaub, M. E., M. Frese, S. Fischer, and M. Hoppe. 2014. "Increasing Personal Initiative in Small Business Managers or Owners Leads to Entrepreneurial Success: A Theory-Based Controlled Randomized Field Intervention for Evidence-Based Management." *Academy of Management Learning and Education* 13 (3): 354–79.

Goldberg, P. K., A. K. Khandelwal, N. Pavcnik, and P. Topalova. 2010. "Imported Intermediate Inputs and Domestic Product Growth: Evidence from India." *Quarterly Journal of Economics* 125 (4): 1727–67.

Gonzalez-Uribe, J., and M. Leatherbee. 2017. "The Effects of Business Accelerators on Venture Performance: Evidence from Start-Up Chile." *Review of Financial Studies* 31 (4): 1566–603.

Görg, H., E. Strobl, and F. Walsh. 2007. "Why Do Foreign-Owned Firms Pay More? The Role of on-the-Job Training." *Review of World Economics* 143 (3): 464–82.

Granovetter, M. 1976. "Network Sampling: Some First Steps." *American Journal of Sociology* 81 (6): 1287–303.

———. 1985. "Economic Action and Social Structure: The Problem of Embeddedness." *American Journal of Sociology* 91 (3): 481–510.

Grimm, M., J. Krueger, and J. Lay. 2011. "Barriers to Entry and Returns to Capital in Informal Activities: Evidence from Sub-Saharan Africa." *Review of Income and Wealth* 57 (Supplement 1): 27–53.

Grover Goswami, A., A. Mattoo, and S. Sáez. 2011. *Exporting Services: A Developing Country Perspective.* Washington, DC: World Bank.

The Hague, Ministry of Economic Affairs of the Netherlands. 2005. "Einvaluatie BioPartner-Programma," by M. B. M. van Dongen, H. T. P. Derksen, and A. E. A. R. van Diemen. Consultant report.

Haltiwanger, J. 2011. "Firm Dynamics and Productivity Growth." EIB Paper 5/2011, European Investment Bank, Luxembourg.

———. 2015. "Top Ten Signs of Declining Business Dynamism and Entrepreneurship in the US." Paper prepared for the Kauffman Foundation New Entrepreneurial Growth Conference, Amelia Island, FL, June 17–19.

———, R. S. Jarmin, and J. Miranda. 2013. "Who Creates Jobs? Small versus Large versus Young." *Review of Economics and Statistics* 95 (2): 347–61.

Harada, N. 2004. "Productivity and Entrepreneurial Chraracteristics in New Japanese Firms." *Small Business Economics* 23 (4): 299–310.

Harris, R., and Q. C. Li. 2007. "Learning-by-Exporting? Firm-Level Evidence for UK Manufacturing and Services Sectors." Working Paper 2007–22, Adam Smith Business School, University of Glasgow, Glasgow.

Henderson, V., A. Kuncoro, and M. Turner. 1995. "Industrial Development in Cities." *Journal of Political Economy* 103 (5): 1067–90.

Henrekson, M., and D. Johansson. 2010. "Gazelles as Job Creators: A Survey and Interpretation of the Evidence." *Small Business Economics* 35 (2): 227–44.

Hoang, H., and B. Antoncic. 2003. "Network-Based Research in Entrepreneurship: A Critical Review." *Journal of Business Venturing* 18 (2): 165–87.

Hoekman, B., and B. Shepherd. 2017. "Services Productivity, Trade Policy and Manufacturing Exports." *World Economy* 40 (3): 499–516.

Hölzl, W. 2009. "Is the R&D Behaviour of Fast-Growing SMEs Different? Evidence from CIS III Data for 16 Countries." *Small Business Economics* 33 (1): 59–75.

———. 2014. "Persistence, Survival, and Growth: A Closer Look at 20 Years of Fast-Growing Firms in Austria." *Industrial and Corporate Change* 12 (1): 199–231.

Hsieh, C.-T., and P. J. Klenow. 2009. "Misallocation and Manufacturing TFP in China and India." *Quarterly Journal of Economics* 124 (4): 1403–48.

———. 2014. "The Life Cycle of Plants in India and Mexico." *Quarterly Journal of Economics* 129 (3): 1035–83.

Hsu, W. T., and H. Zhang. 2014. "The Fundamental Law of Highway Congestion Revisited: Evidence from National Expressways in Japan." *Journal of Urban Economics* 81 (May): 65–76.

Hulsink, W., and T. Elfring. 2000. "Innovatieve Clustervorming: het twinning-concept als voorbeeld." In *Silicon Valley in de Polder*, edited by H. Bouwman and W. Hulsink. Utrecht, the Netherlands: Lemma.

Iacovone, L., G. Calderon, and C. MacGregor. 2018. "Participating or Not? Characteristics of Female Entrepreneurs Participating in and Completing an Entrepreneurial Training Program." *AEA Papers and Proceedings* 108: 246–51.

Isaga, N. 2015. "Owner-Managers' Demographic Characteristics and the Growth of Tanzanian Small and Medium Enterprises." *International Journal of Business and Management* 10 (5): 168.

Isenberg, D. 2010. "The Big Idea: How to Start an Entrepreneurial Revolution." *Harvard Business Review*. June.

———. 2011. "The Entrepreneurship Ecosystem Strategy as a New Paradigm for Economic Policy: Principles for Cultivating Entrepreneurship." Babson Entrepreneurship Ecosystem Project, Babson College, Babson Park, MA.

Jacobs J. 1969. *The Economy of Cities*. New York: Random House.

Jalbert, T., M. Jalbert, and K. Furumo. 2011. "Does AACSB Accreditation Matter? Evidence from Large Firm CEOs." *Journal of Applied Business Research* 27 (3): 93–106.

Javorcik, B. S. 2004. "Does Foreign Direct Investment Increase the Productivity of Domestic Firms? In Search of Spillovers through Backward Linkages." *American Economic Review* 94 (3): 605–27.

Jennings, P. D., R. Greenwood, M. D. Lounsbury, and R. Suddaby. 2013. "Institutions, Entrepreneurs, and Communities: A Special Issue on Entrepreneurship." *Journal of Business Venturing* 28 (1): 1–9.

Jones, G., and B. Macken. 2015. "Questioning Short-Term Memory and Its Measurement: Why Digit Span Measures Long-Term Associative Learning." *Cognition* 144: 1–13.

Kantis, H. D., and J. S. Federico. 2012. "Entrepreneurial Ecosystems in Latin America: The Role of Policies." Paper presented at the Kauffman Foundation's International Research and Policy Roundtable, Liverpool, UK, March 11–12.

Karlan, D., R. Knight, and C. Udry. 2015. "Consulting and Capital Experiments with Microenterprise Tailors in Ghana." *Journal of Economic Behavior and Organization* 118: 281–302.

Karlan, D., and M. Valdivia. 2011. "Teaching Entrepreneurship: Impact of Business Training on Microfinance Clients and Institutions." *Review of Economics and Statistics* 93 (2): 510–27.

Kerr, W. R., R. Nanda, and M. Rhodes-Kropf. 2014. "Entrepreneurship as Experimentation." *Journal of Economic Perspectives* 28 (3): 25–48.

Kerr, S. P., W. R. Kerr, and T. Xu. 2017. "Personality Traits of Entrepreneurs: A Review of Recent Literature." Working Paper 24097, National Bureau of Economic Research, Cambridge, MA.

Khandelwal, A., and M. Teachout. 2016. "Special Economic Zones for Myanmar." Policy Note, International Growth Centre, London School of Economics and Political Science, London.

Kinda, T., and J. L. Loening. 2008. "Small Enterprise Growth and the Rural Investment Climate: Evidence from Tanzania." Policy Research Working Paper 4675, World Bank, Washington, DC.

Klinger, B., L. Castro, P. Szenkman, and A. Khwaja. 2013. "Unlocking SME Finance in Argentina with Psychometrics." Technical Note IDB-TN-532, Inter-American Development Bank, Washington, DC.

Klinger B., A. Khwaja, and J. LaMonte. 2013. "Improving Credit Risk Analysis with Psychometrics in Peru." Technical Note IDB-TN-587, Inter-American Development Bank, Washington, DC.

Klinger, B., and M. Schündeln. 2011. "Can Entrepreneurial Activity Be Taught? Quasi-Experimental Evidence from Central America." *World Development* 39 (9): 1592–610.

Kristiansen, S., B. Furuholt, and F. Wahid. 2003. "Internet Cafe Entrepreneurs: Pioneers in Information Dissemination in Indonesia." *International Journal of Entrepreneurship and Innovation* 4 (4): 251–63.

Lakner, C., and B. Milanovic. 2016. "Response to Adam Corlett's 'Examining an Elephant: Globalisation and the Lower Middle Class of the Rich World.'" Graduate Center Paper, City University of New York, New York.

Lall, S. V., J. V. Henderson, and A. J. Venables. 2017. *Africa's Cities: Opening Doors to the World*. Washington, DC: World Bank.

Lee, N. 2014. "What Holds Back High-Growth Firms? Evidence from UK SMEs." *Small Business Economics* 43 (1): 183–95.

———, P. Sissons, and K. Jones. 2016. "The Geography of Wage Inequality in British Cities." *Regional Studies* 50 (10): 1714–27.

Lerner, J. 2010. "The Future of Public Efforts to Boost Entrepreneurship and Venture Capital." *Small Business Economics* 35 (3): 255–64.

Li, Y., and M. Rama. 2015. "Firm Dynamics, Productivity Growth, and Job Creation in Developing Countries: The Role of Micro- and Small Enterprises." *World Bank Research Observer* 30 (1): 3–38.

Lodefalk, M. 2014. "The Role of Services for Manufacturing Firm Exports." *Review of World Economics* 150 (1): 59–82.

López-García, P., J. M. Montero, and E. Moral-Benito. 2013. "Business Cycles and Investment in Productivity-Enhancing Activities: Evidence from Spanish Firms." *Industry and Innovation* 20 (7): 611–36.

Lucas, R. E., and E. Rossi-Hansberg. 2002. "On the Internal Structure of Cities." *Econometrica* 70 (4): 1445–76.

Lynn, L. H., N. M. Reddy, and J. D. Aram. 1996. "Linking Technology and Institutions: The Innovation Community Framework." *Research Policy* 25 (1): 91–106.

Macours, K., P. Premand, and R. Vakis. 2012. "Transfers, Diversification and Household Risk Strategies: Experimental Evidence with Lessons for Climate Change Adaptation." Policy Research Working Paper 6053, World Bank, Washington, DC.

Malecki, E. J. 2011. "Connecting Local Entrepreneurial Ecosystems to Global Innovation Networks: Open Innovation, Double Networks and Knowledge Integration." *International Journal of Entrepreneurship and Innovation Management* 14 (1): 36–59.

Malerba, F. 2007. "Innovation and the Evolution of Industries." In *Innovation, Industrial Dynamics and Structural Transformation*, edited by Uwe Cantner, 7–27. Berlin: Springer-Verlag.

Mano, Y., A. Iddrisu, Y. Yoshino, and T. Sonobe. 2012. "How Can Micro and Small Enterprises in Sub-Saharan Africa Become More Productive? The Impacts of Experimental Basic Managerial Training." *World Development* 40 (3): 458–68.

Marshall, A. 1890. *Principles of Economics*. London: Macmillan.

Martin, P., T. Mayer, and F. Mayneris. 2011. "Public Support to Clusters: A Firm-Level Study of French 'Local Productive Systems.'" *Regional Science and Urban Economics* 41 (2): 108–23.

Mason, C., and R. Brown. 2013. "Entrepreneurial Ecosystems and Growth-Oriented Entrepreneurship." Background Paper for OECD LEED Program and the Dutch Ministry of Foreign Affairs.

Mason, G., K. Bishop, and C. Robinson. 2009. "Business Growth and Innovation: The Wider Impact of Rapidly-Growing Firms in UK City-Regions." NESTA Research Report, National Endowment for Science, Technology and the Arts, London.

Maxwell, J. R., and D. L. Westerfield. 2002. "Technological Entrepreneurism Characteristics Related to the Adoption of Innovative Technology." *SAM Advanced Management Journal* 67 (1): 9.

Mazzarol, T., T. Volery, N. Doss, and V. Thein. 1999. "Factors Influencing Small Business Start-Ups: A Comparison with Previous Research." *International Journal of Entrepreneurial Behavior and Research* 5 (2): 48–63.

McCline, R. L., S. Bhat, and P. Baj. 2000. "Opportunity Recognition: An Exploratory Investigation of a Component of the Entrepreneurial Process in the Context of the Health Care Industry." *Entrepreneurship Theory and Practice* 25 (2): 81–94.

McKenzie, D. 2015. "Identifying and Spurring High-Growth Entrepreneurship: Experimental Evidence from a Business Plan Competition." Policy Research Working Paper 7391, World Bank, Washington, DC.

———. 2017a. "How Effective Are Active Labor Market Policies in Developing Countries? A Critical Review of Recent Evidence." Policy Research Working Paper 8011, World Bank, Washington, DC.

———. 2017b. "Identifying and Spurring High-Growth Entrepreneurship: Experimental Evidence from a Business Plan Competition." *American Economic Review* 107 (8): 2278–307.

———, Nabila Assaf, and Ana Paula Cusolito. 2016. "The Additionality Impact of a Matching Grant Program for Small Firms: Experimental Evidence from Yemen." Working Paper 7462, World Bank, Washington, DC.

McKenzie, D., and D. Sansone. 2017. "Man vs. Machine in Predicting Successful Entrepreneurs: Evidence from a Business Plan Competition in Nigeria." Policy Research Working Paper 8271, World Bank, Washington, DC.

McKenzie, D., and C. Woodruff. 2008. "Experimental Evidence on Returns to Capital and Access to Finance in Mexico." *World Bank Economic Review* 22 (3): 457–82.

Melitz, M. J., and S. Polanec. 2015. "Dynamic Olley-Pakes Decomposition with Entry and Exit." *RAND Journal of Economics* 46 (2): 362–75.

Milanovic, B. 2002. "The Ricardian Vice: Why Sala-i-Martin's Calculations of World Income Inequality Are Wrong." Unpublished manuscript, Washington, DC.

Moore, J. F. 1993. "Predators and Prey: A New Ecology of Competition." *Harvard Business Review* 71 (3): 75–86.

Mulcahy, D., B. Weeks, and H. S. Bradley. 2012. "We Have Met the Enemy… And He Is US. Lessons from Twenty Years of the Kauffman Foundation's Investments in Venture Capital Funds and the Triumph of Hope over Experience." Kauffman Foundation, Kansas City, MO.

Mungai, E., and S. R. Velamuri. 2010. "Parental Entrepreneurial Role Model Influence on Male Offspring: Is It Always Positive and When Does It Occur?" *Entrepreneurship Theory and Practice* 35 (20): 337–57. http://dx.doi.org/10.1111/j.1540-6520.2009.00363.x.

Nanda, R. 2016. "Financing High-Potential Entrepreneurship." *IZA World of Labor* 252.

———, S. Samila, and O. Sorenson. 2018. "The Persistent Effect of Initial Success: Evidence from Venture Capital." Working Paper 24887, National Bureau of Economic Research, Cambridge, MA.

Napier, G., and C. Hansen. 2011. "Ecosystems for Young Scalable Firms." FORA, Copenhagen.

Neely, A., O. Benedettini, and I. Visnjic. 2011. "The Servitization of Manufacturing: Further Evidence." Paper presented at the 18th European Operations Management Association Conference, Cambridge, July 3–6.

Nightingale, P., and A. Coad. 2014. "Muppets and Gazelles: Political and Methodological Biases in Entrepreneurship Research." *Industrial and Corporate Change* 23 (1): 113–43.

OECD (Organisation for Economic Co-operation and Development). 2003. *Checklist for Foreign Direct Investment Incentive Policies*. Paris: OECD.

Olley, G. S., and A. Pakes. 1996. "The Dynamics of Productivity in the Telecommunications Equipment Industry." *Econometrica* 64 (6): 1263–97.

Rauch, J. E. 1993. "Productivity Gains from Geographic Concentration of Human Capital: Evidence from the Cities." *Journal of Urban Economics* 34 (3): 380–400.

Redding, S. J., and M. A. Turner. 2015. "Transportation Costs and the Spatial Organization of Economic Activity." In *Handbook of Regional and Urban Economics*, vol. 5, 1339–98. Amsterdam: Elsevier.

Rijkers, B., C. Freund, and A. Nucifora. 2017. "All in the Family: State Capture in Tunisia." *Journal of Development Economics* 124 (January): 41–59.

Roberts, M., U. Deichmann, B. Fingleton, and T. Shi. 2012. "Evaluating China's Road to Prosperity: A New Economic Geography Approach." *Regional Science and Urban Economics* 42 (4): 580–94.

Robinson, J. P., P. R. Shaver, and L. S. Wrightsman. 1991. "Criteria for Scale Selection and Evaluation." In *Measures of Personality and Social Psychological Attitudes*, edited by John P. Robinson, Phillip R. Shaver, and Lawrence S. Wrightsman, 1–16. San Diego, CA: Academic Press.

Rotemberg, M., and T. K. White. 2017. "Measuring Cross-Country Differences in Misallocation." Paper presented at the North East Universities Consortium annual conference, Tufts University, Medford, MA, November 4–5.

Ruef, M. 2010. *The Entrepreneurial Group: Social Identities, Relations, and Collective Action.* Princeton, NJ: Princeton University Press.

Saia, A., D. Andrews, and S. Albrizio. 2015. "Productivity Spillovers from the Global Frontier and Public Policy: Industry-Level Evidence." Economics Department Working Paper 1238, OECD Publishing, Paris.

SBA Office of Advocacy. 2008. "High-Impact Firms: Gazelles Revisited," by Z. J. Acs, W. Parsons, and S. Tracy. Small Business Research Summary 328, Washington, DC.

Shane, S. 2009. "Why Encouraging More People to Become Entrepreneurs Is Bad Public Policy." *Small Business Economics* 33 (2): 141–49.

Shittu, A., and Z. Dosunmu. 2014. "Family Background and Entrepreneurial Intention of Fresh Graduates in Nigeria." *Journal of Poverty, Investment and Development* 5: 78–90.

Sinha, T. N. 1996. "Human Factors in Entrepreneurship Effectiveness." *Journal of Entrepreneurship* 5 (1): 23–39.

Storey, D. J. 1994. *Understanding the Small Business Sector.* London: Routledge.

Storeygard, A. 2016. "Farther on Down the Road: Transport Costs, Trade and Urban Growth in Sub-Saharan Africa." *Review of Economic Studies* 83 (3): 1263–95.

Sutton, J. 2012. *Competing in Capabilities: The Globalization Process.* Oxford: Oxford University Press.

Szaszi, B., A. Szollosi, B. Palfi, and B. Aczel. 2017. "The Cognitive Reflection Test Revisited: Exploring the Ways Individuals Solve the Test." *Thinking and Reasoning* 23 (3): 207–34.

Thornton, M. M., and M. J. Flynn. 2006. "Measurement of the Spatial Resolution of a Clinical Volumetric Computed Tomography Scanner Using a Sphere Phantom." In *Medical Imaging 2006: Physics of Medical Imaging*, vol. 6142, 61421Z. Bellingham, WA: International Society for Optics and Photonics.

Thornton, P. H., W. Ocasio, and M. Lounsbury. 2012. *The Institutional Logics Perspective: A New Approach to Culture, Structure, and Process.* Oxford: Oxford University Press.

Toplak, M. E., R. F. West, and K. E. Stanovich. 2011. "The Cognitive Reflection Test as a Predictor of Performance on Heuristics-and-Biases Tasks." *Memory and Cognition* 39 (7): 1275–89.

Tybout, James R. 1996. "Heterogeneity and Productivity Growth: Assessing the Evidence." In *Industrial Evolution in Developing Countries: Micro Patterns of Turnover, Productivity, and Market Structure*, edited by M. J. Roberts and J. R. Tybout, 43–72. New York: Oxford University Press for the World Bank.

Unger, J. M., A. Rauch, M. Frese, and N. Rosenbusch. 2011. "Human Capital and Entrepreneurial Success: A Meta-Analytical Review." *Journal of Business Venturing* 26 (3): 341–58.

Valdivia, M. 2012. "Training or Technical Assistance for Female Entrepreneurship? Evidence from a Field Experiment in Peru." Working Paper, Grupo de Análisis para el Desarollo, Lima, Peru.

Van Assche, A., and J. Van Biesebroeck. 2018. "Functional Upgrading in China's Export Processing Sector." *China Economic Review* 47 (February): 245–62.

Vandermerwe, S., and J. Rada. 1988. "Servitization of Business: Adding Value by Adding Services." *European Management Journal* 6 (4): 314–24.

van der Sluis, J., M. van Praag, and W. Vijverberg. 2008. "Education and Entrepreneurship Selection and Performance: A Review of the Empirical Literature." *Journal of Economic Surveys* 22 (5): 795–841.

Wadhwa, V., K. Holly, R. Aggarwal, and A. Salkever. 2009. "Anatomy of an Entrepreneur: Family Background and Motivation." Kauffman Foundation Small Research Projects Research, Kansas City, MO.

Walker, F. 1887. "The Source of Business Profits." *Quarterly Journal of Economics* 1 (3): 265–288.

Westmore, B. 2013. "R&D, Patenting and Productivity: The Role of Public Policy." Economics Department Working Paper 1046, Organisation for Economic Co-operation and Development, Paris.

Zacharakis, A. L., G. P. West, G. Chandler, T. Nelson, D. Shepherd, and L. Busenitz. 2003. "Entrepreneurship in Emergence: Fifteen Years of Entrepreneurship Research in Management Journals." *Journal of Management* 29 (3): 285–308.

# List of Background Papers

Atiyas, I., O. Bakis, F. de Nicola, and S. W. Tan. 2018. "High-Growth Firms in Turkey."

Banternghansa, C., and K. Samphantharak. 2018. "How Does Ownership Network Affect High-Growth Firms in Thailand."

Bastos, P., and J. Silva. 2018. "The Origins of High-Growth Firms: Evidence from Brazil."

Buba, J., J. Gonzalez, and D. Kokas. 2018. "Entrepreneurship Programs—Screening for Beneficiaries."

Cirera, X., R. Fattal Jaef, and N. Gonne. 2018. "High-Growth Firms and Misallocation in Low-Income Countries: Evidence from Côte d'Ivoire."

Cruz, M., L. Baghdadi, and H. Arouri. 2018. "The Dynamics of High-Growth Firms: Evidence from Tunisia."

Desai, S., E. Olafsen, and P. A. Cook. 2018. "A Scan of Growth Entrepreneurship Policy in Developing Countries."

Ferro, E., and S. Kuriakose. 2018. "Indonesia: High-Growth Firms."

Grover Goswami, A. 2018. "Firms Far Up! Productivity, Agglomeration, and Growth Entrepreneurship in Ethiopia."

Kim, K., and S. Sharma. 2018. "Microenterprise Growth Dynamics: Evidence from India."

Manghnani, R. 2018. "High-Growth Firms and Innovation: Evidence from India."

Muraközy, B., F. de Nicola, and S. W. Tan. 2018. "High-Growth Firms in Hungary."

Reyes, J.-D., A. Grover Goswami, and Y. Abuhashem. 2018. "Financial Sector Development and High-Growth Firms."

Sanchez Bayardo, L. F., and L. Iacovone. 2018. "High-Growth Firms and Spillovers in Mexico."